Water Decrees of Boulder County, Colorado,

Vol 2:

An Annotated Index

Compiled by Dina C. Carson

Water Decrees of Boulder County, Colorado, Vol 2:
An Annotated Index

Indexed by Dina C. Carson

Published by:

Iron Gate Publishing
P.O. Box 999
Niwot, CO 80544
www.irongate.com

Printed in the United States of America

ISBN 978-1-68224-201-8

Introduction

The *Water Decrees of Boulder County, Colorado, Vol 2: An Annotated Index* is an index to the ditches, ditch companies and land owners from Water Districts 5 and 6, the ditches falling in Boulder, Larimer, and Weld Counties, Colorado.

The first section, Ditch Owners, details the filing date (most falling in 1882), followed by the page number reference in the volume (above), the name of the ditch or reservoir, the original appropriation date, the Water District number (5 or 6), and the source of the water (e.g. Boulder Creek).

The following section Ditch and Reservoir Details, gives the Water District Number (5 or 6), which Judicial District the case falls into, the owners, the page number in the volume (above), where the headgate is located, the natural stream, the general course of the ditch, the date of original appropriation, the date when construction began, the grade, when work commenced and when it was completed, when water began running in the ditch or gathering in the reservoir, the length of the ditch, the width at the top and bottom of the ditch, the capacity, how much water was claimed, the acres under irrigation and how many inches of water were appropriated. Not all entries contain complete information.

The original journal is held by the Colorado State Archives and are accessible for research. You can order a copies of pages from this volume by calling the Colorado State Archives, or placing an order through their website.

The first page of the volume (above) reads as follows:

An Act of Feb 1881

Decrees issued beginning 2 June 1882

Pursuant to an Act of the General Assembly of the State of Colorado approved February 11th 1881; An Act to make further provisions for settling the priority of rights to the use of water for irrigation in the District and Supreme Courts, and for making record of each priorities, and for payment of costs and expenses incidental thereto.

In the matter of ... the same being in Water District No. 5 [or 6], which said "Water District No. 5" embraces portions of the counties of Boulder, Larimer and Weld, and is within and under the jurisdiction of the District Court of the First Judicial District of said State sitting at the County of Boulder.

This cause coming on to be heard upon the "statement," filed, and the testimony and proofs heretofore taken, and the arguments of Counsel and of parties interested herein, and an "abstract" of all the testimony and proofs made, and "Findings" thereon, as required by law, which said "Findings" are considered and made part of this Decree.

Referee, James M. North

Judge, Chester C. Carpenter

Clerk, E. J. Morath

Table of Contents

A

Affolter, Fred
filing date: 1882 June 2
Boulder District Court Judgment Book, Water Decrees, Vol 2, District 5-6, 1869-1896, pg 14-15
ditch/reservoir: Beckwith Ditch No. 5
date of original appropriation: 1860 Mar 8
Water District No. 5
Owner of Longmont
water source: St Vrain Creek

Affolter, Fred
filing date: 1882 June 2
Boulder District Court Judgment Book, Water Decrees, Vol 2, District 5-6, 1869-1896, pg 55-56
ditch/reservoir: South Flat Ditch No. 16
date of original appropriation: 1863 May 15
Water District No. 5
Owner of Longmont
water source: St Vrain Creek

Affolter, Fred
filing date: 1882 June 2
Boulder District Court Judgment Book, Water Decrees, Vol 2, District 5-6, 1869-1896, pg 74-75
ditch/reservoir: Island Ditch No. 20 1/2
date of original appropriation: 1864 June 15
Water District No. 5
owner, 1/2 interest, of Longmont
water source: St Vrain Creek

Allison, Caroline S
filing date: 1900 Dec 19
Boulder District Court Judgment Book, Water Decrees, Vol 2, District 5-6, 1869-1896, pg 553
ditch/reservoir: Last Chance Reservoir No. 1 and No. 2
date of original appropriation:
Water District No. 6
Claimant
water source: Coal Creek

Allison, Caroline S
filing date: 1903 Sept 15
Boulder District Court Judgment Book, Water Decrees, Vol 2, District 5-6, 1869-1896, pg 568-569
ditch/reservoir: Last Chance Reservoir No. 1 and No. 2
date of original appropriation:
Water District No. 6
Claimant
water source: Coal Creek

Allison, Robert J
filing date: 1900 Dec 19
Boulder District Court Judgment Book, Water Decrees, Vol 2, District 5-6, 1869-1896, pg 553
ditch/reservoir: Last Chance Reservoir No. 1 and No. 2
date of original appropriation:
Water District No. 6
Claimant
water source: Coal Creek

Allison, Robert J
filing date: 1903 Sept 15
Boulder District Court Judgment Book, Water Decrees, Vol 2, District 5-6, 1869-1896, pg 568-569
ditch/reservoir: Last Chance Reservoir No. 1 and No. 2
date of original appropriation:
Water District No. 6
Claimant
water source: Coal Creek

Altona Ditch Company
filing date: 1882 Dec 2
Boulder District Court Judgment Book, Water Decrees, Vol 2, District 5-6, 1869-1896, pg 411, 413
ditch/reservoir: Altona Ditch No. 11
date of original appropriation: 1865 May 31
Water District No. 5
Owner, of Altona
water source: Left Hand Creek

Anderson Ditch Company
filing date: 1882 June 2
Boulder District Court Judgment Book, Water Decrees, Vol 2, District 5-6, 1869-1896, pg 202
ditch/reservoir: Anderson Ditch No. 4
date of original appropriation: 1860 Oct 1
Water District No. 6
Owner, of Boulder
water source: Boulder Creek

Anderson, Hugo
filing date: 1882 June 2
Boulder District Court Judgment Book, Water Decrees, Vol 2, District 5-6, 1869-1896, pg 162-163
ditch/reservoir: Ullery Ditch No. 66
date of original appropriation: 1874 July 1
Water District No. 5
Owner, of Niwot
water source: St Vrain Creek

Anderson, J Hugo
filing date: 1882 Dec 2
Boulder District Court Judgment Book, Water Decrees, Vol 2, District 5-6, 1869-1896, pg 394, 396
ditch/reservoir: Holland Ditch No. 4
date of original appropriation: 1863 May 1
Water District No. 5
Owner, of NiWot
water source: Left Hand Creek

Anderson, Hugo
filing date: 1902 Oct 2
Boulder District Court Judgment Book, Water Decrees, Vol 2, District 5-6, 1869-1896, pg 567-568
ditch/reservoir: Anderson Ditch
date of original appropriation: 1883
Water District No. 5
Owner, of Longmont
water source: Dry Creek

Anderson, Swan
filing date: 1882 June 2
Boulder District Court Judgment Book, Water Decrees, Vol 2, District 5-6, 1869-1896, pg 162-163
ditch/reservoir: Ullery Ditch No. 66
date of original appropriation: 1874 July 1
Water District No. 5
Owner, of Longmont
water source: St Vrain Creek

Anderson, Swan
filing date: 1902 Oct 2
Boulder District Court Judgment Book, Water Decrees, Vol 2, District 5-6, 1869-1896, pg 567-568
ditch/reservoir: Anderson Ditch
date of original appropriation: 1883
Water District No. 5
Owner, of Longmont
water source: Dry Creek

Arbuthnot, William
filing date: 1882 Dec 2
Boulder District Court Judgment Book, Water Decrees, Vol 2, District 5-6, 1869-1896, pg 398-399
ditch/reservoir: Bader No. 2 Ditch No. 5
date of original appropriation: 1863 May 31
Water District No. 5
Owner, of Boulder
water source: Left Hand Creek

Arbuthnot, William
filing date: 1882 Dec 2
Boulder District Court Judgment Book, Water Decrees, Vol 2, District 5-6, 1869-1896, pg 401
ditch/reservoir: Farmers Ditch No. 6
date of original appropriation: 1863 June 1
Water District No. 5
Owner, of Longmont
water source: Left Hand Creek

Arbuthnot, William
filing date: 1882 Dec 2
Boulder District Court Judgment Book, Water Decrees, Vol 2, District 5-6, 1869-1896, pg 409-410
ditch/reservoir: Bader No. 1 Ditch No. 8
date of original appropriation: 1864 May 1
Water District No. 5
Owner, of NiWot
water source: Left Hand Creek

Arbuthnot, Wm
filing date: 1882 Dec 2
Boulder District Court Judgment Book, Water Decrees, Vol 2, District 5-6, 1869-1896, pg 394. 396
ditch/reservoir: Holland Ditch No. 4
date of original appropriation: 1863 May 1
Water District No. 5
Owner, of NiWot
water source: Left Hand Creek

Atwood, Joseph T
filing date: 1896 Oct 20
Boulder District Court Judgment Book, Water Decrees, Vol 2, District 5-6, 1869-1896, pg 548
ditch/reservoir: Upper Baldwin Ditch
date of original appropriation: 1872 Apr 1
Water District No. 5
Attorney
water source: Dry Creek

Autrey, George
filing date: 1882 June 2
Boulder District Court Judgment Book, Water Decrees, Vol 2, District 5-6, 1869-1896, pg 348
ditch/reservoir: Autry and Eggleston Ditch No, 1
date of original appropriation: 1860 June 1
Water District No. 6
Owner, of Langford
water source: Coal Creek

B

Bacon, J W
filing date: 1882 June 2
Boulder District Court Judgment Book, Water Decrees, Vol 2, District 5-6, 1869-1896, pg 17-18
ditch/reservoir: Bacon's Appropriation No. 7
date of original appropriation: 1861 June 1
Water District No. 5
Owner of Longmont
water source: St Vrain Creek

Bacon, J W
filing date: 1882 Dec 2
Boulder District Court Judgment Book, Water Decrees, Vol 2, District 5-6, 1869-1896, pg 433-434
ditch/reservoir: Bacon (North Side) Ditch No. 86
date of original appropriation: 1881 May 20
Water District No. 5
Owner, of Longmont
water source: Big Hollow tributary of the St Vrain Creek

Bader, George G
filing date: 1882 Dec 2
Boulder District Court Judgment Book, Water Decrees, Vol 2, District 5-6, 1869-1896, pg 409-410
ditch/reservoir: Bader No. 1 Ditch No. 8
date of original appropriation: 1864 May 1
Water District No. 5
Owner, of Altona
water source: Left Hand Creek

Bader, John G
filing date: 1882 Dec 2
Boulder District Court Judgment Book, Water Decrees, Vol 2, District 5-6, 1869-1896, pg 398-399
ditch/reservoir: Bader No. 2 Ditch No. 5
date of original appropriation: 1863 May 31
Water District No. 5
Owner, of Boulder
water source: Left Hand Creek

Bader, John G
filing date: 1882 Dec 2
Boulder District Court Judgment Book, Water Decrees, Vol 2, District 5-6, 1869-1896, pg 440, 442
ditch/reservoir: Crocker Ditch No. 23
date of original appropriation: 1871 May 1
Water District No. 5
Owner, of Altona
water source: Left Hand Creek

Bader, N E Estate
filing date: 1882 Dec 2
Boulder District Court Judgment Book, Water Decrees, Vol 2, District 5-6, 1869-1896, pg 394, 396
ditch/reservoir: Holland Ditch No. 4
date of original appropriation: 1863 May 1
Water District No. 5
Owner, of NiWot
water source: Left Hand Creek

Bader, Nicholas Estate
filing date: 1882 Dec 2
Boulder District Court Judgment Book, Water Decrees, Vol 2, District 5-6, 1869-1896, pg 389, 392
ditch/reservoir: Williamson and Cavey Ditch No. 3
date of original appropriation: 1862 May 31
Water District No. 5
Owner, of NiWot
water source: Left Hand Creek

Baird (Carpenter & Baird)
filing date: 1900 Dec 19
Boulder District Court Judgment Book, Water Decrees, Vol 2, District 5-6, 1869-1896, pg 553
ditch/reservoir: McKay Reservoir and Ditch
date of original appropriation:
Water District No. 6
Attorney
water source: Coal Creek

Baird (Carpenter & Baird)
filing date: 1903 Sept 15
Boulder District Court Judgment Book, Water Decrees, Vol 2, District 5-6, 1869-1896, pg 569
ditch/reservoir: McKay Reservoir and McKay Ditch
date of original appropriation:
Water District No. 6
Attorney
water source: Coal Creek

Baker
filing date: 1882 Dec 2
Boulder District Court Judgment Book, Water Decrees, Vol 2, District 5-6, 1869-1896, pg 423
ditch/reservoir: Toll Gate Ditch No. 20
date of original appropriation: 1870 Apr 1
Water District No. 5
former Referee
water source: Left Hand Creek

Baker, William
filing date: 1882 June 2
Boulder District Court Judgment Book, Water Decrees, Vol 2, District 5-6, 1869-1896, pg 40-41
ditch/reservoir: Montgomery Private Ditch No. 12 1/2
date of original appropriation: 1862 May 15
Water District No. 5
Owner of Longmont
water source: St Vrain Creek

Baker, William
filing date: 1882 June 2
Boulder District Court Judgment Book, Water Decrees, Vol 2, District 5-6, 1869-1896, pg 43-44
ditch/reservoir: Smead Ditch No. 13
date of original appropriation: 1862 Oct 1
Water District No. 5
Owner of Longmont
water source: St Vrain Creek

Baker, William
filing date: 1882 June 2
Boulder District Court Judgment Book, Water Decrees, Vol 2, District 5-6, 1869-1896, pg 95
ditch/reservoir: Goss Private Ditch 1 No. 25
date of original appropriation: 1865 June 30
Water District No. 5
farm owner
water source: St Vrain Creek

Baldwin, Nettie
filing date: 1895 Feb 12
Boulder District Court Judgment Book, Water Decrees, Vol 2, District 5-6, 1869-1896, pg 543
ditch/reservoir: Lower Baldwin Ditch
date of original appropriation: 1873 Apr 1
Water District No. 5
Owner, of Longmont
water source: Dry Creek

Baldwin, Nettie
filing date: 1896 Oct 20
Boulder District Court Judgment Book, Water Decrees, Vol 2, District 5-6, 1869-1896, pg 547
ditch/reservoir: Upper Baldwin Ditch
date of original appropriation: 1872 Apr 1
Water District No. 5
Owner, of Longmont
water source: Dry Creek

Barbour, E A
filing date: 1882 June 2
Boulder District Court Judgment Book, Water Decrees, Vol 2, District 5-6, 1869-1896, pg 223
ditch/reservoir: Green Ditch No. 13
date of original appropriation: 1862 Sept 15
Water District No. 6
Owner
water source: Boulder Creek

Barbour, W R
filing date: 1900 Dec 19
Boulder District Court Judgment Book, Water Decrees, Vol 2, District 5-6, 1869-1896, pg 553
ditch/reservoir: Community Ditch
date of original appropriation:
Water District No. 6
Attorney
water source: Coal Creek

Barbour, W R
filing date: 1903 Sept 15
Boulder District Court Judgment Book, Water Decrees, Vol 2, District 5-6, 1869-1896, pg 569
ditch/reservoir: Community Ditch, Marshall Reservoir, West Lake Reservoir, Section 19 Reservoir, Section 9 Reservoir, Section 15 Reservoir
date of original appropriation:
Water District No. 6
Attorney
water source: Coal Creek

Barker
filing date: 1882 June 2
Boulder District Court Judgment Book, Water Decrees, Vol 2, District 5-6, 1869-1896, pg 317
ditch/reservoir: Enterprise Ditch No. 12
date of original appropriation: 1865 Feb 1
Water District No. 6
landowner
water source: South Boulder Creek

Barker, Ezra K
filing date: 1882 June 2
Boulder District Court Judgment Book, Water Decrees, Vol 2, District 5-6, 1869-1896, pg 247
ditch/reservoir: Leggett Ditch No. 30
date of original appropriation: 1868 May 1 (half constructed by 1 June 1862)
Water District No. 6
Owner, of Boulder
water source: Boulder Creek

Barnes, J W
filing date: 1900 Dec 19
Boulder District Court Judgment Book, Water Decrees, Vol 2, District 5-6, 1869-1896, pg 553
ditch/reservoir: Last Chance Reservoir No. 1 and No. 2
date of original appropriation:
Water District No. 6
Attorney
water source: Coal Creek

Barnes, J W
filing date: 1903 Sept 15
Boulder District Court Judgment Book, Water Decrees, Vol 2, District 5-6, 1869-1896, pg 568-569
ditch/reservoir: Last Chance Reservoir No. 1 and No. 2
date of original appropriation:
Water District No. 6
Attorney
water source: Coal Creek

Barter
filing date: 1882 June 2
Boulder District Court Judgment Book, Water Decrees, Vol 2, District 5-6, 1869-1896, pg 317
ditch/reservoir: Enterprise Ditch No. 12
date of original appropriation: 1865 Feb 1
Water District No. 6
landowner
water source: South Boulder Creek

Baum, Frederick
filing date: 1882 Dec 2
Boulder District Court Judgment Book, Water Decrees, Vol 2, District 5-6, 1869-1896, pg 406-407
ditch/reservoir: Baum and Goyn Ditch No. 7
date of original appropriation: 1863 Sept 26
Water District No. 5
Owner, of NiWot
water source: Left Hand Creek

Beal, Mrs
filing date: 1882 June 2
Boulder District Court Judgment Book, Water Decrees, Vol 2, District 5-6, 1869-1896, pg 314
ditch/reservoir: Andrews and Farwell Ditch No. 11
date of original appropriation: 1864 June 1
Water District No. 6
homeowner
water source: South Boulder Creek

Beasley, James J
filing date: 1882 June 2
Boulder District Court Judgment Book, Water Decrees, Vol 2, District 5-6, 1869-1896, pg 239
ditch/reservoir: Howell and Beasley Ditch No. 23
date of original appropriation: 1865 Mar 1
Water District No. 6
Owner, of Canfield
water source: Boulder Creek

Beckwith, Elmer F
filing date: 1902 Oct 2
Boulder District Court Judgment Book, Water Decrees, Vol 2, District 5-6, 1869-1896, pg 566, 568
ditch/reservoir: Oscar Beckwith Ditch
date of original appropriation: 1878 May
Water District No. 5
Owner, of Longmont
water source: Dry Creek

Beckwith, George C
filing date: 1882 June 2
Boulder District Court Judgment Book, Water Decrees, Vol 2, District 5-6, 1869-1896, pg 14-15
ditch/reservoir: Beckwith Ditch No. 5
date of original appropriation: 1860 Mar 8
Water District No. 5
Owner of Denver
water source: St Vrain Creek

Beckwith, George C
filing date: 1882 June 2
Boulder District Court Judgment Book, Water Decrees, Vol 2, District 5-6, 1869-1896, pg 74-75
ditch/reservoir: Island Ditch No. 20 1/2
date of original appropriation: 1864 June 15
Water District No. 5
owner, 1/2 interest of Denver
water source: St Vrain Creek

Beckwith, George L
filing date: 1882 June 2
Boulder District Court Judgment Book, Water Decrees, Vol 2, District 5-6, 1869-1896, pg 14-15
ditch/reservoir: Beckwith Ditch No. 5
date of original appropriation: 1860 Mar 8
Water District No. 5
Owner of Longmont
water source: St Vrain Creek

Beckwith, George L
filing date: 1882 June 2
Boulder District Court Judgment Book, Water Decrees, Vol 2, District 5-6, 1869-1896, pg 55-56
ditch/reservoir: South Flat Ditch No. 16
date of original appropriation: 1863 May 15
Water District No. 5
Owner, of Longmont
water source: St Vrain Creek

Beckwith, George L
filing date: 1882 June 2
Boulder District Court Judgment Book, Water Decrees, Vol 2, District 5-6, 1869-1896, pg 69, 71
ditch/reservoir: Coffman Ditch No. 20
date of original appropriation: 1864 May 30
Water District No. 5
Owner, of Longmont
water source: St Vrain Creek

Beckwith, Oscar F
filing date: 1902 Oct 2
Boulder District Court Judgment Book, Water Decrees, Vol 2, District 5-6, 1869-1896, pg 566, 568
ditch/reservoir: Oscar Beckwith Ditch
date of original appropriation: 1878 May
Water District No. 5
Owner, of Longmont
water source: Dry Creek

Belcher, Freeman
filing date: 1882 June 2
Boulder District Court Judgment Book, Water Decrees, Vol 2, District 5-6, 1869-1896, pg 189
ditch/reservoir: Bonus Ditch No. 6
date of original appropriation: 1861 Mar 30
Water District No. 5
Owner, of Longmont
water source: St Vrain Creek

Belcher, Freeman
filing date: 1882 June 2
Boulder District Court Judgment Book, Water Decrees, Vol 2, District 5-6, 1869-1896, pg 191
ditch/reservoir: Bonus Ditch No. 6
date of original appropriation: 1861 Mar 30
Water District No. 5
Owner, of Longmont
water source: St Vrain Creek

Belcher, Freeman
filing date: 1895 Feb 12
Boulder District Court Judgment Book, Water Decrees, Vol 2, District 5-6, 1869-1896, pg 532, 534
ditch/reservoir: Bonus Lateral Ditch
date of original appropriation: 1870 Mar 1
Water District No. 5
Owner, of Longmont
water source: Dry Creek

Belcher, Freeman
filing date: 1895 Feb 12
Boulder District Court Judgment Book, Water Decrees, Vol 2, District 5-6, 1869-1896, pg 546
ditch/reservoir: Upper Baldwin Ditch
date of original appropriation: 1872 Apr 1
Water District No. 5
Owner, of Longmont
water source: Dry Creek

Belcher, M S
filing date: 1896 Oct 20
Boulder District Court Judgment Book, Water Decrees, Vol 2, District 5-6, 1869-1896, pg 547
ditch/reservoir: Upper Baldwin Ditch
date of original appropriation: 1872 Apr 1
Water District No. 5
Owner, of Longmont
water source: Dry Creek

Belcher, M S
filing date: 1895 Feb 12
Boulder District Court Judgment Book, Water Decrees, Vol 2, District 5-6, 1869-1896, pg 543
ditch/reservoir: Lower Baldwin Ditch
date of original appropriation: 1873 Apr 1
Water District No. 5
Owner, of Longmont
water source: Dry Creek

Bell, Thomas
filing date: 1894 Apr 28
Boulder District Court Judgment Book, Water Decrees, Vol 2, District 5-6, 1869-1896, pg 529
ditch/reservoir: Kerr Ditch No. 1 and No. 2
date of original appropriation: 1861 Apr 15
Water District No. 6
Owner, of Louisville
water source: Coal Creek

Bennett, C A
filing date: 1903 Sept 15
Boulder District Court Judgment Book, Water Decrees, Vol 2, District 5-6, 1869-1896, pg 568
ditch/reservoir:
date of original appropriation:
Water District No. 6
Judge
water source:

Bennett, Christian A
filing date:
Boulder District Court Judgment Book, Water Decrees, Vol 2, District 5-6, 1869-1896, pg 517
ditch/reservoir: Low Ditch No. 1
date of original appropriation:
Water District No. 5
Judge
water source:

Bennett, Christian A
filing date: 1902 Oct 2
Boulder District Court Judgment Book, Water Decrees, Vol 2, District 5-6, 1869-1896, pg 566, 568
ditch/reservoir: Peck & Metcalf Ditch
date of original appropriation: 1867 May 15
Water District No. 5
Judge
water source: Dry Creek

Berkley
filing date: 1882 June 2
Boulder District Court Judgment Book, Water Decrees, Vol 2, District 5-6, 1869-1896, pg 268
ditch/reservoir: Dry Creek Ditch No. 11
date of original appropriation: 1862 June 1
Water District No. 6
Claimant
water source: Boulder Creek

Berkley, G
filing date: 1882 June 2
Boulder District Court Judgment Book, Water Decrees, Vol 2, District 5-6, 1869-1896, pg 269
ditch/reservoir: Dry Creek Ditch No. 11
date of original appropriation: 1862 June 1
Water District No. 6
Owner, of Boulder
water source: Boulder Creek

Berkley, G
filing date: 1882 June 2
Boulder District Court Judgment Book, Water Decrees, Vol 2, District 5-6, 1869-1896, pg 282-283
ditch/reservoir: Boulder and White Rock Ditch
date of original appropriation: 1862 June 1
Water District No. 6
Claimant
water source: Boulder Creek

Besher, Samuel
filing date: 1882 June 2
Boulder District Court Judgment Book, Water Decrees, Vol 2, District 5-6, 1869-1896, pg 105
ditch/reservoir: Denio & Taylor Ditch No. 28
date of original appropriation: 1865 July 15
Water District No. 5
Owner, of Longmont
water source: St Vrain Creek

Beshor, Daniel
filing date: 1882 June 2
Boulder District Court Judgment Book, Water Decrees, Vol 2, District 5-6, 1869-1896, pg 103
ditch/reservoir: Denio & Taylor Ditch No. 28
date of original appropriation: 1865 July 15
Water District No. 5
Owner, of Longmont
water source: St Vrain Creek

Bestle, David
filing date: 1882 June 2
Boulder District Court Judgment Book, Water Decrees, Vol 2, District 5-6, 1869-1896, pg 103, 105
ditch/reservoir: Denio & Taylor Ditch No. 28
date of original appropriation: 1865 July 15
Water District No. 5
Owner, of Longmont
water source: St Vrain Creek

Bestler, David
filing date: 1882 June 2
Boulder District Court Judgment Book, Water Decrees, Vol 2, District 5-6, 1869-1896, pg 77-78
ditch/reservoir: Zweck & Turner Ditch No. 21
date of original appropriation: 1864 June 30
Water District No. 5
Owner
water source: St Vrain Creek

Birch, Henry H
filing date: 1882 Dec 2
Boulder District Court Judgment Book, Water Decrees, Vol 2, District 5-6, 1869-1896, pg 389, 392. 396
ditch/reservoir: Williamson and Cavey Ditch No. 3
date of original appropriation: 1862 May 31
Water District No. 5
Owner, of NiWot
water source: Left Hand Creek

Birch, Henry H
filing date: 1882 Dec 2
Boulder District Court Judgment Book, Water Decrees, Vol 2, District 5-6, 1869-1896, pg 394, 396
ditch/reservoir: Holland Ditch No. 4
date of original appropriation: 1863 May 1
Water District No. 5
Owner, of NiWot
water source: Left Hand Creek

Bloom, George
filing date: 1902 Oct 2
Boulder District Court Judgment Book, Water Decrees, Vol 2, District 5-6, 1869-1896, pg 567
ditch/reservoir: Wiswall Ditch
date of original appropriation: 1892 Nov 10
Water District No. 5
Owner, of Longmont
water source: Dry Creek

Bond, Fred
filing date: 1882 Dec 2
Boulder District Court Judgment Book, Water Decrees, Vol 2, District 5-6, 1869-1896, pg 394, 396
ditch/reservoir: Holland Ditch No. 4
date of original appropriation: 1863 May 1
Water District No. 5
Owner, of NiWot
water source: Left Hand Creek

Bond, George S
filing date: 1882 Dec 2
Boulder District Court Judgment Book, Water Decrees, Vol 2, District 5-6, 1869-1896, pg 449
ditch/reservoir: Bond's Private Ditch
date of original appropriation:
Water District No. 5
Owner, of Longmont
water source: St Vrain Creek through the Highland and other ditches

Bond, Isaac L
filing date: 1882 Dec 2
Boulder District Court Judgment Book, Water Decrees, Vol 2, District 5-6, 1869-1896, pg 449
ditch/reservoir: Bond's Private Ditch
date of original appropriation:
Water District No. 5
Owner, of Longmont
water source: St Vrain Creek through the Highland and other ditches

Boughton, J H
filing date: 1903 Sept 15
Boulder District Court Judgment Book, Water Decrees, Vol 2, District 5-6, 1869-1896, pg 568
ditch/reservoir:
date of original appropriation:
Water District No. 6
Judge
water source:

Boughton, Jay H
filing date: 1896 Apr 28
Boulder District Court Judgment Book, Water Decrees, Vol 2, District 5-6, 1869-1896, pg 494
ditch/reservoir:
date of original appropriation:
Water District No. 5
Judge
water source:

Boughton, Jay H
filing date: 1895 Feb 12
Boulder District Court Judgment Book, Water Decrees, Vol 2, District 5-6, 1869-1896, pg 533
ditch/reservoir: Bonus Lateral Ditch
date of original appropriation: 1870 Mar 1
Water District No. 5
Judge crossed out
water source: Dry Creek

Boughton, Jay H
filing date: 1895 Feb 12
Boulder District Court Judgment Book, Water Decrees, Vol 2, District 5-6, 1869-1896, pg 534
ditch/reservoir: Bonus Lateral Ditch
date of original appropriation: 1870 Mar 1
Water District No. 5
Judge
water source: Dry Creek

Boughton, Jay H
filing date: 1895 Feb 12
Boulder District Court Judgment Book, Water Decrees, Vol 2, District 5-6, 1869-1896, pg 536
ditch/reservoir: Bonus Lateral Ditch
date of original appropriation: 1870 Mar 1
Water District No. 5
Judge
water source: Dry Creek

Boughton, Jay H
filing date: 1895 Feb 12
Boulder District Court Judgment Book, Water Decrees, Vol 2, District 5-6, 1869-1896, pg 537
ditch/reservoir: Rice Ditch
date of original appropriation: 1872 Mar 1
Water District No. 5
Judge
water source: Dry Creek

Boughton, Jay H
filing date: 1895 Feb 12
Boulder District Court Judgment Book, Water Decrees, Vol 2, District 5-6, 1869-1896, pg 540
ditch/reservoir: John Rice Ditch
date of original appropriation: 1884 Apr 1
Water District No. 5
Judge
water source: Dry Creek

Boughton, Jay H
filing date: 1895 Feb 12
Boulder District Court Judgment Book, Water Decrees, Vol 2, District 5-6, 1869-1896, pg 540
ditch/reservoir: Mill Ditch
date of original appropriation: 1884 May 1
Water District No. 5
Judge
water source: Dry Creek

Boughton, Jay H
filing date: 1895 Feb 12
Boulder District Court Judgment Book, Water Decrees, Vol 2, District 5-6, 1869-1896, pg 543
ditch/reservoir: Lower Baldwin Ditch
date of original appropriation: 1873 Apr 1
Water District No. 5
Judge
water source: Dry Creek

Boughton, Jay H
filing date: 1895 Feb 12
Boulder District Court Judgment Book, Water Decrees, Vol 2, District 5-6, 1869-1896, pg 546
ditch/reservoir: Upper Baldwin Ditch
date of original appropriation: 1872 Apr 1
Water District No. 5
Judge
water source: Dry Creek

Boulder & White Rock Ditch Company
filing date: 1882 June 2
Boulder District Court Judgment Book, Water Decrees, Vol 2, District 5-6, 1869-1896, pg 267
ditch/reservoir: Boulder and White Rock Ditch No. 35
date of original appropriation: 1873 Nov 1
Water District No. 6
Owner, of Boulder
water source: Boulder Creek

Boulder and Left Hand Ditch Company
filing date: 1882 June 2
Boulder District Court Judgment Book, Water Decrees, Vol 2, District 5-6, 1869-1896, pg 282-283
ditch/reservoir: Boulder and White Rock Ditch
date of original appropriation: 1862 June 1
Water District No. 6
Claimant
water source: Boulder Creek

Boulder and Left Hand Ditch Company
filing date: 1882 June 2
Boulder District Court Judgment Book, Water Decrees, Vol 2, District 5-6, 1869-1896, pg 281
ditch/reservoir: Boulder and Left Hand Ditch
date of original appropriation: 1873 Dec 1
Water District No. 6
Owner, of Longmont
water source: Boulder Creek

Brailey, John
filing date: 1902 Oct 2
Boulder District Court Judgment Book, Water Decrees, Vol 2, District 5-6, 1869-1896, pg 567
ditch/reservoir: Wiswall Ditch
date of original appropriation: 1892 Nov 10
Water District No. 5
Owner, of Longmont
water source: Dry Creek

Breach, William
filing date: 1882 June 2
Boulder District Court Judgment Book, Water Decrees, Vol 2, District 5-6, 1869-1896, pg 273
ditch/reservoir: Dry Creek Ditch No. 11, Claim of Wm Breach
date of original appropriation: 1862 June 1
Water District No. 6
Owner, of Boulder
water source: Boulder Creek

Breach, William
filing date: 1882 June 2
Boulder District Court Judgment Book, Water Decrees, Vol 2, District 5-6, 1869-1896, pg 283
ditch/reservoir: Boulder and White Rock Ditch
date of original appropriation: 1862 June 1
Water District No. 6
Claimant
water source: Boulder Creek

Breach, Wm
filing date: 1882 June 2
Boulder District Court Judgment Book, Water Decrees, Vol 2, District 5-6, 1869-1896, pg 273
ditch/reservoir: Dry Creek Ditch No. 11, Claim of Wm Breach
date of original appropriation: 1862 June 1
Water District No. 6
Claimant
water source: Boulder Creek

Breach, Wm
filing date: 1882 June 2
Boulder District Court Judgment Book, Water Decrees, Vol 2, District 5-6, 1869-1896, pg 282
ditch/reservoir: Boulder and White Rock Ditch
date of original appropriation: 1862 June 1
Water District No. 6
Claimant
water source: Boulder Creek

Brown, John W
filing date: 1882 June 2
Boulder District Court Judgment Book, Water Decrees, Vol 2, District 5-6, 1869-1896, pg 361
ditch/reservoir: Last Chance Ditch No. 6
date of original appropriation: 1870 May 1
Water District No. 6
Owner, of Golden
water source: Coal Creek

Budd, Sylvanus
filing date: 1882 Dec 2
Boulder District Court Judgment Book, Water Decrees, Vol 2, District 5-6, 1869-1896, pg 383
ditch/reservoir: Cochran Ditch No. 1
date of original appropriation: 1860 Sept 1
Water District No. 5
Owner, of NiWot
water source: Left Hand Creek

Budd, Sylvanus
filing date: 1882 Dec 2
Boulder District Court Judgment Book, Water Decrees, Vol 2, District 5-6, 1869-1896, pg 385-386
ditch/reservoir: Hornbaker Ditch No. 2
date of original appropriation: 1861 May 15
Water District No. 5
Owner, of NiWot
water source: Left Hand Creek

Budd, Sylvanus
filing date: 1882 Dec 2
Boulder District Court Judgment Book, Water Decrees, Vol 2, District 5-6, 1869-1896, pg 385, 388
ditch/reservoir: Cochran Ditch No. 1
date of original appropriation: 1860 Sept 1
Water District No. 5
Owner, of NiWot
water source: Left Hand Creek

Burke, A G
filing date: 1882 June 2
Boulder District Court Judgment Book, Water Decrees, Vol 2, District 5-6, 1869-1896, pg 298
ditch/reservoir: Howard Ditch No. 3
date of original appropriation: 1860 Apr 1
Water District No. 6
Owner, of Boulder
water source: South Boulder Creek

Burke, A G
filing date: 1882 June 2
Boulder District Court Judgment Book, Water Decrees, Vol 2, District 5-6, 1869-1896, pg 312
ditch/reservoir: Dry Creek No. 2 Ditch No. 9
date of original appropriation: 1864 May 1
Water District No. 6
Owner, of Boulder
water source: South Boulder Creek

Butler, William
filing date: 1895 Feb 12
Boulder District Court Judgment Book, Water Decrees, Vol 2, District 5-6, 1869-1896, pg 543
ditch/reservoir: Lower Baldwin Ditch
date of original appropriation: 1873 Apr 1
Water District No. 5
Owner, of the state of Washington
water source: Dry Creek

Butte Ditch Irrigating and Milling Company
filing date: 1882 June 2
Boulder District Court Judgment Book, Water Decrees, Vol 2, District 5-6, 1869-1896, pg 236
ditch/reservoir: Butte Mill Ditch No. 22
date of original appropriation: 1865 Mar 1
Water District No. 6
Owner, of Boulder
water source: Boulder Creek

Butterworth, Clara C
filing date: 1902 Oct 2
Boulder District Court Judgment Book, Water Decrees, Vol 2, District 5-6, 1869-1896, pg 566
ditch/reservoir: Peck & Metcalf Ditch
date of original appropriation: 1867 May 15
Water District No. 5
Owner, of Longmont
water source: Dry Creek

Butterworth, Clara C
filing date: 1902 Oct 21
Boulder District Court Judgment Book, Water Decrees, Vol 2, District 5-6, 1869-1896, pg 568
ditch/reservoir:
date of original appropriation:
Water District No. 5
Owner
water source:

C

Campbell, C M
filing date: 1900 Dec 19
Boulder District Court Judgment Book, Water Decrees, Vol 2, District 5-6, 1869-1896, pg 553
ditch/reservoir: Allen-Hayden Ditches No. 1 No. 2 No. 3 No. 4
date of original appropriation:
Water District No. 6
Attorney
water source: Coal Creek

Campbell, C M
filing date: 1903 Sept 15
Boulder District Court Judgment Book, Water Decrees, Vol 2, District 5-6, 1869-1896, pg 569
ditch/reservoir: Allen-Hayden Ditches No. 1 No. 2 No. 3 No. 4
date of original appropriation:
Water District No. 6
Attorney
water source: Coal Creek

Carpenter & Baird
filing date: 1900 Dec 19
Boulder District Court Judgment Book, Water Decrees, Vol 2, District 5-6, 1869-1896, pg 553
ditch/reservoir: McKay Reservoir and Ditch
date of original appropriation:
Water District No. 6
Attorney
water source: Coal Creek

Carpenter & Baird
filing date: 1903 Sept 15
Boulder District Court Judgment Book, Water Decrees, Vol 2, District 5-6, 1869-1896, pg 569
ditch/reservoir: McKay Reservoir and McKay Ditch
date of original appropriation:
Water District No. 6
Attorney
water source: Coal Creek

Carr, Stephen H
filing date: 1882 June 2
Boulder District Court Judgment Book, Water Decrees, Vol 2, District 5-6, 1869-1896, pg 205
ditch/reservoir: Godding, Dailey and Plumb Ditch No. 5
date of original appropriation: 1861 Mar 1
Water District No. 6

Owner, of Erie
water source: Boulder Creek

Carr, Stephen H
filing date: 1882 June 2
Boulder District Court Judgment Book, Water Decrees, Vol 2, District 5-6, 1869-1896, pg 234
ditch/reservoir: Carr and Tyler Ditch No. 19
date of original appropriation: 1864 June 1
Water District No. 6
Owner, of Boulder
water source: Boulder Creek

Carter
filing date: 1882 June 2
Boulder District Court Judgment Book, Water Decrees, Vol 2, District 5-6, 1869-1896, pg 48
ditch/reservoir: Clough Tribute (Private) Ditch No. 14
date of original appropriation: 1863 Apr 15
Water District No. 5
former owner
water source: St Vrain Creek

Cavey, Thomas
filing date: 1882 Dec 2
Boulder District Court Judgment Book, Water Decrees, Vol 2, District 5-6, 1869-1896, pg 389, 392
ditch/reservoir: Williamson and Cavey Ditch No. 3
date of original appropriation: 1862 May 31
Water District No. 5
Owner, of Longmont
water source: Left Hand Creek

Chamberlain, W S
filing date: 1882 June 2
Boulder District Court Judgment Book, Water Decrees, Vol 2, District 5-6, 1869-1896, pg 255
ditch/reservoir: Town of Boulder Ditch and Reservoir No. 37
date of original appropriation: 1875 June 17
Water District No. 6
Addition
water source: Boulder Creek

Chapman, Joshua
filing date: 1882 June 2
Boulder District Court Judgment Book, Water Decrees, Vol 2, District 5-6, 1869-1896, pg 116
ditch/reservoir: Oligarchy Ditch No. 32
date of original appropriation: 1866 June 1
Water District No. 5
home owner
water source: St Vrain Creek

Chapman, Joshua E
filing date: 1882 June 2
Boulder District Court Judgment Book, Water Decrees, Vol 2, District 5-6, 1869-1896, pg 22, 24
ditch/reservoir: Chapman and McCaslin Ditch No. 9
date of original appropriation: 1862 Mar 10
Water District No. 5
Owner of Longmont
water source: St Vrain Creek

Chase, Geo F
filing date: 1882 June 2
Boulder District Court Judgment Book, Water Decrees, Vol 2, District 5-6, 1869-1896, pg 298
ditch/reservoir: Howard Ditch No. 3
date of original appropriation: 1860 Apr 1
Water District No. 6
Owner, of Boulder
water source: South Boulder Creek

Chase, Geo F
filing date: 1882 June 2
Boulder District Court Judgment Book, Water Decrees, Vol 2, District 5-6, 1869-1896, pg 312
ditch/reservoir: Dry Creek No. 2 Ditch No. 9
date of original appropriation: 1864 May 1
Water District No. 6
Owner, of Boulder
water source: South Boulder Creek

Christensen, Hans
filing date: 1882 June 2
Boulder District Court Judgment Book, Water Decrees, Vol 2, District 5-6, 1869-1896, pg 156-157
ditch/reservoir: Renner Ditch No. 60
date of original appropriation: 1874 May 1
Water District No. 5
Owner, of Longmont
water source: St Vrain Creek

Church, George H
filing date: 1882 June 2
Boulder District Court Judgment Book, Water Decrees, Vol 2, District 5-6, 1869-1896, pg 363
ditch/reservoir: Church Ditch No. 7
date of original appropriation: 1870 Sept 20
Water District No. 6
Owner, of Denver
water source: Coal Creek

Church, George Henry
filing date: 1900 Dec 19
Boulder District Court Judgment Book, Water Decrees, Vol 2, District 5-6, 1869-1896, pg 553
ditch/reservoir: Church's Upper Lake
date of original appropriation:
Water District No. 6
Claimant
water source: Coal Creek

Church, George Henry
filing date: 1903 Sept 15
Boulder District Court Judgment Book, Water Decrees, Vol 2, District 5-6, 1869-1896, pg 568-569
ditch/reservoir: Church's Upper Lake
date of original appropriation:
Water District No. 6
Claimant
water source: Coal Creek

City of Boulder
filing date: 1882 June 2
Boulder District Court Judgment Book, Water Decrees, Vol 2, District 5-6, 1869-1896, pg 255
ditch/reservoir: Town of Boulder Ditch and Reservoir No. 37
date of original appropriation: 1875 June 17
Water District No. 6
Owner
water source: Boulder Creek

Clough, C E
filing date: 1882 June 2
Boulder District Court Judgment Book, Water Decrees, Vol 2, District 5-6, 1869-1896, pg 96
ditch/reservoir: Goss Private Ditch 1 No. 25
date of original appropriation: 1865 June 30
Water District No. 5
land irrigated
water source: St Vrain Creek

Clough, Charles E
filing date: 1882 June 2
Boulder District Court Judgment Book, Water Decrees, Vol 2, District 5-6, 1869-1896, pg 37-38
ditch/reservoir: Clough and True Private Ditch No. 12
date of original appropriation: 1862 Apr 15
Water District No. 5
Owner of Longmont
water source: St Vrain Creek

Clough, Charles E
filing date: 1882 June 2
Boulder District Court Judgment Book, Water Decrees, Vol 2, District 5-6, 1869-1896, pg 46-47
ditch/reservoir: Clough Tribute (Private) Ditch No. 14
date of original appropriation: 1863 Apr 15
Water District No. 5
Owner of Longmont
water source: St Vrain Creek

Clover Basin Ditch Company
filing date: 1882 June 2
Boulder District Court Judgment Book, Water Decrees, Vol 2, District 5-6, 1869-1896, pg 174-175
ditch/reservoir: Taylor Ditch 1 No. 78
date of original appropriation: 1879 June 1
Water District No. 5
Owner, of Longmont
water source: St Vrain Creek

Clover Basin Ditch Company
filing date: 1882 June 2
Boulder District Court Judgment Book, Water Decrees, Vol 2, District 5-6, 1869-1896, pg 177-178
ditch/reservoir: Taylor Ditch 2 No. 79
date of original appropriation: 1879 June 2
Water District No. 5
Owner, of Longmont
water source: St Vrain Creek

Clover Basin Ditch Company
filing date: 1902 Oct 2
Boulder District Court Judgment Book, Water Decrees, Vol 2, District 5-6, 1869-1896, pg 566, 568
ditch/reservoir: Clover Basin Ditch
date of original appropriation: 1879 June 2
Water District No. 5
Owner, of Longmont
water source: Dry Creek

Coffin, George W
filing date: 1882 June 2
Boulder District Court Judgment Book, Water Decrees, Vol 2, District 5-6, 1869-1896, pg 9-10
ditch/reservoir: Coffin Meadow Ditch No. 3
date of original appropriation: 1860 May 1
Water District No. 5
Owner of Longmont
water source: St Vrain Creek

Coffin, George W
filing date: 1882 June 2
Boulder District Court Judgment Book, Water Decrees, Vol 2, District 5-6, 1869-1896, pg 110, 112
ditch/reservoir: Coffin-Davis Ditch No. 31
date of original appropriation: 1866 June 1
Water District No. 5
Owner, of Longmont
water source: St Vrain Creek

Coffin, M H
filing date: 1882 June 2
Boulder District Court Judgment Book, Water Decrees, Vol 2, District 5-6, 1869-1896, pg 110, 112
ditch/reservoir: Coffin-Davis Ditch No. 31
date of original appropriation: 1866 June 1
Water District No. 5
Owner, of Longmont
water source: St Vrain Creek

Coffman, E J
filing date: 1882 June 2
Boulder District Court Judgment Book, Water Decrees, Vol 2, District 5-6, 1869-1896, pg 103. 105
ditch/reservoir: Denio & Taylor Ditch No. 28
date of original appropriation: 1865 July 15
Water District No. 5
Owner, of Longmont
water source: St Vrain Creek

Coffman, Enoch J
filing date: 1882 June 2
Boulder District Court Judgment Book, Water Decrees, Vol 2, District 5-6, 1869-1896, pg 69, 71
ditch/reservoir: Coffman Ditch No. 20
date of original appropriation: 1864 May 30
Water District No. 5
Owner of Longmont
water source: St Vrain Creek

Cole, Wm
filing date: 1882 June 2
Boulder District Court Judgment Book, Water Decrees, Vol 2, District 5-6, 1869-1896, pg 244
ditch/reservoir: Highland Ditch Southside No. 28
date of original appropriation: 1865 June 1
Water District No. 6
Owner, of Longmont
water source: Boulder Creek

Community Ditch and Reservoir Company
filing date: 1900 Dec 19
Boulder District Court Judgment Book, Water Decrees, Vol 2, District 5-6, 1869-1896, pg 553
ditch/reservoir: Section 9 Reservoir
date of original appropriation:
Water District No. 6
Claimant
water source: Coal Creek

Community Ditch and Reservoir Company
filing date: 1900 Dec 19
Boulder District Court Judgment Book, Water Decrees, Vol 2, District 5-6, 1869-1896, pg 553
ditch/reservoir: Community Ditch
date of original appropriation:
Water District No. 6
Claimant
water source: Coal Creek

Community Ditch and Reservoir Company
filing date: 1900 Dec 19
Boulder District Court Judgment Book, Water Decrees, Vol 2, District 5-6, 1869-1896, pg 553
ditch/reservoir: Marshall Reservoir
date of original appropriation:
Water District No. 6
Claimant
water source: Coal Creek

Community Ditch and Reservoir Company
filing date: 1900 Dec 19
Boulder District Court Judgment Book, Water Decrees, Vol 2, District 5-6, 1869-1896, pg 553
ditch/reservoir: West-Lake Reservoir
date of original appropriation:
Water District No. 6
Claimant
water source: Coal Creek

Community Ditch and Reservoir Company
filing date: 1900 Dec 19
Boulder District Court Judgment Book, Water Decrees, Vol 2, District 5-6, 1869-1896, pg 553
ditch/reservoir: Section 19 Reservoir
date of original appropriation:
Water District No. 6
Claimant
water source: Coal Creek

Community Ditch and Reservoir Company
filing date: 1900 Dec 19
Boulder District Court Judgment Book, Water Decrees, Vol 2, District 5-6, 1869-1896, pg 553
ditch/reservoir: Section 15 Reservoir
date of original appropriation:
Water District No. 6
Claimant
water source: Coal Creek

Community Ditch and Reservoir Company
filing date: 1903 Sept 15
Boulder District Court Judgment Book, Water Decrees, Vol 2, District 5-6, 1869-1896, pg 569
ditch/reservoir: Community Ditch, Marshall Reservoir, West Lake Reservoir, Section 19 Reservoir, Section 9 Reservoir, Section 15 Reservoir
date of original appropriation:
Water District No. 6
Claimant
water source: Coal Creek

Connell, Annie E
filing date: 1894 Apr 28
Boulder District Court Judgment Book, Water Decrees, Vol 2, District 5-6, 1869-1896, pg 526
ditch/reservoir: Moffat Ditch
date of original appropriation: 1889 Feb 4
Water District No. 6
Owner, of Hutchinson, Kansas
water source: Coal Creek

Cottonwood Ditch Company
filing date: 1882 June 2
Boulder District Court Judgment Book, Water Decrees, Vol 2, District 5-6, 1869-1896, pg 307
ditch/reservoir: Cottonwood No. 2 Ditch No. 6
date of original appropriation: 1863 Apr 15
Water District No. 6
Owner, of Valmont
water source: South Boulder Creek

Cottonwood Ditch Company
filing date: 1882 June 2
Boulder District Court Judgment Book, Water Decrees, Vol 2, District 5-6, 1869-1896, pg 328
ditch/reservoir: Cottonwood No.2 Ditch No. 17
date of original appropriation: 1866 Apr 1
Water District No. 6
Owner, of Canfield
water source: South Boulder Creek

Crocker, H H
filing date: 1882 Dec 2
Boulder District Court Judgment Book, Water Decrees, Vol 2, District 5-6, 1869-1896, pg 440
ditch/reservoir: Crocker Ditch No. 23
date of original appropriation: 1871 May 1
Water District No. 5
Owner, of Altona
water source: Left Hand Creek

Crocker, H H
filing date: 1882 Dec 2
Boulder District Court Judgment Book, Water Decrees, Vol 2, District 5-6, 1869-1896, pg 442
ditch/reservoir: Crocker Ditch No. 23
date of original appropriation: 1871 May 1
Water District No. 5
Owner, of Altona
water source: Left Hand Creek

Culver
filing date: 1882 June 2
Boulder District Court Judgment Book, Water Decrees, Vol 2, District 5-6, 1869-1896, pg 275
ditch/reservoir: Harden Ditch
date of original appropriation: 1862 June 1
Water District No. 6
Subdivision
water source: Boulder Creek

Culver
filing date: 1882 June 2
Boulder District Court Judgment Book, Water Decrees, Vol 2, District 5-6, 1869-1896, pg 145
ditch/reservoir: Bear & McCory Ditch No. 45
date of original appropriation: 1871 June 1
Water District No. 5
land owner
water source: St Vrain Creek

Culver, Robert
filing date: 1882 June 2
Boulder District Court Judgment Book, Water Decrees, Vol 2, District 5-6, 1869-1896, pg 272
ditch/reservoir: Dry Creek Ditch No. 11, Claim of Mary S Stoddard et al
date of original appropriation: 1862 June 1
Water District No. 6
Owner, of Boulder
water source: Boulder Creek

Culver, Robert
filing date: 1882 June 2
Boulder District Court Judgment Book, Water Decrees, Vol 2, District 5-6, 1869-1896, pg 187
ditch/reservoir: Lykins Gulch Ditch No. 82
date of original appropriation: 1881 May 15
Water District No. 5
land owner
water source: St Vrain Creek

Culver, Robert
filing date: 1882 June 2
Boulder District Court Judgment Book, Water Decrees, Vol 2, District 5-6, 1869-1896, pg 278
ditch/reservoir: McCarty Ditch No. 11
date of original appropriation: 1862 June 1
Water District No. 6
Owner, of Boulder
water source: Boulder Creek

Culver, Robert
filing date: 1882 June 2
Boulder District Court Judgment Book, Water Decrees, Vol 2, District 5-6, 1869-1896, pg 121
ditch/reservoir: Davis & Downing Ditch No. 33
date of original appropriation: 1866 Nov 1
Water District No. 5
Owner, of Longmont
water source: St Vrain Creek

Culver, Robert
filing date: 1882 June 2
Boulder District Court Judgment Book, Water Decrees, Vol 2, District 5-6, 1869-1896, pg 119
ditch/reservoir: Davis & Downing Ditch No. 33
date of original appropriation: 1866 Nov 1
Water District No. 5
Owner, of Longmont
water source: St Vrain Creek

Culver, Robert
filing date: 1882 June 2
Boulder District Court Judgment Book, Water Decrees, Vol 2, District 5-6, 1869-1896, pg 143
ditch/reservoir: Bear & McCory Ditch No. 45
date of original appropriation: 1871 June 1
Water District No. 5
Owner, of Longmont
water source: St Vrain Creek

Culver, Robert
filing date: 1882 June 2
Boulder District Court Judgment Book, Water Decrees, Vol 2, District 5-6, 1869-1896, pg 197
ditch/reservoir: Smith and Goss Ditch No. 2
date of original appropriation: 1859 Nov 15
Water District No. 6
Owner, of Boulder
water source: Boulder Creek

Culver, Robert
filing date: 1882 June 2
Boulder District Court Judgment Book, Water Decrees, Vol 2, District 5-6, 1869-1896, pg 144
ditch/reservoir: Bear & McCory Ditch No. 45
date of original appropriation: 1871 June 1
Water District No. 5
Owner, of Longmont
water source: St Vrain Creek

Culver, Robert
filing date: 1882 June 2
Boulder District Court Judgment Book, Water Decrees, Vol 2, District 5-6, 1869-1896, pg 282
ditch/reservoir: Boulder and White Rock Ditch
date of original appropriation: 1862 June 1
Water District No. 6
Claimant
water source: Boulder Creek

Cushman, A W
filing date: 1882 June 2
Boulder District Court Judgment Book, Water Decrees, Vol 2, District 5-6, 1869-1896, pg 56
ditch/reservoir: South Flat Ditch No. 16
date of original appropriation: 1863 May 15
Water District No. 5
Owner of Longmont
water source: St Vrain Creek

Cushman, A W
filing date: 1882 June 2
Boulder District Court Judgment Book, Water Decrees, Vol 2, District 5-6, 1869-1896, pg 55
ditch/reservoir: South Flat Ditch No. 16
date of original appropriation: 1863 May 15
Water District No. 5
Owner of Longmont
water source: St Vrain Creek

Cushman, A W
filing date: 1882 June 2
Boulder District Court Judgment Book, Water Decrees, Vol 2, District 5-6, 1869-1896, pg 20
ditch/reservoir: Cushman Ditch No. 8
date of original appropriation: 1861 June 20
Water District No. 5
Owner of Longmont
water source: St Vrain Creek

Cushman, A W
filing date: 1882 June 2
Boulder District Court Judgment Book, Water Decrees, Vol 2, District 5-6, 1869-1896, pg 21
ditch/reservoir: Cushman Ditch No. 8
date of original appropriation: 1861 June 20
Water District No. 5
Owner of Longmont
water source: St Vrain Creek

Cushman, Alfred
filing date: 1882 June 2
Boulder District Court Judgment Book, Water Decrees, Vol 2, District 5-6, 1869-1896, pg 55
ditch/reservoir: South Flat Ditch No. 16
date of original appropriation: 1863 May 15
Water District No. 5
Owner of Longmont
water source: St Vrain Creek

Cushman, Alfred
filing date: 1882 June 2
Boulder District Court Judgment Book, Water Decrees, Vol 2, District 5-6, 1869-1896, pg 56
ditch/reservoir: South Flat Ditch No. 16
date of original appropriation: 1863 May 15
Water District No. 5
Owner of Longmont
water source: St Vrain Creek

D

Dailey, Dennis
filing date: 1882 June 2
Boulder District Court Judgment Book, Water Decrees, Vol 2, District 5-6, 1869-1896, pg 205
ditch/reservoir: Godding, Dailey and Plumb Ditch No. 5
date of original appropriation: 1861 Mar 1
Water District No. 6
Owner, of Erie
water source: Boulder Creek

Davidson Ditch Company
filing date: 1882 June 2
Boulder District Court Judgment Book, Water Decrees, Vol 2, District 5-6, 1869-1896, pg 337
ditch/reservoir: Davidson Ditch No. 26
date of original appropriation: 1872 Apr 15
Water District No. 6
Owner, of Valmont
water source: South Boulder Creek

Davidson, Wm A
filing date: 1882 June 2
Boulder District Court Judgment Book, Water Decrees, Vol 2, District 5-6, 1869-1896, pg 309
ditch/reservoir: Dry Creek Ditch No. 7
date of original appropriation: 1863 May 1
Water District No. 6
Owner, of Valmont
water source: South Boulder Creek

Davidson, Wm A
filing date: 1882 June 2
Boulder District Court Judgment Book, Water Decrees, Vol 2, District 5-6, 1869-1896, pg 309
ditch/reservoir: Dry Creek Ditch No. 7
date of original appropriation: 1863 May 1
Water District No. 6
Claimant
water source: South Boulder Creek

Davis, George F
filing date: 1882 Dec 2
Boulder District Court Judgment Book, Water Decrees, Vol 2, District 5-6, 1869-1896, pg 448
ditch/reservoir: Davis Individual Ditch
date of original appropriation: 1874 May 17
Water District No. 5
Owner, of Longmont
water source: St Vrain Creek by the Highland and Davis Lateral Ditches

Davis, Joseph
filing date: 1882 June 2
Boulder District Court Judgment Book, Water Decrees, Vol 2, District 5-6, 1869-1896, pg 123
ditch/reservoir: Davis & Downing Ditch No. 33
date of original appropriation: 1866 Nov 1
Water District No. 5
grist mill owner
water source: St Vrain Creek

Davis, W L
filing date: 1882 June 2
Boulder District Court Judgment Book, Water Decrees, Vol 2, District 5-6, 1869-1896, pg 189
ditch/reservoir: Bonus Ditch No. 6
date of original appropriation: 1861 Mar 30
Water District No. 5
Owner, of Longmont
water source: St Vrain Creek

Davis, W L
filing date: 1882 June 2
Boulder District Court Judgment Book, Water Decrees, Vol 2, District 5-6, 1869-1896, pg 110
ditch/reservoir: Coffin-Davis Ditch No. 31
date of original appropriation: 1866 June 1
Water District No. 5
Owner, of Longmont
water source: St Vrain Creek

Davis, W L
filing date: 1882 June 2
Boulder District Court Judgment Book, Water Decrees, Vol 2, District 5-6, 1869-1896, pg 112
ditch/reservoir: Coffin-Davis Ditch No. 31
date of original appropriation: 1866 June 1
Water District No. 5
Owner, of Longmont
water source: St Vrain Creek

Davis, W L
filing date: 1882 June 2
Boulder District Court Judgment Book, Water Decrees, Vol 2, District 5-6, 1869-1896, pg 191
ditch/reservoir: Bonus Ditch No. 6
date of original appropriation: 1861 Mar 30
Water District No. 5
Owner, of Longmont
water source: St Vrain Creek

DeBacker
filing date: 1882 June 2
Boulder District Court Judgment Book, Water Decrees, Vol 2, District 5-6, 1869-1896, pg 317
ditch/reservoir: Enterprise Ditch No. 12
date of original appropriation: 1865 Feb 1
Water District No. 6
landowner
water source: South Boulder Creek

Delehant, Daniel
filing date: 1882 June 2
Boulder District Court Judgment Book, Water Decrees, Vol 2, District 5-6, 1869-1896, pg 241
ditch/reservoir: Delehant Ditch No. 25
date of original appropriation: 1865 May 1
Water District No. 6
Owner, of Erie
water source: Boulder Creek

Denio, J W & Co
filing date: 1882 June 2
Boulder District Court Judgment Book, Water Decrees, Vol 2, District 5-6, 1869-1896, pg 103
ditch/reservoir: Denio & Taylor Ditch No. 28
date of original appropriation: 1865 July 15
Water District No. 5
Owner, of Longmont
water source: St Vrain Creek

Denio, J W & Co
filing date: 1882 June 2
Boulder District Court Judgment Book, Water Decrees, Vol 2, District 5-6, 1869-1896, pg 105
ditch/reservoir: Denio & Taylor Ditch No. 28
date of original appropriation: 1865 July 15
Water District No. 5
Owner, of Longmont
water source: St Vrain Creek

Derwood, Alex
filing date: 1882 June 2
Boulder District Court Judgment Book, Water Decrees, Vol 2, District 5-6, 1869-1896, pg 223
ditch/reservoir: Green Ditch No. 13
date of original appropriation: 1862 Sept 15
Water District No. 6
Owner
water source: Boulder Creek

Dewey, William
filing date: 1882 June 1
Boulder District Court Judgment Book, Water Decrees, Vol 2, District 5-6, 1869-1896, pg 2
ditch/reservoir: Hayseed Ditch No. 1
date of original appropriation: 1860 Jan 1
Water District No. 5
Owner of Longmont
water source: St Vrain Creek

Dewey, Wm
filing date: 1882 June 1
Boulder District Court Judgment Book, Water Decrees, Vol 2, District 5-6, 1869-1896, pg 3
ditch/reservoir: Hayseed Ditch No. 1
date of original appropriation: 1860 Jan 1
Water District No. 5
Owner of Longmont
water source: St Vrain Creek

Dickens, William H
filing date: 1902 Oct 2
Boulder District Court Judgment Book, Water Decrees, Vol 2, District 5-6, 1869-1896, pg 567
ditch/reservoir: William H Dickens Ditch
date of original appropriation: 1882 Nov 1
Water District No. 5
Owner, of Longmont
water source: Dry Creek

Dickens, William H
filing date: 1882 June 2
Boulder District Court Judgment Book, Water Decrees, Vol 2, District 5-6, 1869-1896, pg 35
ditch/reservoir: Dickens Private Ditch No. 12
date of original appropriation: 1862 Apr 15
Water District No. 5
Owner of Longmont
water source: St Vrain Creek

Dickens, William H
filing date: 1882 June 2
Boulder District Court Judgment Book, Water Decrees, Vol 2, District 5-6, 1869-1896, pg 166
ditch/reservoir: Denio & Taylor Extension Ditch No. 69
date of original appropriation: 1875 June 1
Water District No. 5
Owner, of Longmont
water source: St Vrain Creek

Dickens, William H
filing date: 1882 June 2
Boulder District Court Judgment Book, Water Decrees, Vol 2, District 5-6, 1869-1896, pg 165
ditch/reservoir: Denio & Taylor Extension Ditch No. 69
date of original appropriation: 1875 June 1
Water District No. 5
Owner, of Longmont
water source: St Vrain Creek

Dickens, William H
filing date: 1902 Oct 21
Boulder District Court Judgment Book, Water Decrees, Vol 2, District 5-6, 1869-1896, pg 568
ditch/reservoir:
date of original appropriation:
Water District No. 5
Owner
water source:

Dickens, Wm H
filing date: 1882 June 2
Boulder District Court Judgment Book, Water Decrees, Vol 2, District 5-6, 1869-1896, pg 183
ditch/reservoir: Dickens Private Ditch No.2 No. 81
date of original appropriation: 1880 Apr 1
Water District No. 5
Owner, of Longmont
water source: St Vrain Creek

Dickens, Wm H
filing date: 1882 June 2
Boulder District Court Judgment Book, Water Decrees, Vol 2, District 5-6, 1869-1896, pg 184
ditch/reservoir: Dickens Private Ditch No.2 No. 81
date of original appropriation: 1880 Apr 1
Water District No. 5
Owner, of Longmont
water source: St Vrain Creek

Dickens, Wm H
filing date: 1882 June 2
Boulder District Court Judgment Book, Water Decrees, Vol 2, District 5-6, 1869-1896, pg 34
ditch/reservoir: Dickens Private Ditch No. 12 Decree
date of original appropriation: 1862 Apr 15
Water District No. 5
Owner of Longmont
water source: St Vrain Creek

Dickens, Wm H
filing date: 1882 June 2
Boulder District Court Judgment Book, Water Decrees, Vol 2, District 5-6, 1869-1896, pg 15
ditch/reservoir: Beckwith Ditch No. 5
date of original appropriation: 1860 Mar 8
Water District No. 5
Owner of Longmont
water source: St Vrain Creek

Dickson, L H
filing date: 1882 June 2
Boulder District Court Judgment Book, Water Decrees, Vol 2, District 5-6, 1869-1896, pg 66
ditch/reservoir: L H Dickson's Ditch No. 19
date of original appropriation: 1864 Feb 28
Water District No. 5
Owner of Longmont
water source: St Vrain Creek

Dickson, L H
filing date: 1882 June 2
Boulder District Court Judgment Book, Water Decrees, Vol 2, District 5-6, 1869-1896, pg 68
ditch/reservoir: L H Dickson's Ditch No. 19
date of original appropriation: 1864 Feb 28
Water District No. 5
Owner of Longmont
water source: St Vrain Creek

Dickson, L H
filing date: 1882 June 2
Boulder District Court Judgment Book, Water Decrees, Vol 2, District 5-6, 1869-1896, pg 14
ditch/reservoir: Beckwith Ditch No. 5
date of original appropriation: 1860 Mar 8
Water District No. 5
Owner of Longmont
water source: St Vrain Creek

Dickson, L H
filing date: 1882 June 2
Boulder District Court Judgment Book, Water Decrees, Vol 2, District 5-6, 1869-1896, pg 191
ditch/reservoir: Bonus Ditch No. 6
date of original appropriation: 1861 Mar 30
Water District No. 5
Owner, of Longmont
water source: St Vrain Creek

Dickson, L H
filing date: 1882 June 2
Boulder District Court Judgment Book, Water Decrees, Vol 2, District 5-6, 1869-1896, pg 189
ditch/reservoir: Bonus Ditch No. 6
date of original appropriation: 1861 Mar 30
Water District No. 5
Owner, of Longmont
water source: St Vrain Creek

Dodd, Barnett
filing date: 1882 Dec 2
Boulder District Court Judgment Book, Water Decrees, Vol 2, District 5-6, 1869-1896, pg 396
ditch/reservoir: Holland Ditch No. 4
date of original appropriation: 1863 May 1
Water District No. 5
Owner, of NiWot
water source: Left Hand Creek

Dodd, Barnett
filing date: 1882 Dec 2
Boulder District Court Judgment Book, Water Decrees, Vol 2, District 5-6, 1869-1896, pg 394
ditch/reservoir: Holland Ditch No. 4
date of original appropriation: 1863 May 1
Water District No. 5
Owner, of NiWot
water source: Left Hand Creek

Doolittle, J K
filing date: 1882 June 2
Boulder District Court Judgment Book, Water Decrees, Vol 2, District 5-6, 1869-1896, pg 189
ditch/reservoir: Bonus Ditch No. 6
date of original appropriation: 1861 Mar 30
Water District No. 5
Owner, of Longmont
water source: St Vrain Creek

Doolittle, J K
filing date: 1882 June 2
Boulder District Court Judgment Book, Water Decrees, Vol 2, District 5-6, 1869-1896, pg 191
ditch/reservoir: Bonus Ditch No. 6
date of original appropriation: 1861 Mar 30
Water District No. 5
Owner, of Longmont
water source: St Vrain Creek

Doran
filing date: 1882 June 2
Boulder District Court Judgment Book, Water Decrees, Vol 2, District 5-6, 1869-1896, pg 292
ditch/reservoir: McGinn Ditch No. 1
date of original appropriation: 1860 May 1
Water District No. 6
landowner
water source: South Boulder Creek

Downer, S S
filing date: 1892 Apr 30
Boulder District Court Judgment Book, Water Decrees, Vol 2, District 5-6, 1869-1896, pg 492
ditch/reservoir:
date of original appropriation:
Water District No. 5
Judge
water source:

Downer, S S
filing date: 1890 Mar 22
Boulder District Court Judgment Book, Water Decrees, Vol 2, District 5-6, 1869-1896, pg 502
ditch/reservoir:
date of original appropriation:
Water District No. 5
Judge
water source:

Downer, S S
filing date: 1890 Mar 22
Boulder District Court Judgment Book, Water Decrees, Vol 2, District 5-6, 1869-1896, pg 505
ditch/reservoir:
date of original appropriation:
Water District No. 5
Judge
water source:

Downer, S S
filing date: 1894 Apr 29
Boulder District Court Judgment Book, Water Decrees, Vol 2, District 5-6, 1869-1896, pg 520
ditch/reservoir: Willis Ditch
date of original appropriation: 1870 May 5
Water District No. 6
Judge
water source: Coal Creek

Downer, S S
filing date: 1894 Apr 28
Boulder District Court Judgment Book, Water Decrees, Vol 2, District 5-6, 1869-1896, pg 522
ditch/reservoir: Eggleston Reservoir No. 2
date of original appropriation: 1870 May 5
Water District No. 6
Judge
water source: Coal Creek

Downer, S S
filing date: 1894 May 5
Boulder District Court Judgment Book, Water Decrees, Vol 2, District 5-6, 1869-1896, pg 528
ditch/reservoir: Moffat Ditch
date of original appropriation: 1889 Feb 4
Water District No. 6
Judge
water source: Coal Creek

Downer, S S
filing date: 1894 Apr 28
Boulder District Court Judgment Book, Water Decrees, Vol 2, District 5-6, 1869-1896, pg 525
ditch/reservoir: Eggleston Reservoir No. 4
date of original appropriation: 1879 Oct 1
Water District No. 6
Judge
water source: Coal Creek

Downer, S S
filing date: 1894 Apr 28
Boulder District Court Judgment Book, Water Decrees, Vol 2, District 5-6, 1869-1896, pg 531
ditch/reservoir: Kerr Ditch No. 1 and No. 2
date of original appropriation: 1861 Apr 15
Water District No. 6
Judge
water source: Coal Creek

Duffy
filing date: 1882 June 2
Boulder District Court Judgment Book, Water Decrees, Vol 2, District 5-6, 1869-1896, pg 317
ditch/reservoir: Enterprise Ditch No. 12
date of original appropriation: 1865 Feb 1
Water District No. 6
landowner
water source: South Boulder Creek

Duncan, Elisha
filing date: 1882 June 1
Boulder District Court Judgment Book, Water Decrees, Vol 2, District 5-6, 1869-1896, pg 3
ditch/reservoir: Hayseed Ditch No. 1
date of original appropriation: 1860 Jan 1
Water District No. 5
Owner, of Longmont
water source: St Vrain Creek

Duncan, Elisha
filing date: 1882 June 1
Boulder District Court Judgment Book, Water Decrees, Vol 2, District 5-6, 1869-1896, pg 2
ditch/reservoir: Hayseed Ditch No. 1
date of original appropriation: 1860 Jan 1
Water District No. 5
Owner of Longmont
water source: St Vrain Creek

Duncan, Sebastian
filing date: 1882 June 2
Boulder District Court Judgment Book, Water Decrees, Vol 2, District 5-6, 1869-1896, pg 44
ditch/reservoir: Smead Ditch No. 13
date of original appropriation: 1862 Oct 1
Water District No. 5
Owner, of Longmont
water source: St Vrain Creek

Duncan, Sebastian
filing date: 1882 June 2
Boulder District Court Judgment Book, Water Decrees, Vol 2, District 5-6, 1869-1896, pg 43
ditch/reservoir: Smead Ditch No. 13
date of original appropriation: 1862 Oct 1
Water District No. 5
Owner, of Longmont
water source: St Vrain Creek

Dunn, Andrew
filing date: 1882 June 2
Boulder District Court Judgment Book, Water Decrees, Vol 2, District 5-6, 1869-1896, pg 295
ditch/reservoir: Schearer Ditch No. 2
date of original appropriation: 1860 June 1
Water District No. 6
Owner, of Boulder
water source: South Boulder Creek

Dunn, P
filing date: 1882 June 2
Boulder District Court Judgment Book, Water Decrees, Vol 2, District 5-6, 1869-1896, pg 295
ditch/reservoir: Schearer Ditch No. 2
date of original appropriation: 1860 June 1
Water District No. 6
landowner
water source: South Boulder Creek

E

East Boulder Ditch Company
filing date: 1882 June 2
Boulder District Court Judgment Book, Water Decrees, Vol 2, District 5-6, 1869-1896, pg 300
ditch/reservoir: East Boulder Ditch No. 4
date of original appropriation: 1862 Apr 1
Water District No. 6
Owner, of Boulder
water source: South Boulder Creek

Eggleston, Geo W
filing date: 1882 June 2
Boulder District Court Judgment Book, Water Decrees, Vol 2, District 5-6, 1869-1896, pg 348
ditch/reservoir: Autry and Eggleston Ditch No. 1
date of original appropriation: 1860 June 1
Water District No. 6
Owner, of Langford
water source: Coal Creek

Eggleston, Geo W
filing date: 1882 June 2
Boulder District Court Judgment Book, Water Decrees, Vol 2, District 5-6, 1869-1896, pg 353
ditch/reservoir: Eggleston No. 2 Ditch No. 3
date of original appropriation: 1862 May 1
Water District No. 6
Owner, of Langford
water source: Coal Creek

Eggleston, Geo W
filing date: 1882 June 2
Boulder District Court Judgment Book, Water Decrees, Vol 2, District 5-6, 1869-1896, pg 358
ditch/reservoir: Eggleston No.1 Ditch No. 5
date of original appropriation: 1869 Oct 1
Water District No. 6
Owner, of Langford
water source: Coal Creek

Eggleston, Geo W
filing date: 1894 Apr 28
Boulder District Court Judgment Book, Water Decrees, Vol 2, District 5-6, 1869-1896, pg 520
ditch/reservoir: Eggleston Reservoir No. 2
date of original appropriation: 1870 May 5
Water District No. 6
Owner, of Louisville
water source: Coal Creek

Eggleston, Geo W
filing date: 1894 Apr 28
Boulder District Court Judgment Book, Water Decrees, Vol 2, District 5-6, 1869-1896, pg 523
ditch/reservoir: Eggleston Reservoir No. 4
date of original appropriation: 1879 Oct 1
Water District No. 6
Owner, of Louisville
water source: Coal Creek

Elsberry, Code
filing date: 1882 June 2
Boulder District Court Judgment Book, Water Decrees, Vol 2, District 5-6, 1869-1896, pg 282
ditch/reservoir: Boulder and White Rock Ditch
date of original appropriation: 1862 June 1
Water District No. 6
original builder of Dry Creek Ditch, 1 June 1862
water source: Boulder Creek

Emmons, A J
filing date: 1882 June 2
Boulder District Court Judgment Book, Water Decrees, Vol 2, District 5-6, 1869-1896, pg 205
ditch/reservoir: Godding, Dailey and Plumb Ditch No. 5
date of original appropriation: 1861 Mar 1
Water District No. 6
Owner, of Longmont
water source: Boulder Creek

Emmons, A J
filing date: 1882 June 2
Boulder District Court Judgment Book, Water Decrees, Vol 2, District 5-6, 1869-1896, pg 231
ditch/reservoir: Smith and Emmons Ditch No. 18
date of original appropriation: 1863 June 1
Water District No. 6
Owner, of Longmont
water source: Boulder Creek

English, W H
filing date: 1894 Apr 28
Boulder District Court Judgment Book, Water Decrees, Vol 2, District 5-6, 1869-1896, pg 523
ditch/reservoir: Eggleston Reservoir No. 4
date of original appropriation: 1879 Oct 1
Water District No. 6
Owner, of Louisville
water source: Coal Creek

Enterprise Irrigating Ditch Company
filing date: 1882 June 2
Boulder District Court Judgment Book, Water Decrees, Vol 2, District 5-6, 1869-1896, pg 317
ditch/reservoir: Enterprise Ditch No. 12
date of original appropriation: 1865 Feb 1
Water District No. 6
Owner, of Boulder
water source: South Boulder Creek

Esteb, Ralph E
filing date: 1902 Oct 21
Boulder District Court Judgment Book, Water Decrees, Vol 2, District 5-6, 1869-1896, pg 568
ditch/reservoir:
date of original appropriation:
Water District No. 5
Attorney
water source:

F

Farmers Ditch Company
filing date: 1882 June 2
Boulder District Court Judgment Book, Water Decrees, Vol 2, District 5-6, 1869-1896, pg 226
ditch/reservoir: Farmers Ditch No. 14
date of original appropriation: 1862 Oct 1
Water District No. 6
Owner, of Boulder
water source: Boulder Creek

Farmers Ditch Company
filing date: 1882 Dec 2
Boulder District Court Judgment Book, Water Decrees, Vol 2, District 5-6, 1869-1896, pg 401
ditch/reservoir: Farmers Ditch No. 6
date of original appropriation: 1863 June 1
Water District No. 5
Owner, of Longmont
water source: Left Hand Creek

Field, I N
filing date: 1882 June 2
Boulder District Court Judgment Book, Water Decrees, Vol 2, District 5-6, 1869-1896, pg 223
ditch/reservoir: Green Ditch No. 13
date of original appropriation: 1862 Sept 15
Water District No. 6
Owner
water source: Boulder Creek

Field, Thomas
filing date: 1882 June 2
Boulder District Court Judgment Book, Water Decrees, Vol 2, District 5-6, 1869-1896, pg 314
ditch/reservoir: Andrews and Farwell Ditch No. 11
date of original appropriation: 1864 June 1
Water District No. 6
Owner, of Denver
water source: South Boulder Creek

G

Gamble, Harry P
filing date: 1900 Dec 19
Boulder District Court Judgment Book, Water Decrees, Vol 2, District 5-6, 1869-1896, pg 553
ditch/reservoir: Low Ditch
date of original appropriation:
Water District No. 6
Attorney
water source: Coal Creek

Gamble, Harry P
filing date: 1903 Sept 15
Boulder District Court Judgment Book, Water Decrees, Vol 2, District 5-6, 1869-1896, pg 569
ditch/reservoir: Low Ditch
date of original appropriation:
Water District No. 6
Attorney
water source: Coal Creek

Garrigues, James E
filing date: 1903 July 13
Boulder District Court Judgment Book, Water Decrees, Vol 2, District 5-6, 1869-1896, pg 507
ditch/reservoir:
date of original appropriation:
Water District No. 5
Judge
water source:

Garrigues, James E
filing date: 1904 Apr 19
Boulder District Court Judgment Book, Water Decrees, Vol 2, District 5-6, 1869-1896, pg 508
ditch/reservoir:
date of original appropriation:
Water District No. 5
Judge
water source:

Goodhue, Abner C
filing date: 1882 June 2
Boulder District Court Judgment Book, Water Decrees, Vol 2, District 5-6, 1869-1896, pg 342
ditch/reservoir: Goodhue Ditch and Reservoir No. 29
date of original appropriation: 1873 June 1
Water District No. 6
Owner, of Louisville
water source: South Boulder Creek

Gooding, T F
filing date: 1882 June 2
Boulder District Court Judgment Book, Water Decrees, Vol 2, District 5-6, 1869-1896, pg 244
ditch/reservoir: Highland Ditch Southside No. 28
date of original appropriation: 1865 June 1
Water District No. 6
Owner, of Longmont
water source: Boulder Creek

Goss, John W
filing date: 1882 June 2
Boulder District Court Judgment Book, Water Decrees, Vol 2, District 5-6, 1869-1896, pg 94
ditch/reservoir: Goss Private Ditch 1 No. 25
date of original appropriation: 1865 June 30
Water District No. 5
Owner, of Longmont
water source: St Vrain Creek

Goss, John W
filing date: 1882 June 2
Boulder District Court Judgment Book, Water Decrees, Vol 2, District 5-6, 1869-1896, pg 47
ditch/reservoir: Clough Tribute (Private) Ditch No. 14
date of original appropriation: 1863 Apr 15
Water District No. 5
land owner
water source: St Vrain Creek

Goss, John W
filing date: 1882 June 2
Boulder District Court Judgment Book, Water Decrees, Vol 2, District 5-6, 1869-1896, pg 96
ditch/reservoir: Goss Private Ditch 1 No. 25
date of original appropriation: 1865 June 30
Water District No. 5
land irrigated
water source: St Vrain Creek

Goss, John W
filing date: 1882 June 2
Boulder District Court Judgment Book, Water Decrees, Vol 2, District 5-6, 1869-1896, pg 95
ditch/reservoir: Goss Private Ditch 1 No. 25
date of original appropriation: 1865 June 30
Water District No. 5
Owner, of Longmont
water source: St Vrain Creek

Goss, John W
filing date: 1882 June 2
Boulder District Court Judgment Book, Water Decrees, Vol 2, District 5-6, 1869-1896, pg 97
ditch/reservoir: Goss Private Ditch 2 No. 25
date of original appropriation: 1865 June 30
Water District No. 5
Owner, of Longmont
water source: St Vrain Creek

Gould, J F
filing date: 1882 Dec 2
Boulder District Court Judgment Book, Water Decrees, Vol 2, District 5-6, 1869-1896, pg 386
ditch/reservoir: Hornbaker Ditch No. 2
date of original appropriation: 1861 May 15
Water District No. 5
Owner, of NiWot
water source: Left Hand Creek

Gould, J F
filing date: 1882 Dec 2
Boulder District Court Judgment Book, Water Decrees, Vol 2, District 5-6, 1869-1896, pg 388
ditch/reservoir: Hornbaker Ditch No. 2
date of original appropriation: 1861 May 15
Water District No. 5
Owner, of NiWot
water source: Left Hand Creek

Gould, Jerome F
filing date: 1882 Dec 2
Boulder District Court Judgment Book, Water Decrees, Vol 2, District 5-6, 1869-1896, pg 389
ditch/reservoir: Williamson and Cavey Ditch No. 3
date of original appropriation: 1862 May 31
Water District No. 5
Owner, of NiWot
water source: Left Hand Creek

Gould, Jerome F
filing date: 1882 Dec 2
Boulder District Court Judgment Book, Water Decrees, Vol 2, District 5-6, 1869-1896, pg 392
ditch/reservoir: Williamson and Cavey Ditch No. 3
date of original appropriation: 1862 May 31
Water District No. 5
Owner, of NiWot
water source: Left Hand Creek

Goyn, Richard
filing date: 1882 Dec 2
Boulder District Court Judgment Book, Water Decrees, Vol 2, District 5-6, 1869-1896, pg 428
ditch/reservoir: Johnson Ditch No. 25
date of original appropriation: 1873 Apr 1
Water District No. 5
Owner, of NiWot
water source: Left Hand Creek

Goyn, Richard
filing date: 1882 Dec 2
Boulder District Court Judgment Book, Water Decrees, Vol 2, District 5-6, 1869-1896, pg 460
ditch/reservoir: Left Hand Reservoir No. 3
date of original appropriation: 1877 Apr 15
Water District No. 5
Owner, of NiWot
water source: Left Hand Creek through the Farmers, Baum & Goyn Ditches

Goyn, Richard
filing date: 1882 Dec 2
Boulder District Court Judgment Book, Water Decrees, Vol 2, District 5-6, 1869-1896, pg 401
ditch/reservoir: Farmers Ditch No. 6
date of original appropriation: 1863 June 1
Water District No. 5
Owner, of Longmont
water source: Left Hand Creek

Goyn, Richard
filing date: 1882 Dec 2
Boulder District Court Judgment Book, Water Decrees, Vol 2, District 5-6, 1869-1896, pg 429
ditch/reservoir: Johnson Ditch No. 25
date of original appropriation: 1873 Apr 1
Water District No. 5
Owner, of NiWot
water source: Left Hand Creek

Goyn, Richard
filing date: 1883 Feb 12
Boulder District Court Judgment Book, Water Decrees, Vol 2, District 5-6, 1869-1896, pg 461
ditch/reservoir: Left Hand Reservoir No. 3
date of original appropriation: 1877 Apr 15
Water District No. 5
Owner, of NiWot
water source: Left Hand Creek through the Farmers, Baum & Goyn Ditches

Goyn, Richard
filing date: 1882 Dec 2
Boulder District Court Judgment Book, Water Decrees, Vol 2, District 5-6, 1869-1896, pg 406
ditch/reservoir: Baum and Goyn Ditch No. 7
date of original appropriation: 1863 Sept 26
Water District No. 5
Owner, of NiWot
water source: Left Hand Creek

Goyn, Richard
filing date: 1882 Dec 2
Boulder District Court Judgment Book, Water Decrees, Vol 2, District 5-6, 1869-1896, pg 407
ditch/reservoir: Baum and Goyn Ditch No. 7
date of original appropriation: 1863 Sept 26
Water District No. 5
Owner, of NiWot
water source: Left Hand Creek

Graham
filing date: 1882 June 2
Boulder District Court Judgment Book, Water Decrees, Vol 2, District 5-6, 1869-1896, pg 252
ditch/reservoir: Boulder and Weld County Ditch No. 33
date of original appropriation: 1871 May 1
Water District No. 6
farm owner
water source: Boulder Creek

Green, Geo
filing date: 1882 June 2
Boulder District Court Judgment Book, Water Decrees, Vol 2, District 5-6, 1869-1896, pg 252
ditch/reservoir: Boulder and Weld County Ditch No. 33
date of original appropriation: 1871 May 1
Water District No. 6
farm owner
water source: Boulder Creek

Green, Geo C
filing date: 1882 June 2
Boulder District Court Judgment Book, Water Decrees, Vol 2, District 5-6, 1869-1896, pg 223
ditch/reservoir: Green Ditch No. 13
date of original appropriation: 1862 Sept 15
Water District No. 6
Owner
water source: Boulder Creek

Greub, Rudolf
filing date: 1882 Dec 2
Boulder District Court Judgment Book, Water Decrees, Vol 2, District 5-6, 1869-1896, pg 388
ditch/reservoir: Hornbaker Ditch No. 2
date of original appropriation: 1861 May 15
Water District No. 5
Owner, of NiWot
water source: Left Hand Creek

Greub, Rudolf
filing date: 1882 Dec 2
Boulder District Court Judgment Book, Water Decrees, Vol 2, District 5-6, 1869-1896, pg 387
ditch/reservoir: Hornbaker Ditch No. 2
date of original appropriation: 1861 May 15
Water District No. 5
landowner
water source: Left Hand Creek

Greub, Rudolf
filing date: 1882 Dec 2
Boulder District Court Judgment Book, Water Decrees, Vol 2, District 5-6, 1869-1896, pg 386
ditch/reservoir: Hornbaker Ditch No. 2
date of original appropriation: 1861 May 15
Water District No. 5
Owner, of NiWot
water source: Left Hand Creek

Grill, M A Mrs
filing date: 1882 Dec 2
Boulder District Court Judgment Book, Water Decrees, Vol 2, District 5-6, 1869-1896, pg 394
ditch/reservoir: Holland Ditch No. 4
date of original appropriation: 1863 May 1
Water District No. 5
Owner, of NiWot
water source: Left Hand Creek

Grill, M A Mrs
filing date: 1882 Dec 2
Boulder District Court Judgment Book, Water Decrees, Vol 2, District 5-6, 1869-1896, pg 396
ditch/reservoir: Holland Ditch No. 4
date of original appropriation: 1863 May 1
Water District No. 5
Owner, of NiWot
water source: Left Hand Creek

Groesbeck
filing date: 1882 June 2
Boulder District Court Judgment Book, Water Decrees, Vol 2, District 5-6, 1869-1896, pg 168
ditch/reservoir: Titus & Goyn Ditch No. 72
date of original appropriation: 1878 Apr 1
Water District No. 5
land owner
water source: St Vrain Creek

Groseclose, Peter
filing date: 1882 June 2
Boulder District Court Judgment Book, Water Decrees, Vol 2, District 5-6, 1869-1896, pg 244
ditch/reservoir: Highland Ditch Southside No. 28
date of original appropriation: 1865 June 1
Water District No. 6
Owner, of Longmont
water source: Boulder Creek

H

Hager, John H
filing date: 1882 June 2
Boulder District Court Judgment Book, Water Decrees, Vol 2, District 5-6, 1869-1896, pg 77
ditch/reservoir: Zweck & Turner Ditch No. 21
date of original appropriation: 1864 June 30
Water District No. 5
Owner
water source: St Vrain Creek

Hager, John H
filing date: 1882 June 2
Boulder District Court Judgment Book, Water Decrees, Vol 2, District 5-6, 1869-1896, pg 78
ditch/reservoir: Zweck & Turner Ditch No. 21
date of original appropriation: 1864 June 30
Water District No. 5
Owner
water source: St Vrain Creek

Hager, John H
filing date: 1882 June 2
Boulder District Court Judgment Book, Water Decrees, Vol 2, District 5-6, 1869-1896, pg 62
ditch/reservoir: Hager's Meadow Ditch No. 18
date of original appropriation: 1864 Jan 1
Water District No. 5
Owner
water source: St Vrain Creek

Hager, John H
filing date: 1882 June 2
Boulder District Court Judgment Book, Water Decrees, Vol 2, District 5-6, 1869-1896, pg 61
ditch/reservoir: Hager's Meadow Ditch No. 18
date of original appropriation: 1864 Jan 1
Water District No. 5
Owner of Longmont
water source: St Vrain Creek

Hager, John Henry
filing date: 1882 June 2
Boulder District Court Judgment Book, Water Decrees, Vol 2, District 5-6, 1869-1896, pg 144
ditch/reservoir: Bear & McCory Ditch No. 45
date of original appropriation: 1871 June 1
Water District No. 5
Owner, of Longmont
water source: St Vrain Creek

Hager, John Henry
filing date: 1882 June 2
Boulder District Court Judgment Book, Water Decrees, Vol 2, District 5-6, 1869-1896, pg 143
ditch/reservoir: Bear & McCory Ditch No. 45
date of original appropriation: 1871 June 1
Water District No. 5
Owner, of Longmont
water source: St Vrain Creek

Hager, Mr
filing date: 1882 June 2
Boulder District Court Judgment Book, Water Decrees, Vol 2, District 5-6, 1869-1896, pg 88
ditch/reservoir: Ni-Wot Ditch No. 24
date of original appropriation: 1865 June 1
Water District No. 5
barns mentioned
water source: St Vrain Creek

Hager, Mr
filing date: 1882 June 2
Boulder District Court Judgment Book, Water Decrees, Vol 2, District 5-6, 1869-1896, pg 89
ditch/reservoir: Ni-Wot Ditch No. 24
date of original appropriation: 1865 June 1
Water District No. 5
barns mentioned
water source: St Vrain Creek

Hahn
filing date: 1882 June 2
Boulder District Court Judgment Book, Water Decrees, Vol 2, District 5-6, 1869-1896, pg 283
ditch/reservoir: Boulder and White Rock Ditch
date of original appropriation: 1862 June 1
Water District No. 6
Claimant
water source: Boulder Creek

Hahn, S B
filing date: 1882 June 2
Boulder District Court Judgment Book, Water Decrees, Vol 2, District 5-6, 1869-1896, pg 276
ditch/reservoir: Wellman, Nichols and Hahn Ditch No. 11
date of original appropriation: 1862 June 1
Water District No. 6
Owner, of Central City
water source: Boulder Creek

Hahn, S B
filing date: 1882 June 2
Boulder District Court Judgment Book, Water Decrees, Vol 2, District 5-6, 1869-1896, pg 282
ditch/reservoir: Boulder and White Rock Ditch
date of original appropriation: 1862 June 1
Water District No. 6
Claimant
water source: Boulder Creek

Hake
filing date: 1882 June 2
Boulder District Court Judgment Book, Water Decrees, Vol 2, District 5-6, 1869-1896, pg 317
ditch/reservoir: Enterprise Ditch No. 12
date of original appropriation: 1865 Feb 1
Water District No. 6
landowner
water source: South Boulder Creek

Hake, Levi
filing date: 1882 June 2
Boulder District Court Judgment Book, Water Decrees, Vol 2, District 5-6, 1869-1896, pg 326
ditch/reservoir: Central Ditch No. 16
date of original appropriation: 1866 May 15
Water District No. 6
Owner, of Boulder
water source: South Boulder Creek

Hake, Levi
filing date: 1882 June 2
Boulder District Court Judgment Book, Water Decrees, Vol 2, District 5-6, 1869-1896, pg 331
ditch/reservoir: South Ditch No. 19
date of original appropriation: 1866 June 1
Water District No. 6
Owner, of Boulder
water source: South Boulder Creek

Hake, William C
filing date: 1882 June 2
Boulder District Court Judgment Book, Water Decrees, Vol 2, District 5-6, 1869-1896, pg 351
ditch/reservoir: William C Hake Ditch No. 2
date of original appropriation: 1861 June 1
Water District No. 6
Owner, of Louisville
water source: Coal Creek

Halderman, Grant E
filing date: 1902 Oct 2
Boulder District Court Judgment Book, Water Decrees, Vol 2, District 5-6, 1869-1896, pg 566
ditch/reservoir: Peck & Metcalf Ditch
date of original appropriation: 1867 May 15
Water District No. 5
Referee
water source: Dry Creek

Halderman, Grant E
filing date: 1902 Oct 21
Boulder District Court Judgment Book, Water Decrees, Vol 2, District 5-6, 1869-1896, pg 568
ditch/reservoir:
date of original appropriation:
Water District No. 5
Referee
water source:

Halderman, Grant E
filing date: 1903 July 13
Boulder District Court Judgment Book, Water Decrees, Vol 2, District 5-6, 1869-1896, pg 506
ditch/reservoir:
date of original appropriation:
Water District No. 5
Referee
water source:

Hamlin, Charles P
filing date: 1882 June 2
Boulder District Court Judgment Book, Water Decrees, Vol 2, District 5-6, 1869-1896, pg 282
ditch/reservoir: Boulder and White Rock Ditch
date of original appropriation: 1862 June 1
Water District No. 6
original builder of Dry Creek Ditch, 1 June 1862
water source: Boulder Creek

Hanna
filing date: 1882 June 2
Boulder District Court Judgment Book, Water Decrees, Vol 2, District 5-6, 1869-1896, pg 307
ditch/reservoir: Cottonwood No. 2 Ditch No. 6
date of original appropriation: 1863 Apr 15
Water District No. 6
landowner
water source: South Boulder Creek

Harden, Elizabeth
filing date: 1882 June 2
Boulder District Court Judgment Book, Water Decrees, Vol 2, District 5-6, 1869-1896, pg 275
ditch/reservoir: Harden Ditch
date of original appropriation: 1862 June 1
Water District No. 6
Heirs and Owners, of Boulder
water source: Boulder Creek

Harden, Elizabeth
filing date: 1882 June 2
Boulder District Court Judgment Book, Water Decrees, Vol 2, District 5-6, 1869-1896, pg 278
ditch/reservoir: McCarty Ditch No. 11
date of original appropriation: 1862 June 1
Water District No. 6
Heirs and Owners, of Boulder
water source: Boulder Creek

Harden, Elizabeth
filing date: 1882 June 2
Boulder District Court Judgment Book, Water Decrees, Vol 2, District 5-6, 1869-1896, pg 272
ditch/reservoir: Dry Creek Ditch No. 11, Claim of Mary S Stoddard et al
date of original appropriation: 1862 June 1
Water District No. 6
Heirs and Owners, of Boulder
water source: Boulder Creek

Harden, Elizabeth
filing date: 1882 June 2
Boulder District Court Judgment Book, Water Decrees, Vol 2, District 5-6, 1869-1896, pg 282
ditch/reservoir: Boulder and White Rock Ditch
date of original appropriation: 1862 June 1
Water District No. 6
Heirs and Claimants
water source: Boulder Creek

Harden, Elizabeth
filing date: 1882 June 2
Boulder District Court Judgment Book, Water Decrees, Vol 2, District 5-6, 1869-1896, pg 283
ditch/reservoir: Boulder and White Rock Ditch
date of original appropriation: 1862 June 1
Water District No. 6
Heirs and Claimants
water source: Boulder Creek

Harris, George
filing date: 1894 Apr 29
Boulder District Court Judgment Book, Water Decrees, Vol 2, District 5-6, 1869-1896, pg 518
ditch/reservoir: Willis Ditch
date of original appropriation: 1870 May 5
Water District No. 6
Owner, of Louisville
water source: Coal Creek

Harris, Thomas
filing date: 1894 Apr 29
Boulder District Court Judgment Book, Water Decrees, Vol 2, District 5-6, 1869-1896, pg 518
ditch/reservoir: Willis Ditch
date of original appropriation: 1870 May 5
Water District No. 6
Owner, of Louisville
water source: Coal Creek

Highland Ditch Company
filing date: 1882 June 2
Boulder District Court Judgment Book, Water Decrees, Vol 2, District 5-6, 1869-1896, pg 148
ditch/reservoir: Highland Ditch No. 46
date of original appropriation: 1871 Nov 30
Water District No. 5
Owner, of Longmont
water source: St Vrain Creek

Highland Ditch Company
filing date: 1882 June 2
Boulder District Court Judgment Book, Water Decrees, Vol 2, District 5-6, 1869-1896, pg 146
ditch/reservoir: Highland Ditch No. 46
date of original appropriation: 1871 Nov 30
Water District No. 5
Owner, of Longmont
water source: St Vrain Creek

Highland Ditch Company
filing date: 1882 June 2
Boulder District Court Judgment Book, Water Decrees, Vol 2, District 5-6, 1869-1896, pg 381
ditch/reservoir: Highland Ditch No. 46 Amended
date of original appropriation: 1871 Nov 30
Water District No. 5
Owner, of Longmont
water source: St Vrain Creek

Highland Reservoir and Ditch Company
filing date: 1883 Feb 21
Boulder District Court Judgment Book, Water Decrees, Vol 2, District 5-6, 1869-1896, pg 480
ditch/reservoir: Highland Reservoir No. 3 No. 8
date of original appropriation: 1881 Nov 15
Water District No. 5
Owner, of Longmont
water source: St Vrain Creek

Highland Reservoir and Ditch Company
filing date: 1883 Feb 21
Boulder District Court Judgment Book, Water Decrees, Vol 2, District 5-6, 1869-1896, pg 478
ditch/reservoir: Highland Reservoir No. 2 No. 8
date of original appropriation: 1881 Nov 15
Water District No. 5
Owner, of Longmont
water source: St Vrain Creek

Highland Reservoir and Ditch Company
filing date: 1883 Feb 21
Boulder District Court Judgment Book, Water Decrees, Vol 2, District 5-6, 1869-1896, pg 473
ditch/reservoir: Highland Reservoir No. 1 No. 6
date of original appropriation: 1879 Nov 15
Water District No. 5
Owner, of Longmont
water source: St Vrain Creek by the Highland Ditch

Highland Reservoir and Ditch Company
filing date: 1883 Feb 21
Boulder District Court Judgment Book, Water Decrees, Vol 2, District 5-6, 1869-1896, pg 472
ditch/reservoir: Highland Reservoir No. 1 No. 6
date of original appropriation: 1879 Nov 15
Water District No. 5
Owner, of Longmont
water source: St Vrain Creek by the Highland Ditch

Highland Reservoir and Ditch Company
filing date: 1883 Feb 21
Boulder District Court Judgment Book, Water Decrees, Vol 2, District 5-6, 1869-1896, pg 479
ditch/reservoir: Highland Reservoir No. 3 No. 8
date of original appropriation: 1881 Nov 15
Water District No. 5
Owner, of Longmont
water source: St Vrain Creek

Highland Reservoir and Ditch Company
filing date: 1883 Feb 21
Boulder District Court Judgment Book, Water Decrees, Vol 2, District 5-6, 1869-1896, pg 477
ditch/reservoir: Highland Reservoir No. 2 No. 8
date of original appropriation: 1881 Nov 15
Water District No. 5
Owner, of Longmont
water source: St Vrain Creek

Hinman, Merritt L
filing date: 1882 Dec 2
Boulder District Court Judgment Book, Water Decrees, Vol 2, District 5-6, 1869-1896, pg 409
ditch/reservoir: Bader No. 1 Ditch No. 8
date of original appropriation: 1864 May 1
Water District No. 5
Owner, of NiWot
water source: Left Hand Creek

Hinman, Merritt L
filing date: 1882 Dec 2
Boulder District Court Judgment Book, Water Decrees, Vol 2, District 5-6, 1869-1896, pg 410
ditch/reservoir: Bader No. 1 Ditch No. 8
date of original appropriation: 1864 May 1
Water District No. 5
Owner, of NiWot
water source: Left Hand Creek

Hinman, P M
filing date: 1882 Dec 2
Boulder District Court Judgment Book, Water Decrees, Vol 2, District 5-6, 1869-1896, pg 388
ditch/reservoir: Hornbaker Ditch No. 2
date of original appropriation: 1861 May 15
Water District No. 5
Owner, of NiWot
water source: Left Hand Creek

Hinman, P M
filing date: 1882 Dec 2
Boulder District Court Judgment Book, Water Decrees, Vol 2, District 5-6, 1869-1896, pg 386
ditch/reservoir: Hornbaker Ditch No. 2
date of original appropriation: 1861 May 15
Water District No. 5
Owner, of NiWot
water source: Left Hand Creek

Hinman, P M
filing date: 1882 Dec 2
Boulder District Court Judgment Book, Water Decrees, Vol 2, District 5-6, 1869-1896, pg 401
ditch/reservoir: Farmers Ditch No. 6
date of original appropriation: 1863 June 1
Water District No. 5
Owner, of Longmont
water source: Left Hand Creek

Hinman, P M
filing date: 1883 Feb 12
Boulder District Court Judgment Book, Water Decrees, Vol 2, District 5-6, 1869-1896, pg 461
ditch/reservoir: Left Hand Reservoir No. 3
date of original appropriation: 1877 Apr 15
Water District No. 5
Owner, of NiWot
water source: Left Hand Creek through the Farmers, Baum & Goyn Ditches

Hinman, P M
filing date: 1882 Dec 2
Boulder District Court Judgment Book, Water Decrees, Vol 2, District 5-6, 1869-1896, pg 460
ditch/reservoir: Left Hand Reservoir No. 3
date of original appropriation: 1877 Apr 15
Water District No. 5
Owner, of NiWot
water source: Left Hand Creek through the Farmers, Baum & Goyn Ditches

Hogan, J
filing date: 1882 June 2
Boulder District Court Judgment Book, Water Decrees, Vol 2, District 5-6, 1869-1896, pg 312
ditch/reservoir: Dry Creek No. 2 Ditch No. 9
date of original appropriation: 1864 May 1
Water District No. 6
Owner, of Boulder
water source: South Boulder Creek

Holland, Granville
filing date: 1882 Dec 2
Boulder District Court Judgment Book, Water Decrees, Vol 2, District 5-6, 1869-1896, pg 396
ditch/reservoir: Holland Ditch No. 4
date of original appropriation: 1863 May 1
Water District No. 5
Owner, of NiWot
water source: Left Hand Creek

Holland, Granville
filing date: 1882 Dec 2
Boulder District Court Judgment Book, Water Decrees, Vol 2, District 5-6, 1869-1896, pg 394
ditch/reservoir: Holland Ditch No. 4
date of original appropriation: 1863 May 1
Water District No. 5
Owner, of NiWot
water source: Left Hand Creek

Hornbaker, H H
filing date: 1882 Dec 2
Boulder District Court Judgment Book, Water Decrees, Vol 2, District 5-6, 1869-1896, pg 386
ditch/reservoir: Hornbaker Ditch No. 2
date of original appropriation: 1861 May 15
Water District No. 5
Owner, of NiWot
water source: Left Hand Creek

Hornbaker, H H
filing date: 1882 Dec 2
Boulder District Court Judgment Book, Water Decrees, Vol 2, District 5-6, 1869-1896, pg 388
ditch/reservoir: Hornbaker Ditch No. 2
date of original appropriation: 1861 May 15
Water District No. 5
Owner, of NiWot
water source: Left Hand Creek

Hornbaker, H H
filing date: 1883 Feb 12
Boulder District Court Judgment Book, Water Decrees, Vol 2, District 5-6, 1869-1896, pg 461
ditch/reservoir: Left Hand Reservoir No. 3
date of original appropriation: 1877 Apr 15
Water District No. 5
Owner, of NiWot
water source: Left Hand Creek through the Farmers, Baum & Goyn Ditches

Hornbaker, H H
filing date: 1882 Dec 2
Boulder District Court Judgment Book, Water Decrees, Vol 2, District 5-6, 1869-1896, pg 460
ditch/reservoir: Left Hand Reservoir No. 3
date of original appropriation: 1877 Apr 15
Water District No. 5
Owner, of NiWot
water source: Left Hand Creek through the Farmers, Baum & Goyn Ditches

Hornbaker, Henry
filing date: 1882 Dec 2
Boulder District Court Judgment Book, Water Decrees, Vol 2, District 5-6, 1869-1896, pg 383
ditch/reservoir: Cochran Ditch No. 1
date of original appropriation: 1860 Sept 1
Water District No. 5
Owner, of NiWot
water source: Left Hand Creek

Hornbaker, Henry
filing date: 1882 Dec 2
Boulder District Court Judgment Book, Water Decrees, Vol 2, District 5-6, 1869-1896, pg 385
ditch/reservoir: Cochran Ditch No. 1
date of original appropriation: 1860 Sept 1
Water District No. 5
Owner, of NiWot
water source: Left Hand Creek

Houck, Robert
filing date: 1882 June 2
Boulder District Court Judgment Book, Water Decrees, Vol 2, District 5-6, 1869-1896, pg 208
ditch/reservoir: Houck No. 2 Ditch No. 6
date of original appropriation: 1861 Apr 1
Water District No. 6
Owner, of Erie
water source: Boulder Creek

Houck, Robert
filing date: 1882 June 2
Boulder District Court Judgment Book, Water Decrees, Vol 2, District 5-6, 1869-1896, pg 229
ditch/reservoir: Houck No. 1 Ditch No. 16
date of original appropriation: 1863 Apr 1
Water District No. 6
Owner, of Erie
water source: Boulder Creek

Howard
filing date: 1882 June 2
Boulder District Court Judgment Book, Water Decrees, Vol 2, District 5-6, 1869-1896, pg 317
ditch/reservoir: Enterprise Ditch No. 12
date of original appropriation: 1865 Feb 1
Water District No. 6
landowner
water source: South Boulder Creek

Howard, N M
filing date: 1882 June 2
Boulder District Court Judgment Book, Water Decrees, Vol 2, District 5-6, 1869-1896, pg 300
ditch/reservoir: East Boulder Ditch No. 4
date of original appropriation: 1862 Apr 1
Water District No. 6
landowner
water source: South Boulder Creek

Howard, N R
filing date: 1882 June 2
Boulder District Court Judgment Book, Water Decrees, Vol 2, District 5-6, 1869-1896, pg 312
ditch/reservoir: Dry Creek No. 2 Ditch No. 9
date of original appropriation: 1864 May 1
Water District No. 6
Owner, of Boulder
water source: South Boulder Creek

Howard, N R
filing date: 1882 June 2
Boulder District Court Judgment Book, Water Decrees, Vol 2, District 5-6, 1869-1896, pg 298
ditch/reservoir: Howard Ditch No. 3
date of original appropriation: 1860 Apr 1
Water District No. 6
Owner, of Boulder
water source: South Boulder Creek

Howard, Nephi
filing date: 1882 June 2
Boulder District Court Judgment Book, Water Decrees, Vol 2, District 5-6, 1869-1896, pg 298
ditch/reservoir: Howard Ditch No. 3
date of original appropriation: 1860 Apr 1
Water District No. 6
landowner
water source: South Boulder Creek

Howell, W R
filing date: 1882 June 2
Boulder District Court Judgment Book, Water Decrees, Vol 2, District 5-6, 1869-1896, pg 210
ditch/reservoir: Jones and Donnelly Ditch No. 7
date of original appropriation: 1860 [1861] May 1
Water District No. 6
Owner, of Erie
water source: Boulder Creek

Howell, William R
filing date: 1882 June 2
Boulder District Court Judgment Book, Water Decrees, Vol 2, District 5-6, 1869-1896, pg 200
ditch/reservoir: Howell Ditch No. 3
date of original appropriation: 1859 Dec 1
Water District No. 6
Owner, of Canfield
water source: Boulder Creek

Howell, Wm R
filing date: 1882 June 2
Boulder District Court Judgment Book, Water Decrees, Vol 2, District 5-6, 1869-1896, pg 247
ditch/reservoir: Leggett Ditch No. 30
date of original appropriation: 1868 May 1 (half constructed by 1 June 1862)
Water District No. 6
Owner, of Erie
water source: Boulder Creek

Howell, Wm R
filing date: 1882 June 2
Boulder District Court Judgment Book, Water Decrees, Vol 2, District 5-6, 1869-1896, pg 239
ditch/reservoir: Howell and Beasley Ditch No. 23
date of original appropriation: 1865 Mar 1
Water District No. 6
Owner, of Canfield
water source: Boulder Creek

Hughes, William
filing date: 1894 Apr 28
Boulder District Court Judgment Book, Water Decrees, Vol 2, District 5-6, 1869-1896, pg 523
ditch/reservoir: Eggleston Reservoir No. 4
date of original appropriation: 1879 Oct 1
Water District No. 6
Owner, of Louisville
water source: Coal Creek

J

Jackson
filing date: 1882 June 2
Boulder District Court Judgment Book, Water Decrees, Vol 2, District 5-6, 1869-1896, pg 317
ditch/reservoir: Enterprise Ditch No. 12
date of original appropriation: 1865 Feb 1
Water District No. 6
landowner
water source: South Boulder Creek

Jacobs, J W
filing date: 1894 Apr 29
Boulder District Court Judgment Book, Water Decrees, Vol 2, District 5-6, 1869-1896, pg 518
ditch/reservoir: Willis Ditch
date of original appropriation: 1870 May 5
Water District No. 6
Owner, of Louisville
water source: Coal Creek

James Ditch Company
filing date: 1882 June 2
Boulder District Court Judgment Book, Water Decrees, Vol 2, District 5-6, 1869-1896, pg 129
ditch/reservoir: James Ditch No. 37
date of original appropriation: 1868 June 30
Water District No. 5
Owner, of Longmont
water source: St Vrain Creek

James Ditch Company
filing date: 1882 June 2
Boulder District Court Judgment Book, Water Decrees, Vol 2, District 5-6, 1869-1896, pg 127
ditch/reservoir: James Ditch No. 37
date of original appropriation: 1868 June 30
Water District No. 5
Owner, of Longmont
water source: St Vrain Creek

Johnson, Anna
filing date: 1882 Dec 2
Boulder District Court Judgment Book, Water Decrees, Vol 2, District 5-6, 1869-1896, pg 429
ditch/reservoir: Johnson Ditch No. 25
date of original appropriation: 1873 Apr 1
Water District No. 5
Owner, of NiWot
water source: Left Hand Creek

Johnson, Anna
filing date: 1882 Dec 2
Boulder District Court Judgment Book, Water Decrees, Vol 2, District 5-6, 1869-1896, pg 428
ditch/reservoir: Johnson Ditch No. 25
date of original appropriation: 1873 Apr 1
Water District No. 5
Owner, of NiWot
water source: Left Hand Creek

Johnson, C A
filing date: 1882 Dec 2
Boulder District Court Judgment Book, Water Decrees, Vol 2, District 5-6, 1869-1896, pg 428
ditch/reservoir: Johnson Ditch No. 25
date of original appropriation: 1873 Apr 1
Water District No. 5
Owner, of NiWot
water source: Left Hand Creek

Johnson, C A
filing date: 1882 Dec 2
Boulder District Court Judgment Book, Water Decrees, Vol 2, District 5-6, 1869-1896, pg 429
ditch/reservoir: Johnson Ditch No. 25
date of original appropriation: 1873 Apr 1
Water District No. 5
Owner, of NiWot
water source: Left Hand Creek

Johnson, Nels
filing date: 1882 June 2
Boulder District Court Judgment Book, Water Decrees, Vol 2, District 5-6, 1869-1896, pg 157
ditch/reservoir: Renner Ditch No. 60
date of original appropriation: 1874 May 1
Water District No. 5
land owner
water source: St Vrain Creek

Johnson, Peter J
filing date: 1882 June 2
Boulder District Court Judgment Book, Water Decrees, Vol 2, District 5-6, 1869-1896, pg 161
ditch/reservoir: Richardson Ditch No. 64
date of original appropriation: 1874 June 15
Water District No. 5
prior owner
water source: St Vrain Creek

Johnson, Swan
filing date: 1882 June 2
Boulder District Court Judgment Book, Water Decrees, Vol 2, District 5-6, 1869-1896, pg 163
ditch/reservoir: Ullery Ditch No. 66
date of original appropriation: 1874 July 1
Water District No. 5
land owner
water source: St Vrain Creek

Jones, Lathan W
filing date: 1894 Apr 28
Boulder District Court Judgment Book, Water Decrees, Vol 2, District 5-6, 1869-1896, pg 526
ditch/reservoir: Moffat Ditch
date of original appropriation: 1889 Feb 4
Water District No. 6
Owner, of Louisville
water source: Coal Creek

Jones, Rosalie W
filing date: 1894 Apr 28
Boulder District Court Judgment Book, Water Decrees, Vol 2, District 5-6, 1869-1896, pg 526
ditch/reservoir: Moffat Ditch
date of original appropriation: 1889 Feb 4
Water District No. 6
Owner, of Louisville
water source: Coal Creek

Jones, Thomas J
filing date: 1882 June 2
Boulder District Court Judgment Book, Water Decrees, Vol 2, District 5-6, 1869-1896, pg 210
ditch/reservoir: Jones and Donnelly Ditch No. 7
date of original appropriation: 1860 [1861] May 1
Water District No. 6
Owner, of Valmont
water source: Boulder Creek

K

Kearns, James
filing date: 1895 Feb 12
Boulder District Court Judgment Book, Water Decrees, Vol 2, District 5-6, 1869-1896, pg 543
ditch/reservoir: Lower Baldwin Ditch
date of original appropriation: 1873 Apr 1
Water District No. 5
Owner, of Longmont
water source: Dry Creek

Kerr, David
filing date: 1894 Apr 28
Boulder District Court Judgment Book, Water Decrees, Vol 2, District 5-6, 1869-1896, pg 529
ditch/reservoir: Kerr Ditch No. 1 and No. 2
date of original appropriation: 1861 Apr 15
Water District No. 6
Owner, of Louisville
water source: Coal Creek

King, Jas A
filing date: 1882 June 2
Boulder District Court Judgment Book, Water Decrees, Vol 2, District 5-6, 1869-1896, pg 314
ditch/reservoir: Andrews and Farwell Ditch No. 11
date of original appropriation: 1864 June 1
Water District No. 6
Owner, of Valmont
water source: South Boulder Creek

Kinnear, John S
filing date: 1882 June 2
Boulder District Court Judgment Book, Water Decrees, Vol 2, District 5-6, 1869-1896, pg 366
ditch/reservoir: Kinnear Ditch and Reservoir No. 8
date of original appropriation: 1872 May 20
Water District No. 6
Owner, of Golden
water source: Coal Creek

Kinnear, John S
filing date: 1900 Dec 19
Boulder District Court Judgment Book, Water Decrees, Vol 2, District 5-6, 1869-1896, pg 554
ditch/reservoir: Kinnear Reservoir
date of original appropriation:
Water District No. 5
Owner
water source: Coal Creek

Kirk, Frank V
filing date: 1895 Feb 12
Boulder District Court Judgment Book, Water Decrees, Vol 2, District 5-6, 1869-1896, pg 545
ditch/reservoir: Lower Baldwin Ditch
date of original appropriation: 1873 Apr 1
Water District No. 5
Witness
water source: Dry Creek

Kirk, Frank V
filing date: 1895 Feb 12
Boulder District Court Judgment Book, Water Decrees, Vol 2, District 5-6, 1869-1896, pg 540
ditch/reservoir: Mill Ditch
date of original appropriation: 1884 May 1
Water District No. 5
Witness
water source: Dry Creek

Kirk, Frank V
filing date: 1895 Feb 12
Boulder District Court Judgment Book, Water Decrees, Vol 2, District 5-6, 1869-1896, pg 541
ditch/reservoir: John Rice Ditch
date of original appropriation: 1884 Apr 1
Water District No. 5
Witness
water source: Dry Creek

Knoth, Conrad W
filing date: 1883 Feb 21
Boulder District Court Judgment Book, Water Decrees, Vol 2, District 5-6, 1869-1896, pg 475
ditch/reservoir: Knoth Reservoir No. 7
date of original appropriation: 1880 Apr 25
Water District No. 5
Owner, of Longmont
water source: St Vrain Creek by the Supply Ditch and Knoth's Private Ditch No. 2

Knoth, Conrad W
filing date: 1883 Feb 21
Boulder District Court Judgment Book, Water Decrees, Vol 2, District 5-6, 1869-1896, pg 474
ditch/reservoir: Knoth Reservoir No. 7
date of original appropriation: 1880 Apr 25
Water District No. 5
Owner, of Longmont
water source: St Vrain Creek by the Supply Ditch and Knoth's Private Ditch No. 2

Knoth, Conrad W
filing date: 1882 Dec 2
Boulder District Court Judgment Book, Water Decrees, Vol 2, District 5-6, 1869-1896, pg 436
ditch/reservoir: Knoth, Streeter & Lake Ditch
date of original appropriation: 1873 Mar 15
Water District No. 5
Owner, of Longmont
water source: St Vrain Creek through the Oligarchy Ditch

Knoth, Conrad W
filing date: 1882 Dec 2
Boulder District Court Judgment Book, Water Decrees, Vol 2, District 5-6, 1869-1896, pg 447
ditch/reservoir: Knoth Private Ditch No. 2
date of original appropriation: 1879 May 1
Water District No. 5
Owner, of Longmont
water source: St Vrain Creek by the Highland and Davis Lateral Ditches

Knoth, Conrad W
filing date: 1882 Dec 2
Boulder District Court Judgment Book, Water Decrees, Vol 2, District 5-6, 1869-1896, pg 445
ditch/reservoir: Knoth Private Ditch No. 1
date of original appropriation: 1875 [1877] May 1
Water District No. 5
Owner, of Longmont
water source: St Vrain Creek by the Supply Ditch

L

Lagerman, Frederick
filing date: 1882 June 2
Boulder District Court Judgment Book, Water Decrees, Vol 2, District 5-6, 1869-1896, pg 180
ditch/reservoir: Lagerman Supply Ditch No. 80
date of original appropriation: 1879 Nov 14
Water District No. 5
Owner, of Niwot
water source: St Vrain Creek

Lagerman, Frederick
filing date: 1882 June 2
Boulder District Court Judgment Book, Water Decrees, Vol 2, District 5-6, 1869-1896, pg 181
ditch/reservoir: Lagerman Supply Ditch No. 80
date of original appropriation: 1879 Nov 14
Water District No. 5
Owner, of Niwot
water source: St Vrain Creek

Lagerman, Frederick
filing date: 1883 Feb 12
Boulder District Court Judgment Book, Water Decrees, Vol 2, District 5-6, 1869-1896, pg 462
ditch/reservoir: Lagerman Reservoir No. 4
date of original appropriation: 1878 Sept 3
Water District No. 5
Owner, of NiWot
water source: Left Hand Creek by Table Mountain Ditch and Spring Gulch

Lagerman, Frederick
filing date: 1883 Feb 12
Boulder District Court Judgment Book, Water Decrees, Vol 2, District 5-6, 1869-1896, pg 463
ditch/reservoir: Lagerman Reservoir No. 4
date of original appropriation: 1878 Sept 3
Water District No. 5
Owner, of NiWot
water source: Left Hand Creek by Table Mountain Ditch and Spring Gulch

Lagerman, Rev Mr
filing date: 1882 June 2
Boulder District Court Judgment Book, Water Decrees, Vol 2, District 5-6, 1869-1896, pg 176
ditch/reservoir: Taylor Ditch 1 No. 78
date of original appropriation: 1879 June 1
Water District No. 5

land owner
water source: St Vrain Creek

Lake Ditch Company
filing date: 1882 Dec 2
Boulder District Court Judgment Book, Water Decrees, Vol 2, District 5-6, 1869-1896, pg 430
ditch/reservoir: Lake Ditch No. 27
date of original appropriation: 1874 Apr 15
Water District No. 5
Owner, of Altona
water source: Left Hand Creek

Lake Ditch Company
filing date: 1882 Dec 2
Boulder District Court Judgment Book, Water Decrees, Vol 2, District 5-6, 1869-1896, pg 432
ditch/reservoir: Lake Ditch No. 27
date of original appropriation: 1874 Apr 15
Water District No. 5
Owner, of Altona
water source: Left Hand Creek

Lake, Charles
filing date: 1882 Dec 2
Boulder District Court Judgment Book, Water Decrees, Vol 2, District 5-6, 1869-1896, pg 436
ditch/reservoir: Knoth, Streeter & Lake Ditch
date of original appropriation: 1873 Mar 15
Water District No. 5
Owner, of Longmont
water source: St Vrain Creek through the Oligarchy Ditch

Last Chance Ditch Company
filing date: 1882 June 2
Boulder District Court Judgment Book, Water Decrees, Vol 2, District 5-6, 1869-1896, pg 151
ditch/reservoir: Last Chance Ditch No. 49
date of original appropriation: 1871 Mar 15
Water District No. 5
Owner, of Plattsville, Weld Co, Colorado
water source: St Vrain Creek

Last Chance Ditch Company
filing date: 1882 June 2
Boulder District Court Judgment Book, Water Decrees, Vol 2, District 5-6, 1869-1896, pg 150
ditch/reservoir: Last Chance Ditch No. 49
date of original appropriation: 1871 Mar 15
Water District No. 5
Owner, of Plattsville, Weld Co, Colorado
water source: St Vrain Creek

Lawson, A P
filing date: 1882 Dec 2
Boulder District Court Judgment Book, Water Decrees, Vol 2, District 5-6, 1869-1896, pg 394
ditch/reservoir: Holland Ditch No. 4
date of original appropriation: 1863 May 1
Water District No. 5
Owner, of NiWot
water source: Left Hand Creek

Lawson, A P
filing date: 1882 Dec 2
Boulder District Court Judgment Book, Water Decrees, Vol 2, District 5-6, 1869-1896, pg 396
ditch/reservoir: Holland Ditch No. 4
date of original appropriation: 1863 May 1
Water District No. 5
Owner, of NiWot
water source: Left Hand Creek

Laybourn, Alice P
filing date: 1902 Oct 2
Boulder District Court Judgment Book, Water Decrees, Vol 2, District 5-6, 1869-1896, pg 567
ditch/reservoir: Wiswall Ditch
date of original appropriation: 1892 Nov 10
Water District No. 5
Owner, of Longmont
water source: Dry Creek

Left Hand Ditch Company
filing date: 1882 June 2
Boulder District Court Judgment Book, Water Decrees, Vol 2, District 5-6, 1869-1896, pg 51
ditch/reservoir: Left Hand Ditch No. 15 1/2
date of original appropriation: 1863 June 1
Water District No. 5
Owner of Niwot
water source: St Vrain Creek

Left Hand Ditch Company
filing date: 1882 June 2
Boulder District Court Judgment Book, Water Decrees, Vol 2, District 5-6, 1869-1896, pg 53
ditch/reservoir: Left Hand Ditch No. 15 1/2
date of original appropriation: 1863 June 1
Water District No. 5
Owner of Niwot
water source: St Vrain Creek

Leggett, Jeremiah
filing date: 1882 June 2
Boulder District Court Judgment Book, Water Decrees, Vol 2, District 5-6, 1869-1896, pg 247
ditch/reservoir: Leggett Ditch No. 30
date of original appropriation: 1868 May 1 (half constructed by 1 June 1862)
Water District No. 6
Owner, of Erie
water source: Boulder Creek

Leyner Ditch Company
filing date: 1882 June 2
Boulder District Court Judgment Book, Water Decrees, Vol 2, District 5-6, 1869-1896, pg 320
ditch/reservoir: Leyner Ditch No. 13
date of original appropriation: 1865 Apr 1
Water District No. 6
Owner, of Boulder
water source: South Boulder Creek

Lockard [Lockhard], Ira
filing date: 1882 June 1
Boulder District Court Judgment Book, Water Decrees, Vol 2, District 5-6, 1869-1896, pg 2
ditch/reservoir: Hayseed Ditch No. 1
date of original appropriation: 1860 Jan 1
Water District No. 5
Owner of Longmont
water source: St Vrain Creek

Lockard [Lockhard], Ira
filing date: 1882 June 1
Boulder District Court Judgment Book, Water Decrees, Vol 2, District 5-6, 1869-1896, pg 3
ditch/reservoir: Hayseed Ditch No. 1
date of original appropriation: 1860 Jan 1
Water District No. 5
Owner of Longmont
water source: St Vrain Creek

Longmont Supply Ditch Company
filing date: 1882 June 2
Boulder District Court Judgment Book, Water Decrees, Vol 2, District 5-6, 1869-1896, pg 81
ditch/reservoir: Longmont Supply Ditch No. 21 1/2
date of original appropriation: 1865 May 1
Water District No. 5
Owner
water source: St Vrain Creek

Longmont Supply Ditch Company
filing date: 1882 June 2
Boulder District Court Judgment Book, Water Decrees, Vol 2, District 5-6, 1869-1896, pg 80
ditch/reservoir: Longmont Supply Ditch No. 21 1/2
date of original appropriation: 1865 May 1
Water District No. 5
Owner
water source: St Vrain Creek

Louisville Coal Mining Company
filing date: 1894 Apr 28
Boulder District Court Judgment Book, Water Decrees, Vol 2, District 5-6, 1869-1896, pg 529
ditch/reservoir: Kerr Ditch No. 1 and No. 2
date of original appropriation: 1861 Apr 15
Water District No. 6
Owner, of Louisville
water source: Coal Creek

Low {Lowe], Samantha
filing date: 1903 Sept 15
Boulder District Court Judgment Book, Water Decrees, Vol 2, District 5-6, 1869-1896, pg 569
ditch/reservoir: Low Ditch
date of original appropriation:
Water District No. 6
Claimant
water source: Coal Creek

Low [Lowe], Samantha
filing date: 1900 Dec 19
Boulder District Court Judgment Book, Water Decrees, Vol 2, District 5-6, 1869-1896, pg 553
ditch/reservoir: Low Ditch
date of original appropriation:
Water District No. 6
Claimant
water source: Coal Creek

Lower Boulder Ditch Company
filing date: 1882 June 2
Boulder District Court Judgment Book, Water Decrees, Vol 2, District 5-6, 1869-1896, pg 194
ditch/reservoir: Lower Boulder Ditch No. 1
date of original appropriation: 1859 Oct 1
Water District No. 6
Owner, of Canfield
water source: Boulder Creek

M

Magni, Swan
filing date: 1882 June 2
Boulder District Court Judgment Book, Water Decrees, Vol 2, District 5-6, 1869-1896, pg 160
ditch/reservoir: Richardson Ditch No. 64
date of original appropriation: 1874 June 15
Water District No. 5
Owner, of Longmont
water source: St Vrain Creek

Magni, Swan
filing date: 1882 June 2
Boulder District Court Judgment Book, Water Decrees, Vol 2, District 5-6, 1869-1896, pg 159
ditch/reservoir: Richardson Ditch No. 64
date of original appropriation: 1874 June 15
Water District No. 5
Owner, of Longmont
water source: St Vrain Creek

Marquette, Frank A
filing date: 1882 June 2
Boulder District Court Judgment Book, Water Decrees, Vol 2, District 5-6, 1869-1896, pg 44
ditch/reservoir: Smead Ditch No. 13
date of original appropriation: 1862 Oct 1
Water District No. 5
Owner of Longmont
water source: St Vrain Creek

Marquette, Frank A
filing date: 1882 June 2
Boulder District Court Judgment Book, Water Decrees, Vol 2, District 5-6, 1869-1896, pg 43
ditch/reservoir: Smead Ditch No. 13
date of original appropriation: 1862 Oct 1
Water District No. 5
Owner of Longmont
water source: St Vrain Creek

Marshallville Ditch Company
filing date: 1882 June 2
Boulder District Court Judgment Book, Water Decrees, Vol 2, District 5-6, 1869-1896, pg 323
ditch/reservoir: Marshallville Ditch No. 14
date of original appropriation: 1865 June 1
Water District No. 6
Owner, Boulder
water source: South Boulder Creek

Mason, J R
filing date: 1882 June 2
Boulder District Court Judgment Book, Water Decrees, Vol 2, District 5-6, 1869-1896, pg 55
ditch/reservoir: South Flat Ditch No. 16
date of original appropriation: 1863 May 15
Water District No. 5
Owner of Longmont
water source: St Vrain Creek

Mason, J R
filing date: 1882 June 2
Boulder District Court Judgment Book, Water Decrees, Vol 2, District 5-6, 1869-1896, pg 56
ditch/reservoir: South Flat Ditch No. 16
date of original appropriation: 1863 May 15
Water District No. 5
Owner of Longmont
water source: St Vrain Creek

Mason, James
filing date: 1882 June 2
Boulder District Court Judgment Book, Water Decrees, Vol 2, District 5-6, 1869-1896, pg 105
ditch/reservoir: Denio & Taylor Ditch No. 28
date of original appropriation: 1865 July 15
Water District No. 5
Owner, of Longmont
water source: St Vrain Creek

Mason, James
filing date: 1882 June 2
Boulder District Court Judgment Book, Water Decrees, Vol 2, District 5-6, 1869-1896, pg 103
ditch/reservoir: Denio & Taylor Ditch No. 28
date of original appropriation: 1865 July 15
Water District No. 5
Owner, of Longmont
water source: St Vrain Creek

Mason, James R
filing date: 1882 June 2
Boulder District Court Judgment Book, Water Decrees, Vol 2, District 5-6, 1869-1896, pg 7
ditch/reservoir: Hayseed Ditch No. 1, Appropriation No. 2
date of original appropriation: 1860 July 31
Water District No. 5
Owner of Longmont
water source: St Vrain Creek

Mason, James R
filing date: 1882 June 2
Boulder District Court Judgment Book, Water Decrees, Vol 2, District 5-6, 1869-1896, pg 8
ditch/reservoir: Hayseed Ditch No. 1, Appropriation No. 2
date of original appropriation: 1860 July 31
Water District No. 5
claimant
water source: St Vrain Creek

Mason, James R
filing date: 1882 June 2
Boulder District Court Judgment Book, Water Decrees, Vol 2, District 5-6, 1869-1896, pg 6
ditch/reservoir: Hayseed Ditch No. 1, Appropriation No. 2
date of original appropriation: 1860 July 31
Water District No. 5
claimant
water source: St Vrain Creek

Mason, James R
filing date: 1882 June 2
Boulder District Court Judgment Book, Water Decrees, Vol 2, District 5-6, 1869-1896, pg 6
ditch/reservoir: Hayseed Ditch No. 1, Appropriation No. 2
date of original appropriation: 1860 July 31
Water District No. 5
claimant, of Longmont
water source: St Vrain Creek

Mason, James R
filing date: 1882 June 2
Boulder District Court Judgment Book, Water Decrees, Vol 2, District 5-6, 1869-1896, pg 5
ditch/reservoir: Hayseed Ditch No. 1
date of original appropriation: 1860 Jan 1
Water District No. 5
claimant
water source: St Vrain Creek

Mathews, Geo W
filing date: 1882 June 2
Boulder District Court Judgment Book, Water Decrees, Vol 2, District 5-6, 1869-1896, pg 287
ditch/reservoir: Mathews Ditch No. 40
date of original appropriation: 1879 Feb 13
Water District No. 6
Owner, of Erie
water source: Boulder Creek

Mathews, Martha M
filing date: 1882 June 2
Boulder District Court Judgment Book, Water Decrees, Vol 2, District 5-6, 1869-1896, pg 212
ditch/reservoir: Martha M Mathews Ditch No. 8
date of original appropriation: 1861 June 1
Water District No. 6
Owner, of Erie
water source: Boulder Creek

Mathews, Milton
filing date: 1882 June 2
Boulder District Court Judgment Book, Water Decrees, Vol 2, District 5-6, 1869-1896, pg 287
ditch/reservoir: Mathews Ditch No. 40
date of original appropriation: 1879 Feb 13
Water District No. 6
Owner, of Erie
water source: Boulder Creek

Mathews, Newton
filing date: 1882 June 2
Boulder District Court Judgment Book, Water Decrees, Vol 2, District 5-6, 1869-1896, pg 287
ditch/reservoir: Mathews Ditch No. 40
date of original appropriation: 1879 Feb 13
Water District No. 6
Owner, of Erie
water source: Boulder Creek

Mathews, Sarah
filing date: 1882 June 2
Boulder District Court Judgment Book, Water Decrees, Vol 2, District 5-6, 1869-1896, pg 287
ditch/reservoir: Mathews Ditch No. 40
date of original appropriation: 1879 Feb 13
Water District No. 6
Owner, of Erie
water source: Boulder Creek

McCaslin, M L
filing date: 1882 June 2
Boulder District Court Judgment Book, Water Decrees, Vol 2, District 5-6, 1869-1896, pg 100
ditch/reservoir: Webster & McCaslin Ditch No. 27
date of original appropriation: 1865 July 5
Water District No. 5
Owner, of Longmont
water source: St Vrain Creek

McCaslin, M L
filing date: 1882 June 2
Boulder District Court Judgment Book, Water Decrees, Vol 2, District 5-6, 1869-1896, pg 101
ditch/reservoir: Webster & McCaslin Ditch No. 27
date of original appropriation: 1865 July 5
Water District No. 5
Owner, of Longmont
water source: St Vrain Creek

McCaslin, M L
filing date: 1882 June 2
Boulder District Court Judgment Book, Water Decrees, Vol 2, District 5-6, 1869-1896, pg 121
ditch/reservoir: Davis & Downing Ditch No. 33
date of original appropriation: 1866 Nov 1
Water District No. 5
Owner, of Longmont
water source: St Vrain Creek

McCaslin, M L
filing date: 1882 June 2
Boulder District Court Judgment Book, Water Decrees, Vol 2, District 5-6, 1869-1896, pg 119
ditch/reservoir: Davis & Downing Ditch No. 33
date of original appropriation: 1866 Nov 1
Water District No. 5
Owner, of Longmont
water source: St Vrain Creek

McCaslin, M L
filing date: 1882 June 2
Boulder District Court Judgment Book, Water Decrees, Vol 2, District 5-6, 1869-1896, pg 105
ditch/reservoir: Denio & Taylor Ditch No. 28
date of original appropriation: 1865 July 15
Water District No. 5
land owner
water source: St Vrain Creek

McCaslin, Matthew L
filing date: 1882 June 2
Boulder District Court Judgment Book, Water Decrees, Vol 2, District 5-6, 1869-1896, pg 24
ditch/reservoir: Chapman and McCaslin Ditch No. 9
date of original appropriation: 1862 Mar 10
Water District No. 5
Owner of Longmont
water source: St Vrain Creek

McCaslin, Matthew L
filing date: 1882 June 2
Boulder District Court Judgment Book, Water Decrees, Vol 2, District 5-6, 1869-1896, pg 23
ditch/reservoir: Chapman and McCaslin Ditch No. 9
date of original appropriation: 1862 Mar 10
Water District No. 5
Owner of Longmont
water source: St Vrain Creek

McCory [McCory], V W
filing date: 1882 June 2
Boulder District Court Judgment Book, Water Decrees, Vol 2, District 5-6, 1869-1896, pg 121
ditch/reservoir: Davis & Downing Ditch No. 33
date of original appropriation: 1866 Nov 1
Water District No. 5
Owner, of Longmont
water source: St Vrain Creek

McCory [McCory], V W
filing date: 1882 June 2
Boulder District Court Judgment Book, Water Decrees, Vol 2, District 5-6, 1869-1896, pg 119
ditch/reservoir: Davis & Downing Ditch No. 33
date of original appropriation: 1866 Nov 1
Water District No. 5
Owner, of Longmont
water source: St Vrain Creek

McCory
filing date: 1882 June 2
Boulder District Court Judgment Book, Water Decrees, Vol 2, District 5-6, 1869-1896, pg 145
ditch/reservoir: Bear & McCory Ditch No. 45
date of original appropriation: 1871 June 1
Water District No. 5
land owner
water source: St Vrain Creek

McGinn Ditch Company
filing date: 1882 June 2
Boulder District Court Judgment Book, Water Decrees, Vol 2, District 5-6, 1869-1896, pg 292
ditch/reservoir: McGinn Ditch No. 1
date of original appropriation: 1860 May 1
Water District No. 6
Owner, of Boulder
water source: South Boulder Creek

McGwire (Secor & McGwire)
filing date: 1902 Oct 21
Boulder District Court Judgment Book, Water Decrees, Vol 2, District 5-6, 1869-1896, pg 568
ditch/reservoir:
date of original appropriation:
Water District No. 5
Attorney
water source:

McKay, Elvina
filing date: 1900 Dec 19
Boulder District Court Judgment Book, Water Decrees, Vol 2, District 5-6, 1869-1896, pg 553
ditch/reservoir: McKay Reservoir and Ditch
date of original appropriation:
Water District No. 6
Claimant
water source: Coal Creek

McKay, Elvina
filing date: 1903 Sept 15
Boulder District Court Judgment Book, Water Decrees, Vol 2, District 5-6, 1869-1896, pg 569
ditch/reservoir: McKay Reservoir and Ditch
date of original appropriation:
Water District No. 6
Claimant
water source: Coal Creek

McKenzie, Neil D
filing date: 1903 Sept 15
Boulder District Court Judgment Book, Water Decrees, Vol 2, District 5-6, 1869-1896, pg 569
ditch/reservoir: Allen-Hayden Ditches No. 1 No. 2 No. 3 No. 4
date of original appropriation:
Water District No. 6
Claimant
water source: Coal Creek

McKenzie, Neil D
filing date: 1900 Dec 19
Boulder District Court Judgment Book, Water Decrees, Vol 2, District 5-6, 1869-1896, pg 553
ditch/reservoir: Allen-Hayden Ditches No. 1 No. 2 No. 3 No. 4
date of original appropriation:
Water District No. 6
Claimant
water source: Coal Creek

McKenzie, William
filing date: 1882 June 2
Boulder District Court Judgment Book, Water Decrees, Vol 2, District 5-6, 1869-1896, pg 356
ditch/reservoir: McKenzie Ditch No. 4
date of original appropriation: 1866 June 1
Water District No. 6
Owner, of Boulder
water source: Coal Creek

Mead, Lorin C
filing date: 1883 Feb 21
Boulder District Court Judgment Book, Water Decrees, Vol 2, District 5-6, 1869-1896, pg 471
ditch/reservoir: Highland Lake Reservoir No. 2
date of original appropriation: 1874 May 31
Water District No. 5
Owner, of Longmont
water source: St Vrain Creek by the Highland Ditch

Mead, Lorin C
filing date: 1883 Feb 21
Boulder District Court Judgment Book, Water Decrees, Vol 2, District 5-6, 1869-1896, pg 470
ditch/reservoir: Highland Lake Reservoir No. 2
date of original appropriation: 1874 May 31
Water District No. 5
Owner, of Longmont
water source: St Vrain Creek by the Highland Ditch

Miller, J A
filing date: 1882 June 2
Boulder District Court Judgment Book, Water Decrees, Vol 2, District 5-6, 1869-1896, pg 103
ditch/reservoir: Denio & Taylor Ditch No. 28
date of original appropriation: 1865 July 15
Water District No. 5
Owner, of Longmont
water source: St Vrain Creek

Miller, J A
filing date: 1882 June 2
Boulder District Court Judgment Book, Water Decrees, Vol 2, District 5-6, 1869-1896, pg 105
ditch/reservoir: Denio & Taylor Ditch No. 28
date of original appropriation: 1865 July 15
Water District No. 5
Owner, of Longmont
water source: St Vrain Creek

Minor, H M
filing date: 1902 Oct 21
Boulder District Court Judgment Book, Water Decrees, Vol 2, District 5-6, 1869-1896, pg 568
ditch/reservoir:
date of original appropriation:
Water District No. 5
Attorney
water source:

Mitchell, John T
filing date: 1882 June 2
Boulder District Court Judgment Book, Water Decrees, Vol 2, District 5-6, 1869-1896, pg 331
ditch/reservoir: South Ditch No. 19
date of original appropriation: 1866 June 1
Water District No. 6
Owner, of Boulder
water source: South Boulder Creek

Mitchell, John T
filing date: 1882 June 2
Boulder District Court Judgment Book, Water Decrees, Vol 2, District 5-6, 1869-1896, pg 326
ditch/reservoir: Central Ditch No. 16
date of original appropriation: 1866 May 15
Water District No. 6
Owner, of Boulder
water source: South Boulder Creek

Moffat, Annie M
filing date: 1894 Apr 28
Boulder District Court Judgment Book, Water Decrees, Vol 2, District 5-6, 1869-1896, pg 526
ditch/reservoir: Moffat Ditch
date of original appropriation: 1889 Feb 4
Water District No. 6
Owner, of Wilkes-Barre, Pennsylvania
water source: Coal Creek

Moffat, George W
filing date: 1894 Apr 28
Boulder District Court Judgment Book, Water Decrees, Vol 2, District 5-6, 1869-1896, pg 526
ditch/reservoir: Moffat Ditch
date of original appropriation: 1889 Feb 4
Water District No. 6
Owner, of Lawrence, Kansas
water source: Coal Creek

Moffat, Martha A
filing date: 1894 Apr 28
Boulder District Court Judgment Book, Water Decrees, Vol 2, District 5-6, 1869-1896, pg 526
ditch/reservoir: Moffat Ditch
date of original appropriation: 1889 Feb 4
Water District No. 6
Owner, of Wilkes-Barre, Pennsylvania
water source: Coal Creek

Moffat, William R
filing date: 1894 Apr 28
Boulder District Court Judgment Book, Water Decrees, Vol 2, District 5-6, 1869-1896, pg 526
ditch/reservoir: Moffat Ditch
date of original appropriation: 1889 Feb 4
Water District No. 6
deceased
water source: Coal Creek

Moffat, William R Jr
filing date: 1894 Apr 28
Boulder District Court Judgment Book, Water Decrees, Vol 2, District 5-6, 1869-1896, pg 526
ditch/reservoir: Moffat Ditch
date of original appropriation: 1889 Feb 4
Water District No. 6
Owner, of Latourelle Falls, Oregon
water source: Coal Creek

Montgomery, Alexander W
filing date: 1882 June 2
Boulder District Court Judgment Book, Water Decrees, Vol 2, District 5-6, 1869-1896, pg 40
ditch/reservoir: Montgomery Private Ditch No. 12 1/2
date of original appropriation: 1862 May 15
Water District No. 5
Owner of Longmont
water source: St Vrain Creek

Montgomery, Alexander W
filing date: 1882 June 2
Boulder District Court Judgment Book, Water Decrees, Vol 2, District 5-6, 1869-1896, pg 41
ditch/reservoir: Montgomery Private Ditch No. 12 1/2
date of original appropriation: 1862 May 15
Water District No. 5
Owner of Longmont
water source: St Vrain Creek

Montgomery, Norton
filing date: 1903 Sept 15
Boulder District Court Judgment Book, Water Decrees, Vol 2, District 5-6, 1869-1896, pg 568
ditch/reservoir:
date of original appropriation:
Water District No. 6
Attorney
water source:

Morath, E J (was the Clerk on the following cases in the order they appear in the book)
filing date: 1882 June 2
True and Webster Ditch No. 11
Butte Mill Ditch No. 22
Green Ditch No. 13
Clough and True Private Ditch No. 12
McCarty Ditch No. 11
Plumb Ditch No. 10
Howell and Beasley Ditch No. 23
Taylor Ditch 1 No. 78
Dickens Private Ditch No. 2 No. 81
Lykins Gulch Ditch No. 82
Carr and Tyler Ditch No. 19
North Boulder Farmers Ditch No. 11
Farmers Ditch No. 14
N K Smith and Tyler Ditch No. 9
Boulder and Left Hand Ditch
Lagerman Supply Ditch No. 80
Hayseed Ditch No. 1
Rural Ditch No. 12
Taylor Ditch 2 No. 79
Dickens Private Ditch No. 12
Dickens Private Ditch No. 2 No. 81
True and Webster Ditch No. 11
Butte Mill Ditch No. 22
Farmers Ditch No. 14
Northwestern Mutual Life Insurance Co, Ditch No. 4
Houck No. 2 Ditch No. 6
Bonus Ditch No. 6
Dry Creek Ditch No. 11, Claim of D H Nichols
Green Ditch No. 13
Beckwith Ditch No. 5
Taylor Ditch No. 31
Lower Boulder Ditch No. 1
Boulder and Weld County Ditch No. 33
Beckwith Ditch No. 5
Pella Ditch No. 10
Smith and Goss Ditch No. 2
Dry Creek Ditch No. 11, Claim of Mary S Stoddard et al
Boulder and Weld County Ditch No. 33
Anderson Ditch No. 4
Smith and Goss Ditch No. 2
Boulder and White Rock Ditch No. 35
Town of Boulder Ditch and Reservoir No. 37
Houck No. 1 Ditch No. 16
Smith and Emmons Ditch No. 18
Bacon's Appropriation No. 7
Anderson Ditch No. 4
Cushman Ditch No. 8
Godding, Dailey and Plumb Ditch No. 5
Jones and Donnelly Ditch No. 7
Wellman, Nichols and Hahn Ditch No. 11
Lykins Gulch Ditch No. 82
Delehant Ditch No. 25
N K Smith and Tyler Ditch No. 9
Highland Ditch Southside No. 28
Town of Boulder Ditch and Reservoir No. 37
Martha M Mathews Ditch No. 8
Harden Ditch
Taylor Ditch No. 31
Coffin Meadow Ditch No. 3
Houck #2 Ditch No. 6
Smith and Emmons Ditch No. 18
Dry Creek Ditch No. 11, Claim of Wm Breach
Chapman and McCaslin Ditch No. 9
Highland Ditch Southside No. 28
Leggett Ditch No. 30
Jones and Donnelly Ditch No. 7
Cushman Ditch No. 8
Northwestern Mutual Life Insurance Co, Ditch No. 4
Delehant Ditch No. 25
Pella Ditch No. 10
Houck No. 1 Ditch No. 16
Davis & Downing Ditch No. 33
James Ditch No. 37
Peck & Metcalf Ditch No. 36
Goss Private Ditch 1 No. 25
South Boulder Canyon Ditch No. 21
Davidson Ditch No. 26
Peck & Metcalf Ditch No. 36
South Ditch No. 19
Davidson Ditch No. 26
Baker & Weese Ditch No. 24
South Boulder and Coal Creek Ditch No. 28
Goodhue Ditch and Reservoir No. 29
Highland Ditch No. 46 Amended
Goss Private Ditch 1 No. 25
Goodhue Ditch and Reservoir No. 29
St Vrain Creek & Palmerton Ditch No. 23
Davis & Downing Ditch No. 33

Rough & Ready Ditch No. 38
Enterprise Ditch No. 12
Swede Ditch No. 44
Montgomery Private Ditch No. 12 1/2
Left Hand Ditch No. 15 1/2
Nelson Ditch No. 39
Marshallville Ditch No. 14
South Boulder Canyon Ditch No. 21
Central Ditch No. 16
Goss Private Ditch 2 No. 25
Ni-Wot Ditch No. 24
Central Ditch No. 16
Rough & Ready Ditch No. 38
Cottonwood No. 2 Ditch No. 17
James Ditch No. 37
South Ditch No. 19
Eggleston No. 1 Ditch No. 5
South Boulder and Rock Creek Ditch No. 30
McKenzie Ditch No. 4
Forbes Ditch No. 2
Coffin-Davis Ditch No. 31
Four Mile Canyon Ditch No. 1
Eggleston No. 2 Ditch No. 3
Six Mile Bottom Ditch No. 1
Kinnear Ditch and Reservoir No. 8
Last Chance Ditch No. 6
Weese Private Ditch No. 29
Denio & Taylor Ditch No. 28
Last Chance Ditch No. 6
Church Ditch No. 7
Kinnear Ditch and Reservoir No. 8
Weese Private Ditch No. 29
William C Hake Ditch No. 2
South Boulder and Rock Creek Ditch No. 30
Oligarchy Ditch No. 32
Autry and Eggleston Ditch, No, 1
Colorado State Mills Ditch
Goss Private Ditch 2 No. 25
Sternberg Ditch No. 34
Webster & McCaslin Ditch No. 27
Forbes Ditch No. 2
North Branch Six Mile Bottom Ditch No. 2
Leyner Ditch No. 13
William C Hake Ditch No. 2
North Branch Six Mile Bottom Ditch No. 2
Eggleston No. 2 Ditch No. 3
Webster & McCaslin Ditch No. 27
Six Mile Bottom Ditch No. 1
Denio & Taylor Ditch No. 28
Autry and Eggleston Ditch, No, 1
Howard Ditch No. 3
St Vrain Creek and Gold Hill Ditch No. 17
McGinn Ditch No. 1
Runyan Ditch No. 15
McGinn Ditch No. 1
Church Ditch No. 7
Schearer Ditch No. 2
Left Hand Ditch No. 15 1/2
Revolution Ditch No. 41
Denio & Taylor Extension Ditch No. 69
Ullery Ditch No. 66
Richardson Ditch No. 64
South Flat Ditch No. 16
Bear & McCory Ditch No. 45
Richardson Ditch No. 64
Titus & Goyn Ditch No. 72
Taylor Ditch 1 No. 78
Supply Ditch No. 75
Montgomery Private Ditch No. 12 1/2
Wellman Ditch No. 39
Smead Ditch No. 13
Ullery Ditch No. 66
Mathews Ditch No. 40
East Boulder Ditch No. 4
Denio & Taylor Extension Ditch No. 69
Clough Tribute (Private) Ditch No. 14
Wellman Ditch No. 39
Highland Ditch No. 46
Last Chance Ditch No. 49
East Boulder Ditch No. 4
Island Ditch No. 20 1/2
Howard Ditch No. 3
Dry Creek No. 2 Ditch No. 9
Zweck & Turner Ditch No. 21
Bear & McCory Ditch No. 45
Andrews and Farwell Ditch No. 11
Enterprise Ditch No. 12
Zweck & Turner Ditch No. 21
Longmont Supply Ditch No. 21 1/2
St Vrain Creek & Palmerton Ditch No. 23
Spring Creek Ditch No. 52
L H Dickson's Ditch No. 19
Dry Creek No. 2 Ditch No. 9
Renner Ditch No. 60
Dry Creek Ditch No. 7
South Boulder and Bear Creek Ditch No. 5
Northwestern Mutual Life Insurance Co Ditch No. 18
Last Chance Ditch No. 49
Hager's Meadow Ditch No. 18
Cottonwood No. 2 Ditch No. 6

South Boulder and Bear Creek Ditch No. 5
Coffman Ditch No. 20
Renner Ditch No. 60

Mower, Samuel
filing date: 1903 Sept 15
Boulder District Court Judgment Book, Water Decrees, Vol 2, District 5-6, 1869-1896, pg 568
ditch/reservoir:
date of original appropriation:
Water District No. 6
Owner
water source:

Mower, Samuel A
filing date: 1900 Dec 19
Boulder District Court Judgment Book, Water Decrees, Vol 2, District 5-6, 1869-1896, pg 553
ditch/reservoir: Kinnear Reservoir
date of original appropriation:
Water District No. 6
Claimant
water source: Coal Creek

Mowrey, Charles
filing date: 1902 Oct 2
Boulder District Court Judgment Book, Water Decrees, Vol 2, District 5-6, 1869-1896, pg 567
ditch/reservoir: Wiswall Ditch
date of original appropriation: 1892 Nov 10
Water District No. 5
Owner, of Longmont
water source: Dry Creek

Mulverhill, John
filing date: 1882 June 1
Boulder District Court Judgment Book, Water Decrees, Vol 2, District 5-6, 1869-1896, pg 2
ditch/reservoir: Hayseed Ditch No. 1
date of original appropriation: 1860 Jan 1
Water District No. 5
Owner of Denver
water source: St Vrain Creek

Mulverhill, John
filing date: 1882 June 1
Boulder District Court Judgment Book, Water Decrees, Vol 2, District 5-6, 1869-1896, pg 3
ditch/reservoir: Hayseed Ditch No. 1
date of original appropriation: 1860 Jan 1
Water District No. 5
Owner of Denver
water source: St Vrain Creek

N

Neikirk, Henry
filing date: 1882 June 2
Boulder District Court Judgment Book, Water Decrees, Vol 2, District 5-6, 1869-1896, pg 312
ditch/reservoir: Dry Creek No. 2 Ditch No. 9
date of original appropriation: 1864 May 1
Water District No. 6
Owner, of Boulder
water source: South Boulder Creek

Neikirk, Henry
filing date: 1882 Dec 2
Boulder District Court Judgment Book, Water Decrees, Vol 2, District 5-6, 1869-1896, pg 444
ditch/reservoir: Neikirk Ditch
date of original appropriation: 1875 May 1
Water District No. 5
Owner, of Boulder
water source: St Vrain Creek by the Highland Ditch

Neikirk, Henry
filing date: 1883 Feb 12
Boulder District Court Judgment Book, Water Decrees, Vol 2, District 5-6, 1869-1896, pg 466
ditch/reservoir: Divide Reservoir No. 5
date of original appropriation: 1879 Mar 1
Water District No. 5
Owner, of Boulder
water source: St Vrain Creek by the Highland and Supply ditches

Neikirk, Henry
filing date: 1883 Feb 12
Boulder District Court Judgment Book, Water Decrees, Vol 2, District 5-6, 1869-1896, pg 465
ditch/reservoir: Divide Reservoir No. 5
date of original appropriation: 1879 Mar 1
Water District No. 5
Owner, of Boulder
water source: St Vrain Creek by the Highland and Supply ditches

Nelson, August
filing date: 1882 June 2
Boulder District Court Judgment Book, Water Decrees, Vol 2, District 5-6, 1869-1896, pg 137
ditch/reservoir: Nelson Ditch No. 39
date of original appropriation: 1869 Apr 1
Water District No. 5

Owner, of Longmont
water source: St Vrain Creek

Nelson, August
filing date: 1882 June 2
Boulder District Court Judgment Book, Water Decrees, Vol 2, District 5-6, 1869-1896, pg 135
ditch/reservoir: Nelson Ditch No. 39
date of original appropriation: 1869 Apr 1
Water District No. 5
Owner, of Longmont
water source: St Vrain Creek

Nelson, Chris
filing date: 1882 Dec 2
Boulder District Court Judgment Book, Water Decrees, Vol 2, District 5-6, 1869-1896, pg 394
ditch/reservoir: Holland Ditch No. 4
date of original appropriation: 1863 May 1
Water District No. 5
Owner, of NiWot
water source: Left Hand Creek

Nelson, Chris
filing date: 1882 Dec 2
Boulder District Court Judgment Book, Water Decrees, Vol 2, District 5-6, 1869-1896, pg 396
ditch/reservoir: Holland Ditch No. 4
date of original appropriation: 1863 May 1
Water District No. 5
Owner, of NiWot
water source: Left Hand Creek

Nelson, Lewis
filing date: 1882 June 2
Boulder District Court Judgment Book, Water Decrees, Vol 2, District 5-6, 1869-1896, pg 178
ditch/reservoir: Taylor Ditch 2 No. 79
date of original appropriation: 1879 June 2
Water District No. 5
land owner
water source: St Vrain Creek

Nichols, D H
filing date: 1882 June 2
Boulder District Court Judgment Book, Water Decrees, Vol 2, District 5-6, 1869-1896, pg 276
ditch/reservoir: Wellman, Nichols and Hahn Ditch No. 11
date of original appropriation: 1862 June 1
Water District No. 6
Owner, of Boulder
water source: Boulder Creek

Nichols, D H
filing date: 1882 June 2
Boulder District Court Judgment Book, Water Decrees, Vol 2, District 5-6, 1869-1896, pg 270
ditch/reservoir: Dry Creek Ditch No. 11, Claim of D H Nichols
date of original appropriation: 1862 June 1
Water District No. 6
Claimant
water source: Boulder Creek

Nichols, D H
filing date: 1882 June 2
Boulder District Court Judgment Book, Water Decrees, Vol 2, District 5-6, 1869-1896, pg 282
ditch/reservoir: Boulder and White Rock Ditch
date of original appropriation: 1862 June 1
Water District No. 6
Claimant
water source: Boulder Creek

Nichols, David H
filing date: 1882 June 2
Boulder District Court Judgment Book, Water Decrees, Vol 2, District 5-6, 1869-1896, pg 270
ditch/reservoir: Dry Creek Ditch No. 11, Claim of D H Nichols
date of original appropriation: 1862 June 1
Water District No. 6
Owner, of Boulder
water source: Boulder Creek

Nichols, David H
filing date: 1882 June 2
Boulder District Court Judgment Book, Water Decrees, Vol 2, District 5-6, 1869-1896, pg 283
ditch/reservoir: Boulder and White Rock Ditch
date of original appropriation: 1862 June 1
Water District No. 6
Claimant
water source: Boulder Creek

Niwot Irrigating Ditch Company
filing date: 1902 Oct 2
Boulder District Court Judgment Book, Water Decrees, Vol 2, District 5-6, 1869-1896, pg 567
ditch/reservoir: Niwot Irrigating Ditch
date of original appropriation: 1889 Oct
Water District No. 5
Owner, of Longmont
water source: Dry Creek

Niwot Irrigating Ditch Company
filing date: 1902 Oct 21
Boulder District Court Judgment Book, Water Decrees, Vol 2, District 5-6, 1869-1896, pg 568
ditch/reservoir:
date of original appropriation:
Water District No. 5
Owner
water source:

Niwot Irrigating Ditch Company
filing date: 1882 June 2
Boulder District Court Judgment Book, Water Decrees, Vol 2, District 5-6, 1869-1896, pg 87
ditch/reservoir: Ni-Wot Ditch No. 24
date of original appropriation: 1865 June 1
Water District No. 5
Owner, of Longmont
water source: St Vrain Creek

Ni-Wot Irrigating Ditch Company
filing date: 1882 June 2
Boulder District Court Judgment Book, Water Decrees, Vol 2, District 5-6, 1869-1896, pg 89
ditch/reservoir: Ni-Wot Ditch No. 24
date of original appropriation: 1865 June 1
Water District No. 5
Owner, of Longmont
water source: St Vrain Creek

Noblit
filing date: 1882 Dec 2
Boulder District Court Judgment Book, Water Decrees, Vol 2, District 5-6, 1869-1896, pg 411
ditch/reservoir: Altona Ditch No. 11
date of original appropriation: 1865 May 31
Water District No. 5
former ditch name
water source: Left Hand Creek

North Boulder Farmers Ditch Company
filing date: 1882 June 2
Boulder District Court Judgment Book, Water Decrees, Vol 2, District 5-6, 1869-1896, pg 283
ditch/reservoir: Boulder and White Rock Ditch
date of original appropriation: 1862 June 1
Water District No. 6
Claimant
water source: Boulder Creek

North Boulder Farmers Ditch Company
filing date: 1882 June 2
Boulder District Court Judgment Book, Water Decrees, Vol 2, District 5-6, 1869-1896, pg 282
ditch/reservoir: Boulder and White Rock Ditch
date of original appropriation: 1862 June 1
Water District No. 6
Claimant
water source: Boulder Creek

North Boulder Farmers Ditch Company
filing date: 1882 June 2
Boulder District Court Judgment Book, Water Decrees, Vol 2, District 5-6, 1869-1896, pg 279
ditch/reservoir: North Boulder Farmers Ditch No. 11
date of original appropriation: 1862 June 1
Water District No. 6
Owner, of Valmont
water source: Boulder Creek

Northwestern Mutual Life Insurance Co
filing date: 1882 June 2
Boulder District Court Judgment Book, Water Decrees, Vol 2, District 5-6, 1869-1896, pg 13
ditch/reservoir: Northwestern Mutual Life Insurance Co, Ditch No. 4
date of original appropriation: 1860 Dec 31
Water District No. 5
claimant, of Milwaukee, WI
water source: St Vrain Creek

Northwestern Mutual Life Insurance Company
filing date: 1882 June 2
Boulder District Court Judgment Book, Water Decrees, Vol 2, District 5-6, 1869-1896, pg 63
ditch/reservoir: Northwestern Mutual Life Insurance Co Ditch No. 18
date of original appropriation: 1864 Jan 1
Water District No. 5
Owner of Milwaukee, WI
water source: St Vrain Creek

Northwestern Mutual Life Insurance Company
filing date: 1882 June 2
Boulder District Court Judgment Book, Water Decrees, Vol 2, District 5-6, 1869-1896, pg 65
ditch/reservoir: Northwestern Mutual Life Insurance Co Ditch No. 18
date of original appropriation: 1864 Jan 1
Water District No. 5
Owner
water source: St Vrain Creek

North, James M (was the Referee for the following cases in the order they appeared in the book)
filing date: 1882 June 2
Leyner Ditch No. 13
South Boulder and Bear Creek Ditch No. 5
East Boulder Ditch No. 4
Cottonwood No. 2 Ditch No. 6
Dry Creek Ditch No. 7
Dry Creek No. 2 Ditch No. 9
Andrews and Farwell Ditch No. 11
Enterprise Ditch No. 12
Leyner Ditch No. 13
Marshallville Ditch No. 14
Revolution Ditch No. 41
McCarty Ditch No. 11
North Boulder Farmers Ditch No. 11
Boulder and Left Hand Ditch
Boulder and White Rock Ditch
Wellman Ditch No. 39
Mathews Ditch No. 40
Schearer Ditch No. 2
East Boulder Ditch No. 4
McGinn Ditch No. 1
Cottonwood No. 2 Ditch No. 17
Central Ditch No. 16
Howard Ditch No. 3
East Boulder Ditch No. 4
Revolution Ditch No. 41
Four Mile Canyon Ditch No. 1
McKenzie Ditch No. 4
Eggleston No. 1 Ditch No. 5
Last Chance Ditch No. 6
Church Ditch No. 7
Kinnear Ditch and Reservoir No. 8
Four Mile Canyon Ditch No. 1
Eggleston No. 2 Ditch No. 3
Houck No. 1 Ditch No. 16
Forbes Ditch No. 2
Boulder and Left Hand Ditch
Six Mile Bottom Ditch No. 1
North Branch Six Mile Bottom Ditch No. 2
Sternberg Ditch No. 34
Colorado State Mills Ditch
Four Mile Canyon Ditch No. 1
Goodhue Ditch and Reservoir No. 29
Central Ditch No. 16
McCarty Ditch No. 11
South Ditch No. 19
South Boulder Canyon Ditch No. 21
Davidson Ditch No. 26
South Boulder and Coal Creek Ditch No. 28
McKenzie Ditch No. 4
Goodhue Ditch and Reservoir No. 29
South Boulder and Rock Creek Ditch No. 30
Autry and Eggleston Ditch, No, 1
William C Hake Ditch No. 2
Eggleston No. 2 Ditch No. 3
Central Ditch No. 16
South Boulder and Coal Creek Ditch No. 28
Smith and Goss Ditch No. 2
Butte Mill Ditch No. 22
N K Smith and Tyler Ditch No. 9
Boulder and White Rock Ditch No. 35
Howell Ditch No. 3
Delehant Ditch No. 25
Plumb Ditch No. 10
Farmers Ditch No. 14
Howell and Beasley Ditch No. 23
Plumb Ditch No. 10
Houck No. 2 Ditch No. 6
Dry Creek Ditch No. 11
Lower Boulder Ditch No. 1
Rural Ditch No. 12
Lower Boulder Ditch No. 1
Dry Creek Ditch No. 11
Anderson Ditch No. 4
Taylor Ditch No. 31
Godding, Dailey and Plumb Ditch No. 5
Boulder and Weld County Ditch No. 33
Town of Boulder Ditch and Reservoir No. 37
Highland Ditch Southside No. 28
Leggett Ditch No. 30
Rural Ditch No. 12
Anderson Ditch No. 4
Leggett Ditch No. 30
Jones and Donnelly Ditch No. 7
Highland Ditch Southside No. 28
Martha M Mathews Ditch No. 8
Jones and Donnelly Ditch No. 7
Harden Ditch
Smith and Emmons Ditch No. 18
Wellman, Nichols and Hahn Ditch No. 11
Farmers Ditch No. 14
Houck No. 1 Ditch No. 16
Smith and Emmons Ditch No. 18
Dry Creek Ditch No. 11, Claim of Wm Breach
Green Ditch No. 13
Dry Creek Ditch No. 11, Claim of Mary S Stoddard et al
Carr and Tyler Ditch No. 19
Rural Ditch No. 12

Carr and Tyler Ditch No. 19
Butte Mill Ditch No. 22
Northwestern Mutual Life Insurance Co, Ditch No. 4

O

Oligarchy Ditch Company
filing date: 1882 June 2
Boulder District Court Judgment Book, Water Decrees, Vol 2, District 5-6, 1869-1896, pg 116
ditch/reservoir: Oligarchy Ditch No. 32
date of original appropriation: 1866 June 1
Water District No. 5
Owner, of Longmont
water source: St Vrain Creek

Oligarchy Ditch Company
filing date: 1882 June 2
Boulder District Court Judgment Book, Water Decrees, Vol 2, District 5-6, 1869-1896, pg 114
ditch/reservoir: Oligarchy Ditch No. 32
date of original appropriation: 1866 June 1
Water District No. 5
Owner, of Longmont
water source: St Vrain Creek

Oligarchy Extension Irrigating Ditch Company
filing date: 1882 Dec 2
Boulder District Court Judgment Book, Water Decrees, Vol 2, District 5-6, 1869-1896, pg 437
ditch/reservoir: Oligarchy Extension Ditch
date of original appropriation: 1871 Apr 1
Water District No. 5
Owner, of Longmont
water source: St Vrain Creek through the Oligarchy Ditch

Ottens, Brunhilde
filing date: 1895 Feb 12
Boulder District Court Judgment Book, Water Decrees, Vol 2, District 5-6, 1869-1896, pg 543
ditch/reservoir: Lower Baldwin Ditch
date of original appropriation: 1873 Apr 1
Water District No. 5
Owner, of Longmont
water source: Dry Creek

Ottens, Brunhilde
filing date: 1895 Feb 12
Boulder District Court Judgment Book, Water Decrees, Vol 2, District 5-6, 1869-1896, pg 537
ditch/reservoir: Mill Ditch
date of original appropriation: 1884 May 1
Water District No. 5
Reputed Owner
water source: Dry Creek

Ottens, Brunhilde
filing date: 1895 Feb 12
Boulder District Court Judgment Book, Water Decrees, Vol 2, District 5-6, 1869-1896, pg 541
ditch/reservoir: John Rice Ditch
date of original appropriation: 1884 Apr 1
Water District No. 5
Owner, of Longmont
water source: Dry Creek

Owen, Thomas R Jr (was the Referee for the following cases in the order they appear in the book)
Farmers Ditch No. 6
Baum and Goyn Ditch No. 7
Bacon (North Side) Ditch No. 86
Knoth, Streeter & Lake Ditch
Bader No. 2 Ditch No. 5
Williamson and Cavey Ditch No. 3
Taylor Private Ditch
Oligarchy Extension Ditch
Holland Ditch No. 4
Crocker Ditch No. 23
Johnson Ditch No. 25
Toll Gate Ditch No. 20
Star Ditch No. 22
Neikirk Ditch
Way Ditch No. 18
Johnson Ditch No. 25
Table Mountain Ditch No. 15
Lake Ditch No. 27
Cochran Ditch No. 1
Bacon (North Side) Ditch No. 86
Hornbaker Ditch No. 2
Altona Ditch No. 11
Bader No. 1 Ditch No. 8
Williamson and Cavey Ditch No. 3
Highland Reservoir No. 2 No. 8
Highland Lake Reservoir No. 2
Divide Reservoir No. 5
Terry Ditch No. 3
Highland Reservoir No. 3 No. 8
Fred Sigley Ditch
Sigley Lateral No. 1 East Ditch
Robert Stephens Claim
Pleasant Valley Reservoir No. 1
Terry Ditch No. 3

Left Hand Reservoir No. 3
Lagerman Reservoir No. 4
Titus & Goyn Ditch No. 72
Divide Reservoir No. 5
Pleasant Valley Reservoir No. 1
Highland Reservoir No. 1 No. 6
Crocker Ditch No. 23
Holland Ditch No. 4
Farmers Ditch No. 6
Knoth Private Ditch No. 1
Highland Reservoir No. 2 No. 8
Knoth Reservoir No. 7
Knoth Private Ditch No. 2
Terry Ditch No. 2
Davis Individual Ditch
Terry Ditch No. 1
Highland Reservoir No. 3 No. 8
Highland Reservoir No. 1 No. 6
Bond's Private Ditch
Chapman and McCaslin Ditch No. 9
Island Ditch No. 20 1/2
Pella Ditch No. 10
Northwestern Mutual Life Insurance Co. Ditch No. 4
Hayseed Ditch No. 1
St Vrain Creek & Palmerton Ditch No. 23
Dickens Private Ditch #2 No. 81
Longmont Supply Ditch No. 21 1/2
Coffin Meadow Ditch No. 3
Beckwith Ditch No. 5
Cushman Ditch No. 8
Zweck & Turner Ditch No. 21
Bacon's Appropriation No. 7
Clough Tribute (Private) Ditch No. 14
Montgomery Private Ditch No. 12 1/2
Hager's Meadow Ditch No. 18
Smead Ditch No. 13
St Vrain Creek and Gold Hill Ditch No. 17
Dickens Private Ditch No. 12
Northwestern Mutual Life Insurance Co Ditch No. 18
Clough Tribute (Private) Ditch No. 14
South Flat Ditch No. 16
Runyan Ditch No. 15
South Flat Ditch No. 16
Left Hand Ditch No. 15 1/2
Smead Ditch No. 13
Pella Ditch No. 10
Coffman Ditch No. 20
True and Webster Ditch No. 11
Dickens Private Ditch No. 12
Montgomery Private Ditch No. 12 1/2

L H Dickson's Ditch No. 19
Hager's Meadow Ditch No. 18
Clough and True Private Ditch No. 12
Left Hand Ditch No. 15 1/2
Clough and True Private Ditch No. 12
Coffman Ditch No. 20
Dickens Private Ditch No. 12
Renner Ditch No. 60
Last Chance Ditch No. 49
Coffin-Davis Ditch No. 31
Weese Private Ditch No. 29
Denio & Taylor Ditch No. 28
Last Chance Ditch No. 49
Ullery Ditch No. 66
Spring Creek Ditch No. 52
Oligarchy Ditch No. 32
Renner Ditch No. 60
Richardson Ditch No. 64
James Ditch No. 37
Highland Ditch No. 46
Webster & McCaslin Ditch No. 27
Spring Creek Ditch No. 52
Davis & Downing Ditch No. 33
Rough & Ready Ditch No. 38
Nelson Ditch No. 39
Peck & Metcalf Ditch No. 36
Swede Ditch No. 44
Bear & McCory Ditch No. 45
Davis & Downing Ditch No. 33
Highland Ditch No. 46
St Vrain Creek & Palmerton Ditch No. 23
Oligarchy Ditch No. 32
Bonus Ditch No. 6
Ni-Wot Ditch No. 24
Taylor Ditch 1 No. 78
Taylor Ditch 2 No. 79
Baker & Weese Ditch No. 24
Goss Private Ditch 1 No. 25
Lykins Gulch Ditch No. 82
Ni-Wot Ditch No. 24
Lagerman Supply Ditch No. 80
Dickens Private Ditch No. 2 No. 81
Baker & Weese Ditch No. 24
Goss Private Ditch 2 No. 25
Denio & Taylor Extension Ditch No. 69
Titus & Goyn Ditch No. 72
Supply Ditch No. 75
Webster & McCaslin Ditch No. 27

P

Parcel, Ruth C
filing date: 1882 June 2
Boulder District Court Judgment Book, Water Decrees, Vol 2, District 5-6, 1869-1896, pg 44
ditch/reservoir: Smead Ditch No. 13
date of original appropriation: 1862 Oct 1
Water District No. 5
Owner who sells to Frank A Marquette
water source: St Vrain Creek

Parcel, Ruth Mrs
filing date: 1882 June 2
Boulder District Court Judgment Book, Water Decrees, Vol 2, District 5-6, 1869-1896, pg 96
ditch/reservoir: Goss Private Ditch 1 No. 25
date of original appropriation: 1865 June 30
Water District No. 5
land irrigated
water source: St Vrain Creek

Peabody, J C
filing date: 1882 June 2
Boulder District Court Judgment Book, Water Decrees, Vol 2, District 5-6, 1869-1896, pg 312
ditch/reservoir: Dry Creek No. 2 Ditch No. 9
date of original appropriation: 1864 May 1
Water District No. 6
Owner, of Boulder
water source: South Boulder Creek

Pease
filing date: 1882 June 2
Boulder District Court Judgment Book, Water Decrees, Vol 2, District 5-6, 1869-1896, pg 314
ditch/reservoir: Andrews and Farwell Ditch No. 11
date of original appropriation: 1864 June 1
Water District No. 6
landowner
water source: South Boulder Creek

Peck, Thomas S
filing date: 1882 June 2
Boulder District Court Judgment Book, Water Decrees, Vol 2, District 5-6, 1869-1896, pg 187
ditch/reservoir: Lykins Gulch Ditch No. 82
date of original appropriation: 1881 May 15
Water District No. 5
Owner, of Longmont
water source: St Vrain Creek

Peck, Thomas S
filing date: 1882 June 2
Boulder District Court Judgment Book, Water Decrees, Vol 2, District 5-6, 1869-1896, pg 186
ditch/reservoir: Lykins Gulch Ditch No. 82
date of original appropriation: 1881 May 15
Water District No. 5
Owner, of Longmont
water source: St Vrain Creek

Peck, Thomas S
filing date: 1882 June 2
Boulder District Court Judgment Book, Water Decrees, Vol 2, District 5-6, 1869-1896, pg 124
ditch/reservoir: Peck & Metcalf Ditch No. 36
date of original appropriation: 1867 May 16
Water District No. 5
Owner, of Longmont
water source: St Vrain Creek

Pella Ditch Company
filing date: 1882 June 2
Boulder District Court Judgment Book, Water Decrees, Vol 2, District 5-6, 1869-1896, pg 26
ditch/reservoir: Pella Ditch No. 10
date of original appropriation: 1862 Mar 20
Water District No. 5
Owner of Longmont
water source: St Vrain Creek

Pella Ditch Company
filing date: 1883 Feb 19
Boulder District Court Judgment Book, Water Decrees, Vol 2, District 5-6, 1869-1896, pg 486
ditch/reservoir: Pella Ditch
date of original appropriation:
Water District No. 5
Owner
water source: St Vrain Creek

Pella Irrigating Ditch Company
filing date: 1882 June 2
Boulder District Court Judgment Book, Water Decrees, Vol 2, District 5-6, 1869-1896, pg 28
ditch/reservoir: Pella Ditch No. 10
date of original appropriation: 1862 Mar 20
Water District No. 5
Owner of Longmont
water source: St Vrain Creek

Peterson, Aaron
filing date: 1882 June 2
Boulder District Court Judgment Book, Water Decrees, Vol 2, District 5-6, 1869-1896, pg 154
ditch/reservoir: Spring Creek Ditch No. 52
date of original appropriation: 1872 June 1
Water District No. 5
Owner, of Niwot
water source: St Vrain Creek

Peterson, Aaron
filing date: 1882 June 2
Boulder District Court Judgment Book, Water Decrees, Vol 2, District 5-6, 1869-1896, pg 153
ditch/reservoir: Spring Creek Ditch No. 52
date of original appropriation: 1872 June 1
Water District No. 5
Owner, of Niwot
water source: St Vrain Creek

Petty
filing date: 1882 June 2
Boulder District Court Judgment Book, Water Decrees, Vol 2, District 5-6, 1869-1896, pg 317
ditch/reservoir: Enterprise Ditch No. 12
date of original appropriation: 1865 Feb 1
Water District No. 6
landowner
water source: South Boulder Creek

Pleasant Valley Reservoir, Fish & Ditch Company
filing date: 1883 Feb 21
Boulder District Court Judgment Book, Water Decrees, Vol 2, District 5-6, 1869-1896, pg 468
ditch/reservoir: Pleasant Valley Reservoir No. 1
date of original appropriation: 1871 June 1
Water District No. 5
Owner, of Longmont
water source: St Vrain Creek by the Rough & Ready Ditch

Pleasant Valley Reservoir, Fish & Ditch Company
filing date: 1883 Feb 12
Boulder District Court Judgment Book, Water Decrees, Vol 2, District 5-6, 1869-1896, pg 467
ditch/reservoir: Pleasant Valley Reservoir No. 1
date of original appropriation: 1871 June 1
Water District No. 5
Owner, of Longmont
water source: St Vrain Creek by the Rough & Ready Ditch

Plumb, S J
filing date: 1882 June 2
Boulder District Court Judgment Book, Water Decrees, Vol 2, District 5-6, 1869-1896, pg 218
ditch/reservoir: Plumb Ditch No. 10
date of original appropriation: 1862 Apr 1
Water District No. 6
Owner, of Erie
water source: Boulder Creek

Plumb, S J
filing date: 1882 June 2
Boulder District Court Judgment Book, Water Decrees, Vol 2, District 5-6, 1869-1896, pg 205
ditch/reservoir: Godding, Dailey and Plumb Ditch No. 5
date of original appropriation: 1861 Mar 1
Water District No. 6
Owner, of Erie
water source: Boulder Creek

Pound, Clarkson A
filing date: 1883 Feb 21
Boulder District Court Judgment Book, Water Decrees, Vol 2, District 5-6, 1869-1896, pg 470
ditch/reservoir: Highland Lake Reservoir No. 2
date of original appropriation: 1874 May 31
Water District No. 5
Owner, of Longmont
water source: St Vrain Creek by the Highland Ditch

Pound, Clarkson A
filing date: 1883 Feb 21
Boulder District Court Judgment Book, Water Decrees, Vol 2, District 5-6, 1869-1896, pg 471
ditch/reservoir: Highland Lake Reservoir No. 2
date of original appropriation: 1874 May 31
Water District No. 5
Owner, of Longmont
water source: St Vrain Creek by the Highland Ditch

R

Ramage, Addie W
filing date: 1894 Apr 28
Boulder District Court Judgment Book, Water Decrees, Vol 2, District 5-6, 1869-1896, pg 526
ditch/reservoir: Moffat Ditch
date of original appropriation: 1889 Feb 4
Water District No. 6
Owner, of Chicago, Illinois
water source: Coal Creek

Randall, J M
filing date: 1902 Oct 2
Boulder District Court Judgment Book, Water Decrees, Vol 2, District 5-6, 1869-1896, pg 567
ditch/reservoir: Wiswall Ditch
date of original appropriation: 1892 Nov 10
Water District No. 5
Owner, of Longmont
water source: Dry Creek

Reed, Andrew
filing date: 1882 June 2
Boulder District Court Judgment Book, Water Decrees, Vol 2, District 5-6, 1869-1896, pg 312
ditch/reservoir: Dry Creek No. 2 Ditch No. 9
date of original appropriation: 1864 May 1
Water District No. 6
Owner, of Boulder
water source: South Boulder Creek

Rees, John
filing date: 1882 June 2
Boulder District Court Judgment Book, Water Decrees, Vol 2, District 5-6, 1869-1896, pg 381
ditch/reservoir: Highland Ditch No. 46 Amended
date of original appropriation: 1871 Nov 30
Water District No. 5
landowner
water source: St Vrain Creek

Reese, John
filing date: 1882 June 2
Boulder District Court Judgment Book, Water Decrees, Vol 2, District 5-6, 1869-1896, pg 148
ditch/reservoir: Highland Ditch No. 46
date of original appropriation: 1871 Nov 30
Water District No. 5
his bridge mentioned
water source: St Vrain Creek

Revolution Ditch Company
filing date: 1882 June 2
Boulder District Court Judgment Book, Water Decrees, Vol 2, District 5-6, 1869-1896, pg 289
ditch/reservoir: Revolution Ditch No. 41
date of original appropriation: 1881 Dec 7
Water District No. 6
Owner, of Longmont
water source: Boulder Creek

Rice, Georgiana
filing date: 1895 Feb 12
Boulder District Court Judgment Book, Water Decrees, Vol 2, District 5-6, 1869-1896, pg 541
ditch/reservoir: John Rice Ditch
date of original appropriation: 1884 Apr 1
Water District No. 5
Owner, of Longmont
water source: Dry Creek

Rice, Georgiana
filing date: 1895 Feb 12
Boulder District Court Judgment Book, Water Decrees, Vol 2, District 5-6, 1869-1896, pg 537
ditch/reservoir: Mill Ditch
date of original appropriation: 1884 May 1
Water District No. 5
Owner, of Longmont
water source: Dry Creek

Rice, Georgiana
filing date: 1895 Feb 12
Boulder District Court Judgment Book, Water Decrees, Vol 2, District 5-6, 1869-1896, pg 537
ditch/reservoir: Rice Ditch
date of original appropriation: 1872 Mar 1
Water District No. 5
Owner, of Longmont
water source: Dry Creek

Rice, John J
filing date: 1882 June 2
Boulder District Court Judgment Book, Water Decrees, Vol 2, District 5-6, 1869-1896, pg 191
ditch/reservoir: Bonus Ditch No. 6
date of original appropriation: 1861 Mar 30
Water District No. 5
Owner, of Longmont
water source: St Vrain Creek

Rice, John J
filing date: 1882 June 2
Boulder District Court Judgment Book, Water Decrees, Vol 2, District 5-6, 1869-1896, pg 189
ditch/reservoir: Bonus Ditch No. 6
date of original appropriation: 1861 Mar 30
Water District No. 5
Owner, of Longmont
water source: St Vrain Creek

Rice, Kate
filing date: 1895 Feb 12
Boulder District Court Judgment Book, Water Decrees, Vol 2, District 5-6, 1869-1896, pg 541
ditch/reservoir: John Rice Ditch
date of original appropriation: 1884 Apr 1
Water District No. 5
Owner, of Longmont
water source: Dry Creek

Rice, Kate
filing date: 1895 Feb 12
Boulder District Court Judgment Book, Water Decrees, Vol 2, District 5-6, 1869-1896, pg 537
ditch/reservoir: Mill Ditch
date of original appropriation: 1884 May 1
Water District No. 5
Owner, of Longmont
water source: Dry Creek

Rice, Kate
filing date: 1895 Feb 12
Boulder District Court Judgment Book, Water Decrees, Vol 2, District 5-6, 1869-1896, pg 537
ditch/reservoir: Rice Ditch
date of original appropriation: 1872 Mar 1
Water District No. 5
Owner, of Longmont
water source: Dry Creek

Rinkis, Charles
filing date: 1882 June 2
Boulder District Court Judgment Book, Water Decrees, Vol 2, District 5-6, 1869-1896, pg 314
ditch/reservoir: Andrews and Farwell Ditch No. 11
date of original appropriation: 1864 June 1
Water District No. 6
Owner, of Valmont
water source: South Boulder Creek

Robinson, T M
filing date: 1903 Sept 15
Boulder District Court Judgment Book, Water Decrees, Vol 2, District 5-6, 1869-1896, pg 568
ditch/reservoir:
date of original appropriation:
Water District No. 6
Referee
water source:

Robinson, T M
filing date: 1903 Sept 15
Boulder District Court Judgment Book, Water Decrees, Vol 2, District 5-6, 1869-1896, pg 568
ditch/reservoir:
date of original appropriation:
Water District No. 6
Attorney
water source:

Robinson, T M
filing date: 1900 Dec 19
Boulder District Court Judgment Book, Water Decrees, Vol 2, District 5-6, 1869-1896, pg 553
ditch/reservoir: Last Chance Reservoir No. 1 and No. 2
date of original appropriation:
Water District No. 6
Referee
water source: Coal Creek

Robinson, T W [M]
filing date: 1888 Sept 28
Boulder District Court Judgment Book, Water Decrees, Vol 2, District 5-6, 1869-1896, pg 490
ditch/reservoir:
date of original appropriation:
Water District No. 5
Judge
water source:

Rough & Ready Irrigating Ditch Company
filing date: 1882 June 2
Boulder District Court Judgment Book, Water Decrees, Vol 2, District 5-6, 1869-1896, pg 133
ditch/reservoir: Rough & Ready Ditch No. 38
date of original appropriation: 1869 Mar 13
Water District No. 5
Owner, of Longmont
water source: St Vrain Creek

Rowland, E
filing date: 1882 June 2
Boulder District Court Judgment Book, Water Decrees, Vol 2, District 5-6, 1869-1896, pg 58
ditch/reservoir: St Vrain Creek and Gold Hill Ditch No. 17
date of original appropriation: 1863 Oct 25
Water District No. 5
Superintendant, of Boulder
water source: St Vrain Creek

Runion [Runyan], Isaac
filing date: 1882 June 2
Boulder District Court Judgment Book, Water Decrees, Vol 2, District 5-6, 1869-1896, pg 105
ditch/reservoir: Denio & Taylor Ditch No. 28
date of original appropriation: 1865 July 15
Water District No. 5
Owner, of Longmont
water source: St Vrain Creek

Runyan, Isaac
filing date: 1882 June 2
Boulder District Court Judgment Book, Water Decrees, Vol 2, District 5-6, 1869-1896, pg 103
ditch/reservoir: Denio & Taylor Ditch No. 28
date of original appropriation: 1865 July 15
Water District No. 5
Owner, of Longmont
water source: St Vrain Creek

Runyan, Isaac
filing date: 1882 June 2
Boulder District Court Judgment Book, Water Decrees, Vol 2, District 5-6, 1869-1896, pg 50
ditch/reservoir: Runyan Ditch No. 15
date of original appropriation: 1863 May 1
Water District No. 5
Owner of Longmont
water source: St Vrain Creek

Runyan, Isaac
filing date: 1882 June 2
Boulder District Court Judgment Book, Water Decrees, Vol 2, District 5-6, 1869-1896, pg 49
ditch/reservoir: Runyan Ditch No. 15
date of original appropriation: 1863 May 1
Water District No. 5
Owner of Longmont
water source: St Vrain Creek

Rural Ditch Company
filing date: 1882 June 2
Boulder District Court Judgment Book, Water Decrees, Vol 2, District 5-6, 1869-1896, pg 220
ditch/reservoir: Rural Ditch No. 12
date of original appropriation: 1862 May 10
Water District No. 6
Owner, of Longmont
water source: Boulder Creek

Rust, G W
filing date: 1882 June 2
Boulder District Court Judgment Book, Water Decrees, Vol 2, District 5-6, 1869-1896, pg 272
ditch/reservoir: Dry Creek Ditch No. 11, Claim of Mary S Stoddard et al
date of original appropriation: 1862 June 1
Water District No. 6
Owner, of Boulder
water source: Boulder Creek

Rust, George W
filing date: 1882 June 2
Boulder District Court Judgment Book, Water Decrees, Vol 2, District 5-6, 1869-1896, pg 278
ditch/reservoir: McCarty Ditch No. 11
date of original appropriation: 1862 June 1
Water District No. 6
Owner, of Boulder
water source: Boulder Creek

Rust, George W
filing date: 1882 June 2
Boulder District Court Judgment Book, Water Decrees, Vol 2, District 5-6, 1869-1896, pg 282
ditch/reservoir: Boulder and White Rock Ditch
date of original appropriation: 1862 June 1
Water District No. 6
Claimant
water source: Boulder Creek

Rust, George W
filing date: 1882 June 2
Boulder District Court Judgment Book, Water Decrees, Vol 2, District 5-6, 1869-1896, pg 283
ditch/reservoir: Boulder and White Rock Ditch
date of original appropriation: 1862 June 1
Water District No. 6
Claimant
water source: Boulder Creek

S

Sawdy [Sawdey], Edgar
filing date: 1882 June 2
Boulder District Court Judgment Book, Water Decrees, Vol 2, District 5-6, 1869-1896, pg 247
ditch/reservoir: Leggett Ditch No. 30
date of original appropriation: 1868 May 1 (half constructed by 1 June 1862)
Water District No. 6
Owner, of Erie
water source: Boulder Creek

Scott, H S
filing date: 1882 June 1
Boulder District Court Judgment Book, Water Decrees, Vol 2, District 5-6, 1869-1896, pg 3
ditch/reservoir: Hayseed Ditch No. 1
date of original appropriation: 1860 Jan 1
Water District No. 5
Owner of Boulder
water source: St Vrain Creek

Scott, H S
filing date: 1882 June 1
Boulder District Court Judgment Book, Water Decrees, Vol 2, District 5-6, 1869-1896, pg 2
ditch/reservoir: Hayseed Ditch No. 1
date of original appropriation: 1860 Jan 1
Water District No. 5
Owner of Boulder
water source: St Vrain Creek

Secor & McGwire
filing date: 1902 Oct 21
Boulder District Court Judgment Book, Water Decrees, Vol 2, District 5-6, 1869-1896, pg 568
ditch/reservoir:
date of original appropriation:
Water District No. 5
Attorney
water source:

Secor, F P
filing date: 1896 Oct 20
Boulder District Court Judgment Book, Water Decrees, Vol 2, District 5-6, 1869-1896, pg 548
ditch/reservoir: Upper Baldwin Ditch
date of original appropriation: 1872 Apr 1
Water District No. 5
Attorney
water source: Dry Creek

See, Ruth R
filing date: 1894 Apr 28
Boulder District Court Judgment Book, Water Decrees, Vol 2, District 5-6, 1869-1896, pg 526
ditch/reservoir: Moffat Ditch
date of original appropriation: 1889 Feb 4
Water District No. 6
Owner, of New York City, New York
water source: Coal Creek

Shanahan, Michael
filing date: 1882 June 2
Boulder District Court Judgment Book, Water Decrees, Vol 2, District 5-6, 1869-1896, pg 295
ditch/reservoir: Schearer Ditch No. 2
date of original appropriation: 1860 June 1
Water District No. 6
Owner, of Boulder
water source: South Boulder Creek

Shelton
filing date: 1882 June 2
Boulder District Court Judgment Book, Water Decrees, Vol 2, District 5-6, 1869-1896, pg 252
ditch/reservoir: Boulder and Weld County Ditch No. 33
date of original appropriation: 1871 May 1
Water District No. 6
farm owner
water source: Boulder Creek

Sigley, Fred C
filing date: 1882 Dec 2
Boulder District Court Judgment Book, Water Decrees, Vol 2, District 5-6, 1869-1896, pg 455
ditch/reservoir: Fred Sigley Ditch
date of original appropriation: 1878 May 15
Water District No. 5
Owner, of Longmont
water source: St Vrain Creek through the Highland Ditch

Sigley, W B
filing date: 1882 Dec 2
Boulder District Court Judgment Book, Water Decrees, Vol 2, District 5-6, 1869-1896, pg 456
ditch/reservoir: Sigley Lateral No. 1 East Ditch
date of original appropriation: 1874 Apr 1
Water District No. 5
Owner, of Longmont
water source: St Vrain Creek through the Highland & Supply Ditches

Smart, Francis
filing date: 1903 Sept 15
Boulder District Court Judgment Book, Water Decrees, Vol 2, District 5-6, 1869-1896, pg 568
ditch/reservoir:
date of original appropriation:
Water District No. 6
Owner deceased
water source:

Smart, Francis
filing date: 1900 Dec 19
Boulder District Court Judgment Book, Water Decrees, Vol 2, District 5-6, 1869-1896, pg 553
ditch/reservoir: Kinnear Reservoir
date of original appropriation:
Water District No. 6
Claimant
water source: Coal Creek

Smead
filing date: 1882 June 2
Boulder District Court Judgment Book, Water Decrees, Vol 2, District 5-6, 1869-1896, pg 48
ditch/reservoir: Clough Tribute (Private) Ditch No. 14
date of original appropriation: 1863 Apr 15
Water District No. 5
former owner
water source: St Vrain Creek

Smead, C L
filing date: 1882 June 2
Boulder District Court Judgment Book, Water Decrees, Vol 2, District 5-6, 1869-1896, pg 40
ditch/reservoir: Montgomery Private Ditch No. 12 1/2
date of original appropriation: 1862 May 15
Water District No. 5
Owner, of Longmont
water source: St Vrain Creek

Smead, C L
filing date: 1882 June 2
Boulder District Court Judgment Book, Water Decrees, Vol 2, District 5-6, 1869-1896, pg 43
ditch/reservoir: Smead Ditch No. 13
date of original appropriation: 1862 Oct 1
Water District No. 5
Owner, of Longmont
water source: St Vrain Creek

Smead, C L
filing date: 1882 June 2
Boulder District Court Judgment Book, Water Decrees, Vol 2, District 5-6, 1869-1896, pg 41
ditch/reservoir: Montgomery Private Ditch No. 12 1/2
date of original appropriation: 1862 May 15
Water District No. 5
Owner, of Longmont
water source: St Vrain Creek

Smead, C L
filing date: 1882 June 2
Boulder District Court Judgment Book, Water Decrees, Vol 2, District 5-6, 1869-1896, pg 44
ditch/reservoir: Smead Ditch No. 13
date of original appropriation: 1862 Oct 1
Water District No. 5
Owner, of Longmont
water source: St Vrain Creek

Smead, Chester
filing date: 1882 June 2
Boulder District Court Judgment Book, Water Decrees, Vol 2, District 5-6, 1869-1896, pg 141
ditch/reservoir: Swede Ditch No. 44
date of original appropriation: 1871 May 1
Water District No. 5
land owner
water source: St Vrain Creek

Smith
filing date: 1882 June 2
Boulder District Court Judgment Book, Water Decrees, Vol 2, District 5-6, 1869-1896, pg 268
ditch/reservoir: Dry Creek Ditch No. 11
date of original appropriation: 1862 June 1
Water District No. 6
Claimant
water source: Boulder Creek

Smith, Daniel Mrs
filing date: 1882 June 2
Boulder District Court Judgment Book, Water Decrees, Vol 2, District 5-6, 1869-1896, pg 249
ditch/reservoir: Taylor Ditch No. 31
date of original appropriation: 1870 Apr 1
Water District No. 6
Owner, of Longmont
water source: Boulder Creek

Smith, M G
filing date: 1882 June 2
Boulder District Court Judgment Book, Water Decrees, Vol 2, District 5-6, 1869-1896, pg 197
ditch/reservoir: Smith and Goss Ditch No. 2
date of original appropriation: 1859 Nov 15
Water District No. 6
Owner, of Boulder
water source: Boulder Creek

Smith, M G
filing date: 1882 June 2
Boulder District Court Judgment Book, Water Decrees, Vol 2, District 5-6, 1869-1896, pg 269
ditch/reservoir: Dry Creek Ditch No. 11, claims of Berkley and Smith
date of original appropriation: 1862 June 1
Water District No. 6
Owner, of Boulder
water source: Boulder Creek

Smith, M G
filing date: 1882 June 2
Boulder District Court Judgment Book, Water Decrees, Vol 2, District 5-6, 1869-1896, pg 283
ditch/reservoir: Boulder and White Rock Ditch
date of original appropriation: 1862 June 1
Water District No. 6
Claimant
water source: Boulder Creek

Smith, M G
filing date: 1882 June 2
Boulder District Court Judgment Book, Water Decrees, Vol 2, District 5-6, 1869-1896, pg 282
ditch/reservoir: Boulder and White Rock Ditch
date of original appropriation: 1862 June 1
Water District No. 6
Claimant
water source: Boulder Creek

Smith, M G
filing date: 1882 June 2
Boulder District Court Judgment Book, Water Decrees, Vol 2, District 5-6, 1869-1896, pg 255
ditch/reservoir: Town of Boulder Ditch and Reservoir No. 37
date of original appropriation: 1875 June 17
Water District No. 6
Addition
water source: Boulder Creek

Smith, Milton
filing date: 1900 Dec 19
Boulder District Court Judgment Book, Water Decrees, Vol 2, District 5-6, 1869-1896, pg 553
ditch/reservoir: Kinnear Reservoir
date of original appropriation:
Water District No. 6
Attorney
water source: Coal Creek

Smith, Milton
filing date: 1903 Sept 15
Boulder District Court Judgment Book, Water Decrees, Vol 2, District 5-6, 1869-1896, pg 569
ditch/reservoir: Kinnear Reservoir
date of original appropriation:
Water District No. 6
Attorney
water source: Coal Creek

Smith, R N
filing date: 1882 June 2
Boulder District Court Judgment Book, Water Decrees, Vol 2, District 5-6, 1869-1896, pg 231
ditch/reservoir: Smith and Emmons Ditch No. 18
date of original appropriation: 1863 June 1
Water District No. 6
Owner, of Longmont
water source: Boulder Creek

Smith, R N
filing date: 1882 June 2
Boulder District Court Judgment Book, Water Decrees, Vol 2, District 5-6, 1869-1896, pg 244
ditch/reservoir: Highland Ditch Southside No. 28
date of original appropriation: 1865 June 1
Water District No. 6
Owner, of Longmont
water source: Boulder Creek

Solander, D
filing date: 1882 June 2
Boulder District Court Judgment Book, Water Decrees, Vol 2, District 5-6, 1869-1896, pg 317
ditch/reservoir: Enterprise Ditch No. 12
date of original appropriation: 1865 Feb 1
Water District No. 6
landowner
water source: South Boulder Creek

South Boulder and Bear Creek Ditch Company
filing date: 1882 June 2
Boulder District Court Judgment Book, Water Decrees, Vol 2, District 5-6, 1869-1896, pg 303
ditch/reservoir: South Boulder and Bear Creek Ditch No. 5
date of original appropriation: 1862 May 25
Water District No. 6
Owner, of Boulder
water source: South Boulder Creek

South Boulder and Coal Creek Ditch Company
filing date: 1882 June 2
Boulder District Court Judgment Book, Water Decrees, Vol 2, District 5-6, 1869-1896, pg 340
ditch/reservoir: South Boulder and Coal Creek Ditch No. 28
date of original appropriation: 1872 June 1
Water District No. 6
Owner, of Louisville
water source: South Boulder Creek

South Boulder and Rock Creek Ditch Company
filing date: 1882 June 2
Boulder District Court Judgment Book, Water Decrees, Vol 2, District 5-6, 1869-1896, pg 345
ditch/reservoir: South Boulder and Rock Creek Ditch No. 30
date of original appropriation: 1873 June 1
Water District No. 6
Owner, of Louisville
water source: South Boulder Creek

South Boulder Canyon Ditch Company
filing date: 1882 June 2
Boulder District Court Judgment Book, Water Decrees, Vol 2, District 5-6, 1869-1896, pg 334
ditch/reservoir: South Boulder Canyon Ditch No. 21
date of original appropriation: 1870 May 15
Water District No. 6
Owner, of Boulder
water source: South Boulder Creek

Squires (Tourtellot & Squires)
filing date: 1882 June 2
Boulder District Court Judgment Book, Water Decrees, Vol 2, District 5-6, 1869-1896, pg 255
ditch/reservoir: Town of Boulder Ditch and Reservoir No. 37
date of original appropriation: 1875 June 17
Water District No. 6
Addition
water source: Boulder Creek

St Vrain Creek and Gold Hill Ditch Company, Inc.
filing date: 1882 June 2
Boulder District Court Judgment Book, Water Decrees, Vol 2, District 5-6, 1869-1896, pg 58
ditch/reservoir: St Vrain Creek and Gold Hill Ditch No. 17
date of original appropriation: 1863 Oct 25
Water District No. 5
Owner
water source: St Vrain Creek

St Vrain Creek and Palmerton Ditch Company
filing date: 1882 June 2
Boulder District Court Judgment Book, Water Decrees, Vol 2, District 5-6, 1869-1896, pg 85
ditch/reservoir: St Vrain Creek & Palmerton Ditch No. 23
date of original appropriation: 1865 May 31
Water District No. 5
Owner
water source: St Vrain Creek

St Vrain Creek and Palmerton Ditch Company
filing date: 1882 June 2
Boulder District Court Judgment Book, Water Decrees, Vol 2, District 5-6, 1869-1896, pg 83
ditch/reservoir: St Vrain Creek & Palmerton Ditch No. 23
date of original appropriation: 1865 May 31
Water District No. 5
Owner, of Longmont
water source: St Vrain Creek

Standart, S H
filing date: 1895 Feb 12
Boulder District Court Judgment Book, Water Decrees, Vol 2, District 5-6, 1869-1896, pg 546
ditch/reservoir: Upper Baldwin Ditch
date of original appropriation: 1872 Apr 1
Water District No. 5
Owner, of 301 Boston Building, Denver, CO
water source: Dry Creek

Standley, Joseph
filing date: 1903 Sept 15
Boulder District Court Judgment Book, Water Decrees, Vol 2, District 5-6, 1869-1896, pg 569
ditch/reservoir: Kinnear Reservoir
date of original appropriation:
Water District No. 6

Claimant
water source: Coal Creek

Standley, Joseph
filing date: 1900 Dec 19
Boulder District Court Judgment Book, Water Decrees, Vol 2, District 5-6, 1869-1896, pg 553
ditch/reservoir: Kinnear Reservoir
date of original appropriation:
Water District No. 6
Claimant
water source: Coal Creek

Standley, Joseph
filing date: 1903 Sept 15
Boulder District Court Judgment Book, Water Decrees, Vol 2, District 5-6, 1869-1896, pg 568
ditch/reservoir:
date of original appropriation:
Water District No. 6
Owner
water source:

Standley, Joseph
filing date: 1900 Dec 19
Boulder District Court Judgment Book, Water Decrees, Vol 2, District 5-6, 1869-1896, pg 553
ditch/reservoir: Kinnear Reservoir
date of original appropriation:
Water District No. 6
Claimant
water source: Coal Creek

Staples
filing date: 1882 June 2
Boulder District Court Judgment Book, Water Decrees, Vol 2, District 5-6, 1869-1896, pg 317
ditch/reservoir: Enterprise Ditch No. 12
date of original appropriation: 1865 Feb 1
Water District No. 6
landowner
water source: South Boulder Creek

Star Ditch Company
filing date: 1882 Dec 2
Boulder District Court Judgment Book, Water Decrees, Vol 2, District 5-6, 1869-1896, pg 425
ditch/reservoir: Star Ditch No. 22
date of original appropriation: 1871 Apr 1
Water District No. 5
Owner, of Longmont
water source: Left Hand Creek

Star Ditch Company
filing date: 1882 Dec 2
Boulder District Court Judgment Book, Water Decrees, Vol 2, District 5-6, 1869-1896, pg 426
ditch/reservoir: Star Ditch No. 22
date of original appropriation: 1871 Apr 1
Water District No. 5
Owner, of Longmont
water source: Left Hand Creek

Stephens, Robert
filing date: 1882 Dec 2
Boulder District Court Judgment Book, Water Decrees, Vol 2, District 5-6, 1869-1896, pg 457
ditch/reservoir: Robert Stephens Claim
date of original appropriation: 1874 June 10
Water District No. 5
Owner, of Longmont
water source: St Vrain Creek through the Highland Ditch

Sternberg, D K
filing date: 1882 June 2
Boulder District Court Judgment Book, Water Decrees, Vol 2, District 5-6, 1869-1896, pg 312
ditch/reservoir: Dry Creek No. 2 Ditch No. 9
date of original appropriation: 1864 May 1
Water District No. 6
Owner, of Boulder
water source: South Boulder Creek

Sternberg, D K
filing date: 1882 June 2
Boulder District Court Judgment Book, Water Decrees, Vol 2, District 5-6, 1869-1896, pg 298
ditch/reservoir: Howard Ditch No. 3
date of original appropriation: 1860 Apr 1
Water District No. 6
Owner, of Boulder
water source: South Boulder Creek

Sternberg, Jay
filing date: 1882 June 2
Boulder District Court Judgment Book, Water Decrees, Vol 2, District 5-6, 1869-1896, pg 378
ditch/reservoir: Sternberg Ditch No. 34
date of original appropriation: 1872 Nov 28
Water District No. 6
Owner, of Boulder
water source: Boulder Creek

Stevens, Sarah C
filing date: 1894 Apr 28
Boulder District Court Judgment Book, Water Decrees, Vol 2, District 5-6, 1869-1896, pg 526
ditch/reservoir: Moffat Ditch
date of original appropriation: 1889 Feb 4
Water District No. 6
Owner, of Wilkes-Barre, Pennsylvania
water source: Coal Creek

Stoddard, Mary S
filing date: 1882 June 2
Boulder District Court Judgment Book, Water Decrees, Vol 2, District 5-6, 1869-1896, pg 272
ditch/reservoir: Dry Creek Ditch No. 11, Claim of Mary S Stoddard et al
date of original appropriation: 1862 June 1
Water District No. 6
Owner, of Boulder
water source: Boulder Creek

Stoddard, Mary S
filing date: 1882 June 2
Boulder District Court Judgment Book, Water Decrees, Vol 2, District 5-6, 1869-1896, pg 271
ditch/reservoir: Dry Creek Ditch No. 11, Claim of Mary S Stoddard et al
date of original appropriation: 1862 June 1
Water District No. 6
Claimant
water source: Boulder Creek

Stoddard, Mary S
filing date: 1882 June 2
Boulder District Court Judgment Book, Water Decrees, Vol 2, District 5-6, 1869-1896, pg 282
ditch/reservoir: Boulder and White Rock Ditch
date of original appropriation: 1862 June 1
Water District No. 6
Claimant
water source: Boulder Creek

Stoddard, Mary S
filing date: 1882 June 2
Boulder District Court Judgment Book, Water Decrees, Vol 2, District 5-6, 1869-1896, pg 278
ditch/reservoir: McCarty Ditch No. 11
date of original appropriation: 1862 June 1
Water District No. 6
Owner, of Boulder
water source: Boulder Creek

Stoner, Peter
filing date: 1882 June 2
Boulder District Court Judgment Book, Water Decrees, Vol 2, District 5-6, 1869-1896, pg 78
ditch/reservoir: Zweck & Turner Ditch No. 21
date of original appropriation: 1864 June 30
Water District No. 5
Owner
water source: St Vrain Creek

Stoner, Peter
filing date: 1882 June 2
Boulder District Court Judgment Book, Water Decrees, Vol 2, District 5-6, 1869-1896, pg 77
ditch/reservoir: Zweck & Turner Ditch No. 21
date of original appropriation: 1864 June 30
Water District No. 5
Owner
water source: St Vrain Creek

Stott
filing date: 1882 June 2
Boulder District Court Judgment Book, Water Decrees, Vol 2, District 5-6, 1869-1896, pg 298
ditch/reservoir: Howard Ditch No. 3
date of original appropriation: 1860 Apr 1
Water District No. 6
landowner
water source: South Boulder Creek

Streeter, Reinzi
filing date: 1882 Dec 2
Boulder District Court Judgment Book, Water Decrees, Vol 2, District 5-6, 1869-1896, pg 436
ditch/reservoir: Knoth, Streeter & Lake Ditch
date of original appropriation: 1873 Mar 15
Water District No. 5
Owner, of Longmont
water source: St Vrain Creek through the Oligarchy Ditch

Supply Ditch Company
filing date: 1882 June 2
Boulder District Court Judgment Book, Water Decrees, Vol 2, District 5-6, 1869-1896, pg 172
ditch/reservoir: Supply Ditch No. 75
date of original appropriation: 1878 May 31
Water District No. 5
Owner, of Longmont
water source: St Vrain Creek

Swede Ditch Company
filing date: 1882 June 2
Boulder District Court Judgment Book, Water Decrees, Vol 2, District 5-6, 1869-1896, pg 141
ditch/reservoir: Swede Ditch No. 44
date of original appropriation: 1871 May 1
Water District No. 5
Owner, of Longmont
water source: St Vrain Creek

Swede Ditch Company
filing date: 1882 June 2
Boulder District Court Judgment Book, Water Decrees, Vol 2, District 5-6, 1869-1896, pg 139
ditch/reservoir: Swede Ditch No. 44
date of original appropriation: 1871 May 1
Water District No. 5
Owner, of Longmont
water source: St Vrain Creek

T

Table Mountain Ditch Company
filing date: 1882 Dec 2
Boulder District Court Judgment Book, Water Decrees, Vol 2, District 5-6, 1869-1896, pg 417
ditch/reservoir: Table Mountain Ditch No. 15
date of original appropriation: 1866 June 25
Water District No. 5
[Owner], of NiWot, CO
water source: Left Hand Creek

Table Mountain Ditch Company
filing date: 1882 Dec 2
Boulder District Court Judgment Book, Water Decrees, Vol 2, District 5-6, 1869-1896, pg 414
ditch/reservoir: Table Mountain Ditch No. 15
date of original appropriation: 1866 June 25
Water District No. 5
Owner, of NiWot
water source: Left Hand Creek

Taylor, D C
filing date: 1882 June 2
Boulder District Court Judgment Book, Water Decrees, Vol 2, District 5-6, 1869-1896, pg 29
ditch/reservoir: Pella Ditch No. 10
date of original appropriation: 1862 Mar 20
Water District No. 5
witness
water source: St Vrain Creek

Taylor, David C
filing date: 1882 Dec 2
Boulder District Court Judgment Book, Water Decrees, Vol 2, District 5-6, 1869-1896, pg 439
ditch/reservoir: Taylor Private Ditch
date of original appropriation: 1872 May 10
Water District No. 5
Owner, of Longmont
water source: St Vrain Creek through the Peck Lateral Ditch

Taylor, Florence
filing date: 1882 June 2
Boulder District Court Judgment Book, Water Decrees, Vol 2, District 5-6, 1869-1896, pg 249
ditch/reservoir: Taylor Ditch No. 31
date of original appropriation: 1870 Apr 1
Water District No. 6
Owner, of Longmont
water source: Boulder Creek

Taylor, James H
filing date: 1882 June 2
Boulder District Court Judgment Book, Water Decrees, Vol 2, District 5-6, 1869-1896, pg 249
ditch/reservoir: Taylor Ditch No. 31
date of original appropriation: 1870 Apr 1
Water District No. 6
Owner, of Longmont
water source: Boulder Creek

Templeton, Andrew
filing date: 1882 June 2
Boulder District Court Judgment Book, Water Decrees, Vol 2, District 5-6, 1869-1896, pg 244
ditch/reservoir: Highland Ditch Southside No. 28
date of original appropriation: 1865 June 1
Water District No. 6
Owner, of Longmont
water source: Boulder Creek

Terry, Seth
filing date: 1882 Dec 2
Boulder District Court Judgment Book, Water Decrees, Vol 2, District 5-6, 1869-1896, pg 451
ditch/reservoir: Terry Ditch No. 1
date of original appropriation: 1873 May 15
Water District No. 5
Owner, of Longmont
water source: St Vrain Creek through the Highland & Supply Ditches

Terry, Seth
filing date: 1882 Dec 2
Boulder District Court Judgment Book, Water Decrees, Vol 2, District 5-6, 1869-1896, pg 453
ditch/reservoir: Terry Ditch No. 3
date of original appropriation: 1878 May 1
Water District No. 5
Owner, of Longmont
water source: St Vrain Creek through the Highland Ditch

Terry, Seth
filing date: 1882 Dec 2
Boulder District Court Judgment Book, Water Decrees, Vol 2, District 5-6, 1869-1896, pg 452
ditch/reservoir: Terry Ditch No. 2
date of original appropriation: 1877 May 1
Water District No. 5
Owner, of Longmont
water source: St Vrain Creek through the Highland Ditch

Thorne, George H
filing date: 1902 Oct 21
Boulder District Court Judgment Book, Water Decrees, Vol 2, District 5-6, 1869-1896, pg 568
ditch/reservoir:
date of original appropriation:
Water District No. 5
Attorney
water source:

Titus, Albert
filing date: 1883 May 7
Boulder District Court Judgment Book, Water Decrees, Vol 2, District 5-6, 1869-1896, pg 482
ditch/reservoir: Titus & Goyn Ditch No. 72
date of original appropriation: 1878 Apr 1
Water District No. 5
Owner, of Boulder
water source: Dry Creek, a tributary of St Vrain Creek

Titus, Albert
filing date: 1882 June 2
Boulder District Court Judgment Book, Water Decrees, Vol 2, District 5-6, 1869-1896, pg 169
ditch/reservoir: Titus & Goyn Ditch No. 72
date of original appropriation: 1878 Apr 1
Water District No. 5
Owner, of Boulder
water source: St Vrain Creek

Titus, Albert
filing date: 1882 June 2
Boulder District Court Judgment Book, Water Decrees, Vol 2, District 5-6, 1869-1896, pg 168
ditch/reservoir: Titus & Goyn Ditch No. 72
date of original appropriation: 1878 Apr 1
Water District No. 5
Owner, of Boulder
water source: St Vrain Creek

Toll Gate Ditch Company
filing date: 1882 Dec 2
Boulder District Court Judgment Book, Water Decrees, Vol 2, District 5-6, 1869-1896, pg 423
ditch/reservoir: Toll Gate Ditch No. 20
date of original appropriation: 1870 Apr 1
Water District No. 5
Owner, of Altona
water source: Left Hand Creek

Toll Gate Ditch Company
filing date: 1882 Dec 2
Boulder District Court Judgment Book, Water Decrees, Vol 2, District 5-6, 1869-1896, pg 421
ditch/reservoir: Toll Gate Ditch No. 20
date of original appropriation: 1870 Apr 1
Water District No. 5
Owner, of Altona
water source: Left Hand Creek

Tourtellot & Squires
filing date: 1882 June 2
Boulder District Court Judgment Book, Water Decrees, Vol 2, District 5-6, 1869-1896, pg 255
ditch/reservoir: Town of Boulder Ditch and Reservoir No. 37
date of original appropriation: 1875 June 17
Water District No. 6
Addition
water source: Boulder Creek

True, C C
filing date: 1882 June 2
Boulder District Court Judgment Book, Water Decrees, Vol 2, District 5-6, 1869-1896, pg 38
ditch/reservoir: Clough and True Private Ditch No. 12
date of original appropriation: 1862 Apr 15
Water District No. 5
Owner of Longmont
water source: St Vrain Creek

True, C C
filing date: 1882 June 2
Boulder District Court Judgment Book, Water Decrees, Vol 2, District 5-6, 1869-1896, pg 31
ditch/reservoir: True and Webster Ditch No. 11
date of original appropriation: 1862 Apr 1
Water District No. 5
Owner of Longmont
water source: St Vrain Creek

True, C C
filing date: 1882 June 2
Boulder District Court Judgment Book, Water Decrees, Vol 2, District 5-6, 1869-1896, pg 37
ditch/reservoir: Clough and True Private Ditch No. 12
date of original appropriation: 1862 Apr 15
Water District No. 5
Owner of Longmont
water source: St Vrain Creek

True, C C
filing date: 1882 June 2
Boulder District Court Judgment Book, Water Decrees, Vol 2, District 5-6, 1869-1896, pg 32
ditch/reservoir: True and Webster Ditch No. 11
date of original appropriation: 1862 Apr 1
Water District No. 5
Owner of Longmont
water source: St Vrain Creek

Turner, T A
filing date: 1882 June 2
Boulder District Court Judgment Book, Water Decrees, Vol 2, District 5-6, 1869-1896, pg 78
ditch/reservoir: Zweck & Turner Ditch No. 21
date of original appropriation: 1864 June 30
Water District No. 5
Owner
water source: St Vrain Creek

Turner, T A
filing date: 1882 June 2
Boulder District Court Judgment Book, Water Decrees, Vol 2, District 5-6, 1869-1896, pg 77
ditch/reservoir: Zweck & Turner Ditch No. 21
date of original appropriation: 1864 June 30
Water District No. 5
Owner
water source: St Vrain Creek

Tyler, Clinton M
filing date: 1882 Dec 2
Boulder District Court Judgment Book, Water Decrees, Vol 2, District 5-6, 1869-1896, pg 440
ditch/reservoir: Crocker Ditch No. 23
date of original appropriation: 1871 May 1
Water District No. 5
Owner, of Boulder
water source: Left Hand Creek

Tyler, Clinton M
filing date: 1882 June 2
Boulder District Court Judgment Book, Water Decrees, Vol 2, District 5-6, 1869-1896, pg 205
ditch/reservoir: Godding, Dailey and Plumb Ditch No. 5
date of original appropriation: 1861 Mar 1
Water District No. 6
Owner, of Boulder
water source: Boulder Creek

Tyler, Clinton M
filing date: 1882 June 2
Boulder District Court Judgment Book, Water Decrees, Vol 2, District 5-6, 1869-1896, pg 371
ditch/reservoir: Forbes Ditch No. 2
date of original appropriation: 1878 Apr 1
Water District No. 6
Owner, Boulder
water source: Four Mile Canyon Creek

Tyler, Clinton M
filing date: 1882 Dec 2
Boulder District Court Judgment Book, Water Decrees, Vol 2, District 5-6, 1869-1896, pg 442
ditch/reservoir: Crocker Ditch No. 23
date of original appropriation: 1871 May 1
Water District No. 5
Owner, of Boulder
water source: Left Hand Creek

Tyler, Clinton M
filing date: 1882 June 2
Boulder District Court Judgment Book, Water Decrees, Vol 2, District 5-6, 1869-1896, pg 376
ditch/reservoir: North Branch Six Mile Bottom Ditch No. 2
date of original appropriation: 1875 Apr 1
Water District No. 6
Owner, of Boulder
water source: Jains Gulch a tributary of Left Hand Creek

Tyler, Clinton M
filing date: 1882 June 2
Boulder District Court Judgment Book, Water Decrees, Vol 2, District 5-6, 1869-1896, pg 234
ditch/reservoir: Carr and Tyler Ditch No. 19
date of original appropriation: 1864 June 1
Water District No. 6
Owner, of Boulder
water source: Boulder Creek

Tyler, Clinton M
filing date: 1882 June 2
Boulder District Court Judgment Book, Water Decrees, Vol 2, District 5-6, 1869-1896, pg 368
ditch/reservoir: Four Mile Canyon Ditch No. 1
date of original appropriation: 1875 Apr 1
Water District No. 6
Owner, of Boulder
water source: Four Mile Canyon Creek

Tyler, Clinton M
filing date: 1882 June 2
Boulder District Court Judgment Book, Water Decrees, Vol 2, District 5-6, 1869-1896, pg 215
ditch/reservoir: N K Smith and Tyler Ditch No. 9
date of original appropriation: 1861 June 1
Water District No. 6
Owner, of Boulder
water source: Boulder Creek

V

Valker, R F
filing date: 1882 Dec 2
Boulder District Court Judgment Book, Water Decrees, Vol 2, District 5-6, 1869-1896, pg 428
ditch/reservoir: Johnson Ditch No. 25
date of original appropriation: 1873 Apr 1
Water District No. 5
Owner, of NiWot
water source: Left Hand Creek

Valker, R F
filing date: 1882 Dec 2
Boulder District Court Judgment Book, Water Decrees, Vol 2, District 5-6, 1869-1896, pg 429
ditch/reservoir: Johnson Ditch No. 25
date of original appropriation: 1873 Apr 1
Water District No. 5
Owner, of NiWot
water source: Left Hand Creek

Viele
filing date: 1882 June 2
Boulder District Court Judgment Book, Water Decrees, Vol 2, District 5-6, 1869-1896, pg 317
ditch/reservoir: Enterprise Ditch No. 12
date of original appropriation: 1865 Feb 1
Water District No. 6
landowner
water source: South Boulder Creek

Viele, J B
filing date: 1882 June 2
Boulder District Court Judgment Book, Water Decrees, Vol 2, District 5-6, 1869-1896, pg 309
ditch/reservoir: Dry Creek Ditch No. 7
date of original appropriation: 1863 May 1
Water District No. 6
landowner
water source: South Boulder Creek

Virden, John
filing date: 1882 June 2
Boulder District Court Judgment Book, Water Decrees, Vol 2, District 5-6, 1869-1896, pg 77
ditch/reservoir: Zweck & Turner Ditch No. 21
date of original appropriation: 1864 June 30
Water District No. 5
Owner
water source: St Vrain Creek

Virden, John
filing date: 1882 June 2
Boulder District Court Judgment Book, Water Decrees, Vol 2, District 5-6, 1869-1896, pg 78
ditch/reservoir: Zweck & Turner Ditch No. 21
date of original appropriation: 1864 June 30
Water District No. 5
Owner
water source: St Vrain Creek

W

Way, Enoch
filing date: 1882 Dec 2
Boulder District Court Judgment Book, Water Decrees, Vol 2, District 5-6, 1869-1896, pg 420
ditch/reservoir: Way Ditch No. 18
date of original appropriation: 1868 May 1
Water District No. 5
Owner, of NiWot
water source: Left Hand Creek

Way, Enoch
filing date: 1882 Dec 2
Boulder District Court Judgment Book, Water Decrees, Vol 2, District 5-6, 1869-1896, pg 418
ditch/reservoir: Way Ditch No. 18
date of original appropriation: 1868 May 1
Water District No. 5
Owner, of NiWot
water source: Left Hand Creek

Way [Woy], George W
filing date: 1882 June 2
Boulder District Court Judgment Book, Water Decrees, Vol 2, District 5-6, 1869-1896, pg 239
ditch/reservoir: Howell and Beasley Ditch No. 23
date of original appropriation: 1865 Mar 1
Water District No. 6
Owner, of Canfield
water source: Boulder Creek

Webb
filing date: 1882 Dec 2
Boulder District Court Judgment Book, Water Decrees, Vol 2, District 5-6, 1869-1896, pg 392
ditch/reservoir: Williamson and Cavey Ditch No. 3
date of original appropriation: 1862 May 31
Water District No. 5
Owner, of Boulder
water source: Left Hand Creek

Webb
filing date: 1882 Dec 2
Boulder District Court Judgment Book, Water Decrees, Vol 2, District 5-6, 1869-1896, pg 389
ditch/reservoir: Williamson and Cavey Ditch No. 3
date of original appropriation: 1862 May 31
Water District No. 5
Owner, of Boulder
water source: Left Hand Creek

Webster, George W
filing date: 1882 June 2
Boulder District Court Judgment Book, Water Decrees, Vol 2, District 5-6, 1869-1896, pg 32
ditch/reservoir: True and Webster Ditch No. 11
date of original appropriation: 1862 Apr 1
Water District No. 5
Owner of Longmont
water source: St Vrain Creek

Webster, George W
filing date: 1882 June 2
Boulder District Court Judgment Book, Water Decrees, Vol 2, District 5-6, 1869-1896, pg 31
ditch/reservoir: True and Webster Ditch No. 11
date of original appropriation: 1862 Apr 1
Water District No. 5
Owner
water source: St Vrain Creek

Webster, George W
filing date: 1882 June 2
Boulder District Court Judgment Book, Water Decrees, Vol 2, District 5-6, 1869-1896, pg 101
ditch/reservoir: Webster & McCaslin Ditch No. 27
date of original appropriation: 1865 July 5
Water District No. 5
Owner, of Longmont
water source: St Vrain Creek

Webster, George W
filing date: 1882 June 2
Boulder District Court Judgment Book, Water Decrees, Vol 2, District 5-6, 1869-1896, pg 100
ditch/reservoir: Webster & McCaslin Ditch No. 27
date of original appropriation: 1865 July 5
Water District No. 5
Owner
water source: St Vrain Creek

Weese, Columbus C
filing date: 1882 June 2
Boulder District Court Judgment Book, Water Decrees, Vol 2, District 5-6, 1869-1896, pg 92
ditch/reservoir: Baker & Weese Ditch No. 24
date of original appropriation: 1865 June 1
Water District No. 5
Owner, of Longmont
water source: St Vrain Creek

Weese, Columbus C
filing date: 1882 June 2
Boulder District Court Judgment Book, Water Decrees, Vol 2, District 5-6, 1869-1896, pg 107
ditch/reservoir: Weese Private Ditch No. 29
date of original appropriation: 1865 Sept 1
Water District No. 5
Owner, of Longmont
water source: St Vrain Creek

Weese, Columbus C
filing date: 1882 June 2
Boulder District Court Judgment Book, Water Decrees, Vol 2, District 5-6, 1869-1896, pg 91
ditch/reservoir: Baker & Weese Ditch No. 24
date of original appropriation: 1865 June 1
Water District No. 5
Owner, of Longmont
water source: St Vrain Creek

Weese, Columbus C
filing date: 1882 June 2
Boulder District Court Judgment Book, Water Decrees, Vol 2, District 5-6, 1869-1896, pg 81
ditch/reservoir: Longmont Supply Ditch No. 21 1/2
date of original appropriation: 1865 May 1
Water District No. 5
land owner
water source: St Vrain Creek

Wellman Ditch Company
filing date: 1882 June 2
Boulder District Court Judgment Book, Water Decrees, Vol 2, District 5-6, 1869-1896, pg 284
ditch/reservoir: Wellman Ditch No. 39
date of original appropriation: 1878 May 1
Water District No. 6
Owner, of Boulder
water source: Boulder Creek

Wellman, S
filing date: 1882 June 2
Boulder District Court Judgment Book, Water Decrees, Vol 2, District 5-6, 1869-1896, pg 283
ditch/reservoir: Boulder and White Rock Ditch
date of original appropriation: 1862 June 1
Water District No. 6
Claimant
water source: Boulder Creek

Wellman, Sylvanus
filing date: 1882 June 2
Boulder District Court Judgment Book, Water Decrees, Vol 2, District 5-6, 1869-1896, pg 275
ditch/reservoir: Harden Ditch
date of original appropriation: 1862 June 1
Water District No. 6
Owner, of Boulder
water source: Boulder Creek

Wellman, Sylvanus
filing date: 1882 June 2
Boulder District Court Judgment Book, Water Decrees, Vol 2, District 5-6, 1869-1896, pg 276
ditch/reservoir: Wellman, Nichols and Hahn Ditch No. 11
date of original appropriation: 1862 June 1
Water District No. 6
Owner, of Boulder
water source: Boulder Creek

Wellman, Sylvanus
filing date: 1882 June 2
Boulder District Court Judgment Book, Water Decrees, Vol 2, District 5-6, 1869-1896, pg 282
ditch/reservoir: Boulder and White Rock Ditch
date of original appropriation: 1862 June 1
Water District No. 6
Claimant
water source: Boulder Creek

Wells, John H
filing date: 1902 Oct 21
Boulder District Court Judgment Book, Water Decrees, Vol 2, District 5-6, 1869-1896, pg 568
ditch/reservoir:
date of original appropriation:
Water District No. 5
Attorney
water source:

Whipple, Everett
filing date: 1902 Oct 2
Boulder District Court Judgment Book, Water Decrees, Vol 2, District 5-6, 1869-1896, pg 567
ditch/reservoir: Wiswall Ditch
date of original appropriation: 1892 Nov 10
Water District No. 5
Owner, of Longmont
water source: Dry Creek

Whipple, W D
filing date: 1902 Oct 2
Boulder District Court Judgment Book, Water Decrees, Vol 2, District 5-6, 1869-1896, pg 567
ditch/reservoir: Wiswall Ditch
date of original appropriation: 1892 Nov 10
Water District No. 5
Owner, of Longmont
water source: Dry Creek

White, Eben
filing date: 1882 June 2
Boulder District Court Judgment Book, Water Decrees, Vol 2, District 5-6, 1869-1896, pg 29
ditch/reservoir: Pella Ditch No. 10
date of original appropriation: 1862 Mar 20
Water District No. 5
tabulated statement
water source: St Vrain Creek

White, Perry
filing date: 1882 June 2
Boulder District Court Judgment Book, Water Decrees, Vol 2, District 5-6, 1869-1896, pg 282
ditch/reservoir: Boulder and White Rock Ditch
date of original appropriation: 1862 June 1
Water District No. 6
Claimant
water source: Boulder Creek

White, Perry
filing date: 1882 June 2
Boulder District Court Judgment Book, Water Decrees, Vol 2, District 5-6, 1869-1896, pg 272
ditch/reservoir: Dry Creek Ditch No. 11, Claim of Mary S Stoddard et al
date of original appropriation: 1862 June 1
Water District No. 6
Owner, of Boulder
water source: Boulder Creek

White, Perry
filing date: 1882 June 2
Boulder District Court Judgment Book, Water Decrees, Vol 2, District 5-6, 1869-1896, pg 278
ditch/reservoir: McCarty Ditch No. 11
date of original appropriation: 1862 June 1
Water District No. 6
Owner, of Boulder
water source: Boulder Creek

White, Perry
filing date: 1882 June 2
Boulder District Court Judgment Book, Water Decrees, Vol 2, District 5-6, 1869-1896, pg 283
ditch/reservoir: Boulder and White Rock Ditch
date of original appropriation: 1862 June 1
Water District No. 6
Claimant
water source: Boulder Creek

Wilder, Eugene
filing date: 1895 Feb 12
Boulder District Court Judgment Book, Water Decrees, Vol 2, District 5-6, 1869-1896, pg 540
ditch/reservoir: John Rice Ditch
date of original appropriation: 1884 Apr 1
Water District No. 5
Referee
water source: Dry Creek

Wilder, Eugene
filing date: 1895 Feb 12
Boulder District Court Judgment Book, Water Decrees, Vol 2, District 5-6, 1869-1896, pg 540
ditch/reservoir: Mill Ditch
date of original appropriation: 1884 May 1
Water District No. 5
Referee
water source: Dry Creek

Wilder, Eugene
filing date: 1895 Feb 12
Boulder District Court Judgment Book, Water Decrees, Vol 2, District 5-6, 1869-1896, pg 545
ditch/reservoir: Lower Baldwin Ditch
date of original appropriation: 1873 Apr 1
Water District No. 5
Referee
water source: Dry Creek

Wilder, Eugene
filing date: 1895 Feb 12
Boulder District Court Judgment Book, Water Decrees, Vol 2, District 5-6, 1869-1896, pg 534
ditch/reservoir: Bonus Lateral Ditch
date of original appropriation: 1870 Mar 1
Water District No. 5
Referee
water source: Dry Creek

Wilder, Eugene
filing date: 1895 Feb 12
Boulder District Court Judgment Book, Water Decrees, Vol 2, District 5-6, 1869-1896, pg 546
ditch/reservoir: Upper Baldwin Ditch
date of original appropriation: 1872 Apr 1
Water District No. 5
Referee
water source: Dry Creek

Williams, Urial
filing date: 1882 June 2
Boulder District Court Judgment Book, Water Decrees, Vol 2, District 5-6, 1869-1896, pg 119
ditch/reservoir: Davis & Downing Ditch No. 33
date of original appropriation: 1866 Nov 1
Water District No. 5
Owner, of Longmont
water source: St Vrain Creek

Williams, Urial
filing date: 1882 June 2
Boulder District Court Judgment Book, Water Decrees, Vol 2, District 5-6, 1869-1896, pg 121
ditch/reservoir: Davis & Downing Ditch No. 33
date of original appropriation: 1866 Nov 1
Water District No. 5
Owner, of Longmont
water source: St Vrain Creek

Williamson, Sam
filing date: 1882 Dec 2
Boulder District Court Judgment Book, Water Decrees, Vol 2, District 5-6, 1869-1896, pg 394
ditch/reservoir: Holland Ditch No. 4
date of original appropriation: 1863 May 1
Water District No. 5
Owner, of NiWot
water source: Left Hand Creek

Williamson, Sam
filing date: 1882 Dec 2
Boulder District Court Judgment Book, Water Decrees, Vol 2, District 5-6, 1869-1896, pg 396
ditch/reservoir: Holland Ditch No. 4
date of original appropriation: 1863 May 1
Water District No. 5
Owner, of NiWot
water source: Left Hand Creek

Williamson, Samuel
filing date: 1882 Dec 2
Boulder District Court Judgment Book, Water Decrees, Vol 2, District 5-6, 1869-1896, pg 392
ditch/reservoir: Williamson and Cavey Ditch No. 3
date of original appropriation: 1862 May 31
Water District No. 5
Owner, of NiWot
water source: Left Hand Creek

Williamson, Samuel
filing date: 1882 Dec 2
Boulder District Court Judgment Book, Water Decrees, Vol 2, District 5-6, 1869-1896, pg 389
ditch/reservoir: Williamson and Cavey Ditch No. 3
date of original appropriation: 1862 May 31
Water District No. 5
Owner, of NiWot
water source: Left Hand Creek

Willis, W A
filing date: 1894 Apr 29
Boulder District Court Judgment Book, Water Decrees, Vol 2, District 5-6, 1869-1896, pg 518
ditch/reservoir: Willis Ditch
date of original appropriation: 1870 May 5
Water District No. 6
Owner, of Louisville
water source: Coal Creek

Wilson, Henry C
filing date: 1882 June 2
Boulder District Court Judgment Book, Water Decrees, Vol 2, District 5-6, 1869-1896, pg 314
ditch/reservoir: Andrews and Farwell Ditch No. 11
date of original appropriation: 1864 June 1
Water District No. 6
Owner, of Valmont
water source: South Boulder Creek

Wiswall, F
filing date: 1900 Dec 19
Boulder District Court Judgment Book, Water Decrees, Vol 2, District 5-6, 1869-1896, pg 566
ditch/reservoir: Peck & Metcalf Ditch
date of original appropriation: 1867 May 15
Water District No. 5
Petitioner
water source: Dry Creek

Wiswall, F
filing date: 1902 Oct 21
Boulder District Court Judgment Book, Water Decrees, Vol 2, District 5-6, 1869-1896, pg 568
ditch/reservoir:
date of original appropriation:
Water District No. 5
Owner
water source:

Wiswall, F
filing date: 1902 Oct 2
Boulder District Court Judgment Book, Water Decrees, Vol 2, District 5-6, 1869-1896, pg 567
ditch/reservoir: Wiswall Ditch
date of original appropriation: 1892 Nov 10
Water District No. 5
Owner, of Longmont
water source: Dry Creek

Witter, Daniel
filing date: 1882 June 2
Boulder District Court Judgment Book, Water Decrees, Vol 2, District 5-6, 1869-1896, pg 103
ditch/reservoir: Denio & Taylor Ditch No. 28
date of original appropriation: 1865 July 15
Water District No. 5
Owner, of Longmont
water source: St Vrain Creek

Witter, Daniel
filing date: 1882 June 2
Boulder District Court Judgment Book, Water Decrees, Vol 2, District 5-6, 1869-1896, pg 69
ditch/reservoir: Coffman Ditch No. 20
date of original appropriation: 1864 May 30
Water District No. 5
Owner of Longmont
water source: St Vrain Creek

Witter, Daniel
filing date: 1882 June 2
Boulder District Court Judgment Book, Water Decrees, Vol 2, District 5-6, 1869-1896, pg 105
ditch/reservoir: Denio & Taylor Ditch No. 28
date of original appropriation: 1865 July 15
Water District No. 5
Owner, of Longmont
water source: St Vrain Creek

Witter, Daniel
filing date: 1882 June 2
Boulder District Court Judgment Book, Water Decrees, Vol 2, District 5-6, 1869-1896, pg 71
ditch/reservoir: Coffman Ditch No. 20
date of original appropriation: 1864 May 30
Water District No. 5
Owner of Longmont
water source: St Vrain Creek

Woy, George W, see Way, George W

Y

Yount, Ella B Mrs
filing date: 1882 June 2
Boulder District Court Judgment Book, Water Decrees, Vol 2, District 5-6, 1869-1896, pg 380
ditch/reservoir: Colorado State Mills Ditch
date of original appropriation: 1860 Apr 1
Water District No. 6
Owner, of Boulder
water source: Boulder Creek

Z

Zweck, George
filing date: 1882 June 2
Boulder District Court Judgment Book, Water Decrees, Vol 2, District 5-6, 1869-1896, pg 78
ditch/reservoir: Zweck & Turner Ditch No. 21
date of original appropriation: 1864 June 30
Water District No. 5
owner
water source: St Vrain Creek

Zweck, George
filing date: 1882 June 2
Boulder District Court Judgmnt Book, Water Decrees, Vol 2, District 5-6, 1869-1896, pg 77
ditch/reservoir: Zweck & Turner Ditch No. 21
date of original appropriation: 1864 June 30
Water District No. 5
Owner
water source: St Vrain Creek

WATER DISTRICT NO. 5

Hayseed Ditch No. 1

Water District No. 5
Jurisdiction, Boulder, Larimer, Weld Counties
First Judicial District
Owner, John Mulverhill of Denver, Elisha Duncan, Ira Lockard, William Dewey of Longmont, and H S Scott of Boulder
Boulder District Court Judgment Book, Water Decrees, Vol 2, District 5-6, 1869-1896, pg 2
Headgate located, Sec 34, T3N R68W
Natural Stream, St Vrain Creek
General Course, north easterly
Original Appropriation, 1 Jan 1860
Construction, 1860
Grade, 1/4 inch per rod
Work commenced, 10 May 1880
Work completed, 30 Sept 1880
Water running, 20 June 1880
Length, 2.5 miles
Bottom width, 6.5 feet
Top width, 7.5 feet
Depth, 24 inches
Capacity, 2016 customary inches
Water Claimed, 2200 inches
Acres under irrigation, 420 acres hay land
Water appropriated, 1680 customary inches

Hayseed Ditch, No. 2

Water District No. 5
Jurisdiction, Boulder, Larimer, Weld Counties
First Judicial District
Owner, James R Mason of Longmont
Boulder District Court Judgment Book, Water Decrees, Vol 2, District 5-6, 1869-1896, pg 6
Original appropriation, 31 July 1860
Appropriation by virtue of original construction, 250 customary inches
Grade, 1/2 inch per rod
Known as: James R Mason's meadow claim
Natural Stream, St Vrain Creek
Acres under irrigation, 50 acres, meadow requiring 200 inches per acre

Coffin Meadow Ditch, No. 3

Water District No. 5
Jurisdiction, Boulder, Larimer, Weld Counties
First Judicial District
Owner, George W Coffin of Longmont
Boulder District Court Judgment Book, Water Decrees, Vol 2, District 5-6, 1869-1896, pg 8
written in the margin, see Decrees in files, No. 1325]
Head located Sec 8, T2N R68W in Boulder County
Natural Stream, St Vrain Creek
General Course, easterly
Appropriation No. 3
Original Appropriation, 1 May 1860 [originally written as 1880 - corrected]
Appropriation, 300 customary inches
Grade, 1/4 inch per rod
Known as: Coffin's Meadow Ditch
Work commenced, 1 May 1880
Work completed, 1 June 1880
Length, 1.5 miles
Width, 1.5 feet
Depth, 30 inches
Nature of construction, heavy grass sod, easy to construct
Capacity, 540 customary inches
Appropriation claimed, 300 inches
Original Appropriation relates back to 1 Sept 1860
Acres under irrigation, 90 acres, meadow requiring 300 inches to irrigate

Northwestern Mutual Life Insurance Co Ditch, No 4

Water District No. 5
Jurisdiction, Boulder, Larimer and Weld Counties
First Judicial District
Owner, Northwestern Mutual Life Insurance Company of Wisconsin
Boulder District Court Judgment Book, Water Decrees, Vol 2, District 5-6, 1869-1896, pg 11
Natural stream, Left Hand Creek
Original Appropriation, 1 Dec 1860
Original construction, 200 customary inches
Grade, 1/2 inch per rod
Known as: NWMLI Co's Meadow claim on the Dwight and Kinney land
Acres under irrigation, 90 acres, meadow requiring 300 inches to irrigate

Beckwith Ditch No 5

Water District No. 5
Jurisdiction, Boulder, Larimer and Weld Counties
First Judicial District
Owner, Fred Affolter, George L Beckwith, L H Dickson of Longmont, and George C Beckwith of Denver
Boulder District Court Judgment Book, Water Decrees, Vol 2, District 5-6, 1869-1896, pg 14
Head located in Sec 5, T2N R69W in Boulder County
Natural stream, St Vrain Creek
General course, easterly

Original Appropriation, 8 Mar 1861
Appropriation, 540 customary inches
Grade, 1/2 inch per rod
Work commenced, 8 Mar 1861
Work completed, 31 July 1861
Length, 2.75 miles
Width bottom, 4 feet
Width top, 5 feet
Depth, 12 inches
Capacity, 648 customary inches
Acres under irrigation, 400 acres
Actual irrigation, 240 acres, 155 acres of meadow, 85 acres of cultivated
Land requires, 2 1/4 inches of water per acre, totalling 540 customary inches

Bacon's Appropriation, No. 7
Water District No. 5
Jurisdiction, Boulder, Larimer and Weld Counties
First Judicial District
Owner, J W Bacon, of Longmont
Boulder District Court Judgment Book, Water Decrees, Vol 2, District 5-6, 1869-1896, pg 17
Land located in Sec 3 T2N R68W in Weld County
Natural stream, St Vrain Creek
Original Appropriation, 1 June 1861
Appropriation, 1165 customary inches
Acres under irrigation, 233 acres
Grade, 1/4 inch per rod

Cushman Ditch, No. 8
Water District No. 5
Jurisdiction, Boulder, Larimer and Weld Counties
First Judicial District
Owner, A W Cushman of Longmont
Boulder District Court Judgment Book, Water Decrees, Vol 2, District 5-6, 1869-1896, pg 19
Head located, Sec 5, T2N R69W in Boulder County
Natural Stream, St Vrain Creek
General course, easterly
Original Appropriation, 20 June 1861
Appropriation, 440 customary inches
Grade, 3/4 inch per rod
Work began, 20 June 1861
Work completed, 2 July 1861
Length, 1/2 mile
Width bottom, 2 1/5 feet
Width top, 3 feet
Depth, 24 inches
Original claim, 720 customary inches
Acres under irrigation, 120 acres, 12 acres cultivated, 98 acres meadow
Requires 4 inches of water per acre to irrigate

Chapman and McCaslin Ditch, No. 9
Water District No. 5
Jurisdiction, Boulder, Larimer and Weld Counties
First Judicial District
Owner, A W Cushman and Matthew L McCaslin of Longmont
Boulder District Court Judgment Book, Water Decrees, Vol 2, District 5-6, 1869-1896, pg 22
Head located, Sec 22 T3N R70W in Boulder County
General Course, easterly
Original appropriation, 10 Mar 1862
Natural stream, St Vrain Creek
Work commenced 31 Aug 1862
Work completed, 31 Aug 1862
Length, 2.5 miles
Width, top and bottom, 6 feet
Depth, 30 inches
Grade, 1 inch per rod
Depth of water, 15 inches
Original capacity, 2160 customary inches
Original claim, 1800 inches
Acres under irrigation, 500 acres, 2/3 creek bottom, 1/3 bottom
Requires 4 inches per acre
Original appropriation, 2000 customary inches

Pella Ditch, No. 10
Water District No. 5
Jurisdiction, Boulder, Larimer and Weld counties
First Judicial District
Owner, Pella Ditch Company of Longmont
Boulder District Court Judgment Book, Water Decrees, Vol 2, District 5-6, 1869-1896, pg 25
Head Located in Sec 36, T3N, R70W in Boulder County, 600 yards above the Pella bridge
Natural Stream, St Vrain Creek by the Pella, Peck Lateral and Clover Basin Ditches
General Course, easterly
Original appropriation, 20 Mar 1862
Original construction, 150 customary inches
Grade, 1/4 inch per rod
First Enlargement - Peck Lateral, 10 May 1867
First Enlargement, No. 35 for the Peck Lateral
Additional enlargement, 822 customary inches, total 972 customary inches
Grade, 1 inch per rod
Second Enlargment - Clover Basin, 1 June 1873

Second Enlargement, No. 56 for Clover Basin
Additional enlargement, 1072 customary inches, total 2044 customary inches
Work began, 20 Mar 1862
Work completed, 1 June 1862
Length, 1.5 miles
Width, 3 feet
Depth, 18 inches
Original capacity, 648 inches
Amount claimed, 175 inches
Enlargement work commenced, 10 May 1867
Enlargement work completed, 1 June 1867
Length, blank
Width bottom, 4 feet
width top, 5 feet
Depth, 1.5 feet
Grade 1/4 inch per rod
Increased capacity, 324 customary inches, total 972 inches
Increased water claim ed, 1296 inches
Enlargement made by the Peck Lateral Ditch under contract to the Pella Ditch Co
Pella Ditch entitled to 350 inches, Peck Lateral to 568 inches
Enlargement work commenced, 1 June 1873
Enlargement work completed, 1 June 1875
Length, not given
Width, 9 feet
depth, 3 feet
Grade, 1/4 inch to rod
Depth of water, 18 inches
Increased capacity 2912 inches, total 3884 inches
Acres under irrigation, 2215 acres, actually irrigated 1635 acres
Claimed 1944 customary inches
Entitlements, Pella 350 inches, Peck Lateral 944 inches, Clover Basin 750 inches

True and Webster Ditch, No. 11
Water District No. 5
Jurisdiction, Boulder, Larimer and Weld Counties
First Judicial District
Owner, George W Webster and C C True, of Longmont
Boulder District Court Judgment Book, Water Decrees, Vol 2, District 5-6, 1869-1896, pg 30
Head located, Sec 27, T3N, R70W in Boulder County
Natural Stream, St Vrain Creek
Course, south easterly
Original Appropriation, 1 Apr 1862
Water appropriated, 320 customary inches
Grade, 1 inch per rod
Work commenced, 1 Apr 1862
Work completed, 1 June 1862
Length, 3/4 miles
Width, 28th inches
Depth, 26 inches
Water Depth, 15 inches
Ditch capacity, 728 customary inches
Water claim, 420 customary inches
Acres under irrigation, 80 acres, sandy creek bottom, requires 4 inches per acre
Water appropriation, 320 inches

Dickens Private Ditch, No. 12
Water District No. 5
First Judicial District
Owner, Wm H Dickens of Longmont
Boulder District Court Judgment Book, Water Decrees, Vol 2, District 5-6, 1869-1896, pg 33
Head located, Sec 9, T2N, R69W in Boulder County
Natural Stream, St Vrain Creek
General Course, easterly
Original Appropriation, 15 Apr 1862
Water Appropriated, 500 customary inches
Grade, 3/4 inch per rod
Work commenced, 15 Apr 1862
Work completed, 1 June 1862
Length, 1 1/4 miles
Bottom Width, 3 feet
Top Width, 4 1/2 feet
Depth, 24 inches
Depth of water, 18 inches
Capacity, 1080 inches
Water claimed, 500 inches
Acres under irrigation, 330 acres, sandy, requires 2 inches per acre

Clough and True Private Ditch, No. 12
Water District No. 5
Jurisdiction, Boulder, Larimer and Weld Counties
First Judicial District
Owner, Charles E Clough and C C True of Longmont
Boulder District Court Judgment Book, Water Decrees, Vol 2, District 5-6, 1869-1896, pg 36
Head located, Sec 27, T3N, R70W in Boulder County
Natural stream, St Vrain Creek
Course, south easterly
Original Appropriation, 15 Apr 1862
Water Appropriated, 320 customary inches
Grade, 3/4 inch per rod
Work commenced, 15 Apr 1862
Work completed, 1 June 1862

Length, 1 mile
Width, 3 feet
Depth, 18 inches
Depth of Water, 12 inches
Capacity, 648 customary inches
Water claimed, 400 inches
Acres under irrigation, 80 acres, creek bottom, requires 4 inches per acre

Montgomery Private Ditch, No. 12 1/2
Water District No. 5
First Judicial District
Owner, Alexander Montgomery, William Baker & C L Smead of Longmont
Boulder District Court Judgment Book, Water Decrees, Vol 2, District 5-6, 1869-1896, pg 39
Jurisdiction, Boulder, Larimer and Weld Counties
Head located, Sec 20, T3N, R70W in Boulder County
Natural stream, St Vrain Creek
General course, south of east
Original Appropriation, 15 May 1862
Water Appropriated, 200 customary inches
Grade, 1/2 inch per rod
Work commenced, 10 May 1862
Work completed 15 June 1862
Length, 3/4 mile
Width, 2 feet
Depth, 24 inches
Capacity, 576 customary inches
Acres under irrigation, 120 acres, requires 2 inches per acre
Water approprited, 200 customary inches

Smead Ditch, No. 13
Water District No. 5
Jurisdiction, Boulder, Larimer and Weld Counties
First Judicial District
Owner, C L Smead, Sebastian Duncan, William Baker and Frank A Marquette of Longmont
Boulder District Court Judgment Book, Water Decrees, Vol 2, District 5-6, 1869-1896, pg 42
Head located, Sec 20, T3N, R70W, in Boulder County
Natural stream, St Vrain Creek
General course, south easterly
Original Appropriation, 1 Oct 1862
Water Appropriated 600 customary inches
Grade, 1/2 inch per rod
Work commenced,
Work completed, 1 Oct 1862
Length, 2 miles
Bottom width, 2 1/2 feet
Top Width, 4 feet
Depth, 30 inches
Water Depth, 12 inches
Capacity, 1170 customary inches
Water claim, 864 inches
Acres under irrigation, 470 acres, 103 cultivated, 165 meadow, requiring 6 inches per acre

Clough Tribute Ditch, No. 14
Water District No. 5
First Judicial District
Jurisdiction, Boulder, Larimer and Weld Counties
Owner, Charles E Clough of Longmont
Boulder District Court Judgment Book, Water Decrees, Vol 2, District 5-6, 1869-1896, pg 45
Head located, Sec 27, T3N, R70W in Boulder County
Natural Stream, St Vrain Creek
General course, south easterly
Original Appropriation, 15 Apr 1863
Water appropriated, 320 customary inches
Grade, 1 inch per rod
Work completed, 15 Apr 1863
Length, 3/4 mile
Width, 2 1/2 feet
Depth, 24 inches
Capacity, 720 customary inches
Water claim, 300 customary inches
Acres under irrigation, 80 acres, meadow, creek bottom subsoild of sand and boulders, requiring 4 inches of water per acre
This is the same as the Smead & Carter Ditch, which was taken out by them, the above date to water their lands, C E Clough now owning and occupying the land then owned by said Carter, and having changed the headgate of said ditch.

Runyan Ditch, No. 15
Water District No. 5
First Judicial District
Jurisdiction, Boulder, Larimer and Weld Counties
Owner, Isaac Runyan of Longmont
Boulder District Court Judgment Book, Water Decrees, Vol 2, District 5-6, 1869-1896, pg 48
Head located, Sec 35, T3N R70W, of Boulder County
Natural Stream, St Vrain Creek
Original Appropriation, 1 May 1863
Water appropriated, 576 customary inches
Grade, 1/4 inch per rod
Work commenced, 1 May 1863
Work completed, 1 June 1863
Length, 1/2 mile

Width, 2 feet
Depth, 24 inches
Water depth, 24 inches
Acres under irrigation, 110 acres, meadow and farm land

Left Hand Ditch, No. 15 1/2
Water District No. 5
First Judicial District
Jurisdiction, Boulder, Larimer and Weld Counties
Owner, Left Hand Ditch Company of Niwot
Boulder District Court Judgment Book, Water Decrees, Vol 2, District 5-6, 1869-1896, pg 51
Head located on the south fork of the St Vrain Creek
Natural Stream, St Vrain Creek via James Creek into and through Left Hand Creek
Original Appropriation, 1 June 1863
Water appropriation, 800 customary inches
Grade 1 1/2 inch per rod
First Enlargement, 1 June 1870, appropriation number 41
Additional water appropriation, 7264 customary inches, total 8064 customary inches
Grade, 1 1/2 inches per rod
Work commenced, 1 June 1863
Work completed, 30 June 1863
Length, 1/2 mile
Bottom width, 3 feet
Top width, 5 feet
Depth, 36 inches
Water depth, 24 inches
Capacity, 1728 inches
Original water claim, 864 inches
Acres under irrigation, not given, land requiring 2 inches per acre
Work on enlargement commenced, 1 June 1870
Work on enlargement completed, 15 June 1870
Length, not given
Bottom width, 14 feet
Top Width, 22 feet
Depth, 4 feet
Grade 1 1/2 inch per rod
Water depth, 42 inches
Capacity increased by 8640 inches, total 10368 inches
Acres under irrigation, 45,020 acres requiring 1 inche per acre

South Flat Ditch, No. 16
Water District No. 5
First Judicial District
Jurisdiction, Boulder, Larimer and Weld Counties
Owner, J R Mason, A W Cushman, Alfred Cushman, Fred Affolter and George L Beckwith of Longmont
Boulder District Court Judgment Book, Water Decrees, Vol 2, District 5-6, 1869-1896, pg 55
Head located, Sec 6, T2N R69W in Boulder County
Natural Stream, St Vrain Creek
General Course, south easterly
Original Appropriation, 15 May 1863
Water Appropriation, 1670 customary inches
Grade, 3/4 inch per rod
Work commenced, 15 May 1863
Work completed, 15 June 1863
Length, 3 1/2 miles
Bottom width, 4 feet
Top width, 5 feet
Depth, 36 inches
Capacity, 1944 inches
Water claimed, 1728 inches
Acres under irrigation, 870 acres, 1st and 2nd bottom land, requires 2 inches of water per acre
Water appropriated, 1670 customary inches

St Vrain and Gold Hill Ditch, No. 17
Water District No. 5
First Judicial District
Jurisdiction, Boulder, Larimer and Weld Counties
Owner, St Vrain and Gold Hill Ditch Company, Inc. of Boulder
Boulder District Court Judgment Book, Water Decrees, Vol 2, District 5-6, 1869-1896, pg 58
Head located, Sec 24 or 25, T2N R73W in Boulder, CO
Natural Stream, south fork of St Vrain Creek
General Course, south easterly
Original Appropriation, 25 Oct 1863
Water appropriated, 594 customary inches
Work commenced, 25 Oct 1863
Work completed, 10 May 1864
water running in the ditch, 1 July 1864
Length, 7 1/4 miles
Bottom width, 3 1/2 feet
Top Width, 2 feet ??
Depth, 18 inches
Grade, 1 inch per rod
Water depth, 18 inches
Capacity, 574 inches
Water claimed, 700 inches

Hager's Meadow Ditch, No. 18
Water District No. 5
First Judicial District
Jurisdiction, Boulder, Larimer and Weld counties

Owner, John H Hager of Longmont
Boulder District Court Judgment Book, Water Decrees, Vol 2, District 5-6, 1869-1896, pg 61
Head located, Secs 3&6, Twps 2&3 N, R69W
Natural Stream, St Vrain Creek
Original Appropriation, 1 Jan 1864
Water appropriated, 140 customary inches
Grade, 1/2 inch per rod
Water claimed, 500 inches
Acres under irrigation, 35 acres, meadow
Direct draw from the creek

Northwestern Mutal Life Insurance Co's Meadow Claim Ditch, No. 18
Water District No. 5
First Judicial District
Jurisdiction, Boulder, Larimer and Weld counties
Owner, Northwestern Mutual Life Insurance Company of Milwaukee
Boulder District Court Judgment Book, Water Decrees, Vol 2, District 5-6, 1869-1896, pg 63
Head located, Sec 6, Tsp 2N, R 69W
Natural Stream, St Vrain Creek
Original appropriation, 1 Jan 1864
Water appropriated, 260 customary inches
Grade, 1/2 inch per rod
Water claimed, 300 inches
Land under irrigation, 65 acres, meadow, requiring 260 inches of water to irrigate
Direct draw from the creek

L H Dickson's Ditch, No. 19
Water District No. 5
First Judicial District
Jurisdiction, Boulder, Larimer and Weld counties
Owner, L H Dickson of Longmont
Boulder District Court Judgment Book, Water Decrees, Vol 2, District 5-6, 1869-1896, pg 66
Head located, Sec 12, T2N, R69W
Natural Stream, St Vrain Creek
Original apropriation, 28 Feb 1864
Water appropriated, 500 customery inches
Grade, 1/4 inch per rod
Water claimed, 500 inches
Land under irrigation, 108 acres, hay and meadow land
Water now used through and by means of the Bemis and the Dixon and Bacon Mill Race Ditches

Coffman Ditch, No. 20
Water District No. 5
First Judicial District
Jurisdiction, Boulder, Larimer and Weld counties
Owner, Enoch J Coffman, George L Beckwith and Daniel Witter of Longmont
Boulder District Court Judgment Book, Water Decrees, Vol 2, District 5-6, 1869-1896, pg 69
Head located, Sec 4, T2N, R69W
Natural Stream, St Vrain Creek
General Course, easterly
Original appropriation, 30 May 1864
Water appropriated, 200 customary inches
Lenth, 1/2 mile
Bottom width, 2 feet
Top width, 2 1/2 feet
Depth, 12 inches
Original capacity, 486 inches
Grade, 1/2 Inch per rod
First enlargement, 20 Mar 1866
Work began, 10 May 1866
Work completed, 30 May 1866
Additional water claim, 400 customary inches (600 total)
Grade, 1/2 inch per rod
Land under irrigation, 300 acres that require 2 inches per acre to irrigate
Second enlargement, 1 May 1867
Additional water claim, 60 inches (660 inches)
Grade, 1/2 inch per rod
Land under irrigation, 130 acres, sandy loam, requires 2 1/2 inches per acre to irrigate
Additional enlargement, 1 Mar 1869
Work began, 1 Mar 1869
Work completed, 1 Apr 1869
Enlarged length 2 1/4 miles
Enlarged bottom width, 4 1/2 feet
Enlarged top width, 5 1/2 feet
Enlarged depth, 20 inches
Enlarged grade, 1/2 inch per rod
Acres under irrigation, 360 acres that require 2 inches for 300 acres and 1 inch for 60 acres to irrigate
Additional enlargement, 1 May 1872
Extended Length, 2 1/4 miles
Enlarged Bottom width, 6 feet
Enlarged top width, 9 1/2 feet
Enlarged depth, 2 feet
Grade, 1/2 inch per rod
Work commenced, 1 May 1872
Work completed, 30 June 1872
Enlarged capacity, 674 inches (2160 inches total)
Acres under irrigation, 640 acres, sandy loam requiring 2 1/2 inches per acre to irrigate

Island Ditch, No. 20 1/2
Water District No. 5
First Judicial District
Jurisdiction, Boulder, Larimer and Weld counties
Owner, George C Beckwith and Fred Affolter of Longmont
Boulder District Court Judgment Book, Water Decrees, Vol 2, District 5-6, 1869-1896, pg 74
Head located in Sec 4, T2N, R69W, NW 1/4 of the SW 1/4
Natural Stream St Vrain Creek, south bank middle fork
General Course, south easterly
Original appropriation, 15 June 1864
Water appropriated 288 customary inches
Grade, 1/4 inch per rod
Length 200 rods
Bottom width 2 1/2 feet
Top width 3 1/2 feet
Depth 20 inches
Original capacity, 720 inches
Acres under irrigation, 100 acres of alluvial with sand and gravel, requiring 5 inches to irrigate

Zweck & Turner Ditch, No. 21
Water District No. 5
First Judicial District
Jurisdiction, Boulder, Larimer and Weld counties
Owner, George Zweck, T A Turner, John H Hager, David Bestler, Peter Stoner and John Virden
Boulder District Court Judgment Book, Water Decrees, Vol 2, District 5-6, 1869-1896, pg 76
Head located in Sec 36, T3N, R70W, NW 1/4 of the SW 1/4
Natural stream, St Vrain Creek
Course is southwest
Original appropriation, 30 June 1864
Water appropriated, 2200 customary inches
Grade 1/2 inch per rod
Work completed 30 June 1864
Length 40 rods
Width 4 feet
Depth 48 inches
Original capacity 2304 customary inches
Acres irrigated 840, 440 actually irrigated, 210 acres meadow and hay, 230 acres cultivated, requiring 5 inches of water to irrigate

Longmont Supply Ditch, No. 21 1/2
Water District No. 5
First Judicial District
Jurisdiction, Boulder, Larimer and Weld counties
Owner, Longmont Supply Ditch Company
Boulder District Court Judgment Book, Water Decrees, Vol 2, District 5-6, 1869-1896, pg 79
Head located in Sec 27, T3N, R70W, E 1/2, north side on the farm of Columbus C Weese
Natural stream, St Vrain Creek
Course is easterly
Original appropriation, 1 May 1865
Water appropriated, 2500 customary inches
Grade, 1/3 inch per rod
Work commenced, 5 Mar 1865
Work completed, 15 July 1865
Water running, 18 July 1865
Length, 9 miles
Bottom width, 7 ft
Top width, 9 ft
Depth, 30 inches
Original capacity, 2880 inches
Acres under irrigation, 2500, 1800 actually irrigated, requiring 1 inch to irrigate
This ditch an extension of the Pleasant Valley Ditch, abandoned at the lower end
Extended the abandoned portion on 15 May 1878

St Vrain & Palmerton Ditch, No. 23
Water District No. 5
First Judicial District
Jurisdiction, Boulder, Larimer and Weld counties
Owner, St Vrain and Palmerton Ditch Company
Boulder District Court Judgment Book, Water Decrees, Vol 2, District 5-6, 1869-1896, pg 83
Head located in Sec 20, T3N, R70W, north side of the creek
Natural stream, St Vrain Creek
Course, easterly
Original appropriation, 31 May 1865
Water running, 10 June 1865
Water appropriated, 900 customary inches
Grade, 3/4 inch per rod
Length, 2 miles
Width, 3 ft
Depth, 18 inches, water running 12 inches
Original capacity, 648 inches
Water appropriated 420 inches
Acres under irrigation, 300 requiring 30 inches to irrigate
First Enlargement, 31 May 1866
Approprition, No 30
Water appropriated, 1200 customary inches
Ditch total 2100 customary inches
Work commenced and completed, Spring 1866

Length, 2 1/2 miles
Width, 8 1/2 ft
Depth, 2 1/2 ft, water depth 24 inches
Grade, 1 inch per rod
Increased capacity, 2412 inches
Ditch total, 3060 customary inches
Acres under irrigation, 700 requiring 3 inches to irrigate
Water claimed, 2500 customary inches
Second Enlargement, 30 June 1874
Length 7 1/4 miles
Width, 10 ft
Depth, 3 1/2 ft
Grade 1/4 inch per rod
Water appropriated, 1980 customary inches
Ditch total, 5040 customary inches
Acres under irrigation, 1436 requiring 3 inches of water to irrigate
Water claimed 400 customary inches
Total appropriated 4000 inches

Ni-Wot Ditch, No. 24
Water District No. 5
First Judicial District
Jurisdiction, Boulder, Larimer and Weld counties
Owner, Niwot Irrigating Ditch Company of Longmont
Boulder District Court Judgment Book, Water Decrees, Vol 2, District 5-6, 1869-1896, pg 87
Head located 1/4 mile NW of Mr Hager's Barns in his field.
Natural Stream St Vrain Creek
General course is southeast
Date of original appropriation 1 June 1865
Amount of water appropriated is 960 customary inches
Grade 1/2 inch fall per rod
Width, blank
Depth, blank
Acres under irrigation 1122, 679 actually irrigated, requiring 2 inches of water to irrigate
First Enlargement, 1 June 1869
Appropriation, No 39 1/2
Water appropriated 398 customary inches
Grade of 1/2 inch per rod
Total appropriated 1358 customary inches
Length, blank
Bottom Width, 8 ft
Top Width, 5 ft
Depth, 2 ft
Grade 1/2 in fall per rod
Total 1872 inches
Acres proposed to be under irrigation, 1122 requiring 2 in of water per acre to irrigate
Acres under irrigation, 679
Water claimed 1800 inches

Baker & Weese Ditch, No. 24
Water District No. 5
First Judicial District
Jurisdiction, Boulder, Larimer and Weld counties
Owner, Columbus C Weese of Longmont
Boulder District Court Judgment Book, Water Decrees, Vol 2, District 5-6, 1869-1896, pg 91
Head located Sec 22, T3N, R70W, 60 rods NE of the SW corner of the section
Natural Stream St Vrain Creek
General course is south easterly
Date of original appropriation 1 June 1865
Amount of water appropriated 150 customary inches
Grade 1/2 inch fall per rod
Length, 80 rods
Width, 2 1/2 ft
Depth, 12 in
Acres under irrigation 50

Goss Private Ditch 1, No. 25
Water District No. 5
First Judicial District
Jurisdiction, Boulder, Larimer and Weld counties
Owner, John W Goss of Longmont
Boulder District Court Judgment Book, Water Decrees, Vol 2, District 5-6, 1869-1896, pg 94
Head is in Sec 27, T3N R70W, Boulder Co, on the south side of the creek, on the farm of Wm Baker
Natural Stream St Vrain Creek
General course is easterly
Date of original appropriateion 30 June 1865
Amount of water appropriated 640 customary inches
Length, 1 mi
Bottom Width, 2 1/2 ft
Top Width, 3 ft
Depth, 12 in
Grade, 1 in fall to the rod
Amount of water appropriated 396 inches
Amount of water claimed by original construction 864 inches
Acres under irrigation 300, creek bottom land, requiring 4 inches per acre to irrigate
Land irrigated, John W Goss, C E Clough, Mrs Ruth Parcels

Goss Private Ditch No. 2, No. 25
Water District No. 5
First Judicial District
Jurisdiction, Boulder, Larimer and Weld counties

Owner, John W Goss of Longmont
Boulder District Court Judgment Book, Water Decrees, Vol 2, District 5-6, 1869-1896, pg 97
Head is located in Sec 27, T3N R70W, Boulder Co, on the farm of William Baker, on the north side of the south fork of the creek
Natural Stream St Vrain Creek
General Course is east
Date of original appropriation is 30 June 1865
Amount of water appropriated is 160 customary inches
Grade, 1 in fall per rod
Length, 3/4 mi
Width, 3 ft
Depth, 12 in
Capacity, 432 customary inches
Water claimed by original construction is 200 inches
Acres proposed to be irrigated, 80
Acres under irrigation, 40 of meadow land and gravel subsoil, requiring 4 inches per acre to irrigate
The testimony claims 200 inches. The statement claims 440 inches. The amount shown to be appropriated is 160 inches

Webster & McCaslin Ditch, No 27
Water District No. 5
First Judicial District
Jurisdiction, Boulder, Larimer and Weld counties
Owner, M L McCaslin of Longmont
Boulder District Court Judgment Book, Water Decrees, Vol 2, District 5-6, 1869-1896, pg 100
Head is located in Sec 26, T3N R70W, Boulder Co, in the SW 1/4 of the SW 1/4 on the south side of the creek on the land of George Webster
Natural stream is St Vrain Creek
General Course is easterly
Date of original appropriation is 5 July 1865
Amount of water appropriated is 432 customary inches
Grade, 3/4 in fall per rod
Length, 3/4 mi
Width, 3 ft
Depth, 26 in
Capacity is 936 customary inches
Acres irrigated, 125 of creek bottom of meadow lands with sandy, porous subsoil

Denio & Taylor Ditch, No. 28
Water District No. 5
First Judicial District
Jurisdiction, Boulder, Larimer and Weld counties
Owner, J W Denio & Co, David Bestler, E J Coffman, James Mason, J A Miller, Isaac Runyan, Daniel Witter and Daniel Bashor of Longmont
Boulder District Court Judgment Book, Water Decrees, Vol 2, District 5-6, 1869-1896, pg 103
Head is located in Sec 35, T3N R70W, Boulder Co, on the E 1/2 of the section, on the north side of the creek in M L McCaslin's field
Natural stream is St Vrain Creek
General Course is easterly
Date of original appropriation is 15 July 1865
Water appropriated is 500 customary inches
Grade, 1 1/2 in per rod
Length, 7 mi
Width, 3 1/2 ft
Depth, 24 in
Capacity, 1008 customary inches
First Enlargement, 15 Oct 1873
Appropriation No. 57
Additional appropriation is 300 customary inches
Grade, 1/2 in per rod
Total amount appropriated 800 customary inches
Length, 7 mi
Bottom Width, 7 ft
Top Width, 9 1/2 ft
Depth, 3 ft
Grade, 1/2 in per rod
Increased capacity was 2556 inches
Total of 3564 inches
Acres under irrigation 800 requiring 1 inch of water per acre to irrigate
An earlier appropriation is claimed, but the claims and testimony are so conflicting and the data so vague and indefinite, it would be impossible to base a decree thereon.

Weese Private Ditch, No. 29
Water District No. 5
First Judicial District
Jurisdiction, Boulder, Larimer and Weld counties
Owner, Columbus C Weese of Longmont
Boulder District Court Judgment Book, Water Decrees, Vol 2, District 5-6, 1869-1896, pg 107
Head is located in Sec 21, T3N R70W, Boulder Co, 80 rods NW of the SE corner of said section
Natural stream is St Vrain Creek
Date of original appropriation is 1 Sept 1865
Water appropriated is 200 customary inches
Grade, 1/2 in per rod
General Course is easterly
Work commenced 15 May 1875 [??], with water flowing on 1 June 1875 [??]
Length, 160 rods
Bottom Width, 2 ft

Top Width, 2 1/2 feet
Depth, 18 in
Capacity, 486 customary inches
Acres under irrigation, 70 of meadow or hay land, sandy subsoil and very porous, requiring 4 inches of water to irrigate

Coffin-Davis Ditch, No. 31
Water District No. 5
First Judicial District
Jurisdiction, Boulder, Larimer and Weld counties
Owner, George W Coffin, W L Davis and M H Coffin of Longmont
Boulder District Court Judgment Book, Water Decrees, Vol 2, District 5-6, 1869-1896, pg 110
Head is located Sec 12, T2N R69W, Boulder County on the south bank of the creek about 40 rods north of the SE corner of the SE 1/4 of said section
Natural Stream is St Vrain Creek
Date of original appropriation is 1 June 1866
Amount appropriated was 1200 customary inches
Grade, 1/4 in to the rod
Length, 1 3/4 mi
Width, 3 ft
Depth, 12 in
Capacity, 432 in
First enlargement, 1 June 1871
Appropriation No. 45
Additional amount of water is, blank
Grade, 1/4 in per rod
Length, 2 1/2 miles long
Bottom width, 6 ft
Top Width, 8 ft
Depth, 2 ft
Capacity, 1584 in
Total appropriation 2016 inches
Acres under proposed irrigation is 500, there being 145 cultivated, 195 meadow, 120 very sandy, the balance is clay loam
Acres actually irrigated is 340

Oligarchy Ditch, No. 32
Water District No. 5
First Judicial District
Jurisdiction, Boulder, Larimer and Weld counties
Owner, Oligarchy Ditch Company of Longmont
Boulder District Court Judgment Book, Water Decrees, Vol 2, District 5-6, 1869-1896, pg 114
Head is located in Sec 27, T3N R70W, Boulder County on the north side of the creek near Joshua Chapman's house
Natural Stream is St Vrain Creek
General Course is easterly
Date of original appropriation is 1 June 1866
Water appropriated 1000 customary inches
Grade, 1 in per rod
Length, 2 1/2 mi
Bottom Width, 5 ft
Top Width, 7 ft
Depth, 18 in
Capacity, 1296 customary inches
First enlargement, 1 Dec 1870
Appropriation is No. 42
Additional water appropriated is 1880 customary inches
Grade, 1 in per rod
Length, 2 1/2 mi
Bottom Width, 8 ft
Top Width, 8 1/2 ft
Depth, 3o in
Grade, 1 in per rod
Increased capacity was 1674 inches
Total capacity of 2970 customary inches
Second enlargement, 1 Mar 1872
Appropriation is No. 48
Additional water appropriated is 870 customary inches
Total amount appropriated is 3700 customary inches
Bottom Width, 10 ft
Top Width, 11 ft
Depth, 30 in
Grade, 1 in per rod
Increased capacity was 810 inches
Total capacity of 3780 inches
166 families use water from the ditch for domestic purposes
Third enlargment, 1 Apr 1874
Appropriation is No. 59
Additional water appropriated is 1250 customary inches
Grade, 1 in per rod
Bottom Width, 12 ft
Top Width, 13 ft
Depth, 36 in
Grade, 1 in per rod
Increased capacity was 1620 inches
Total appropriation of 5400 inches

Davis & Downing Ditch, No. 33
Water District No. 5
First Judicial District
Jurisdiction, Boulder, Larimer and Weld counties
Owner, M L McCaslin, Urial Williams, Robert Culver and V W McCory of Longmont

Boulder District Court Judgment Book, Water Decrees, Vol 2, District 5-6, 1869-1896, pg 118
Head is located in Sec 35, T3N R70W, Boulder County on the south bank of the creek on land now owned by M L McCaslin
Natural Stream is St Vrain Creek
General Course is south of east
Date of original appropriation was 1 Nov 1866
Water appropriated was "enough to run one set of small corn burrs"
Length, 1/2 mi
Bottom Width, 3 ft
Top Width, 4 ft
Depth, 18 in
Grade, 1/3 in per rod
Capacity, 756 inches
Acres under irrigation is not given
This ditch was originally taken out for Mill purposes
First enlargement, 1 May 1867
Appropriation is No. 34
Additional amount appropriated is 324 customary inches
Grade, 1/3 in per rod
Length, 1/2 mi
Width, 5 ft
Depth, 18 in
Grade, 1/3 in per rod
Capacity, 1080 inches
As enlarged it used as a Mill race
Second enlargement, 15 Mar 1870
Appropriation is No. 40
Additional amount appropriated is 432 customary inches
Grade, 1/3 in per rod
Length, 2 1/2 mi
Bottom Width, 4 1/2 ft
Top Width, 6 ft
Depth, 2 ft
Grade, 1/3 in per rod
Increased capacity was 432 inches
Total of 1512 inches
Total amount of water run at that time was 756 inches
Acres under irrigation, not given
Third enlargement, 1 May 1874
Appropriation is, not shown
Bottom Width, 6 ft
Top Width, 8 ft
Depth, 20 in
Grade, 1/8 in per rod
Nothing to show that any additional water was appropriated
Fourth enlargement, 1 Oct 1876
Appropriation is No. 69 1/2
Additional water appropriated is 104 customary inches
Grade, 1/3 in per rod
Total appropriated 860 customary inches
Length, 2 1/2 mi
Bottom Width, 8 ft
Top Width, 12 ft
Depth, 3 ft
Grade, 1/3 in per rod
Increased capacity was 2808 inches
Total appropriation of 4320 inches
Water being run at the time was 2880 inches
Acres under irrigation, 860 cultivated or pasture land, requiring 1 inch per acre to irrigate
Water claimed is 2304 customary inches

Peck & Metcalf Ditch, No. 36
Water District No. 5
First Judicial District
Jurisdiction, Boulder, Larimer and Weld counties
Owner, Thomas S Peck of Longmont
Boulder District Court Judgment Book, Water Decrees, Vol 2, District 5-6, 1869-1896, pg 124
Head is located in Sec 7, T7N R69W, Boulder County one is near the east line and the other near the west line of the SE 1/4 of said section
Natural stream is Dry Creek No. 2 a tributary to St Vrain Creek
Date of original appropriation was 16 May 1867
Water appropriated was 180 customary inches
General Course is east
Lenth, 3/4 mi
Bottom Width, 3 ft
Top Width, 3 1/2 ft
Depth, 24 in
Grade, 1/2 in per rod
Capacity was 936 customary inches
Water claimed was 400 inches
Acres under irrigation is 90, requiring 2 inches of water per acre to irrigate

James Ditch, No. 37
Water District No. 5
First Judicial District
Jurisdiction, Boulder, Larimer and Weld counties
Owner, James Ditch Company of Longmont
Boulder District Court Judgment Book, Water Decrees, Vol 2, District 5-6, 1869-1896, pg 127
Head is located Sec 27, T3N R70W, Boulder County on the south side of the creek

Natural stream is St Vrain Creek
General Course is south easterly
Date of original appropriation was 30 June 1868
Water appropriated was 480 customary inches
Grade, 1/4 in per rod
Acres under irrigation, not given
First enlargement, 30 Dec 1871
Appropriation No. 47
Additional water appropriated was 360 customary inches
Grade 1/4 in per rod
Total appropriated 840 customary inches
Width, 3 1/2 ft
Depth, 20 in
Increased capacity was 360 inches
Total capacity of 840 inches
Second enlargment, 1 Apr 1877
Appropriation No. 70
Additional water appropriated was 648 customary inches
Grade, 1/4 in per rod
Length, 10 mi
Bottom Width, 6 ft
Top Width, 7 1/2 ft
Depth, 1 1/2 ft
Grade, 1/4 in per rod
Increased capacity was 618 inches
Total capacity of 1458 inches
Acres under irrigation, 1500 of cultivated or meadow land, requiring 1 inch per acre to irrigate

Rough & Ready Ditch, No 38
Water District No. 5
First Judicial District
Jurisdiction, Boulder, Larimer and Weld counties
Owner, Rough & Ready Irrigating Ditch Company
Boulder District Court Judgment Book, Water Decrees, Vol 2, District 5-6, 1869-1896, pg 131
Head is located in Section __, T __ R __, Boulder County about 1/8 of a mile above the mouth of St Vrain Canon
Natural stream is St Vrain Creek
General Course is easterly
Date of original appropriation was 13 Mar 1869
Water appropriated was 1500 customary inches
Length, 15 mi
Width, 7 ft
Depth, 20 in
Grade, 1/3 in per rod
Capacity was 1680 customary inches
Acres proposed under irrigation, 5460
Acres actually udner irrigation, 1410, requiring 1500 inches of water to irrigate
First enlargement, 4 Mar 1873
Appropriation No. 55 1/2
Additional appropriation is 1500 customary inches
Grade, 1/3 in per rod
Width, 12 ft
Depth, 3 ft
Increased capacity 3504 customary inches
Total capacity 5184 customary inches
Acres under irrigation, 5460
The statement claims another enlargement and 500 additional inches by virtue thereof, but the testimony shows it to have been only a cleaning out and strengthening of the ditch, and nothing to show any additional appropriation of water.

Nelson Ditch, No. 39
Water District No. 5
First Judicial District
Jurisdiction, Boulder, Larimer and Weld counties
Owner, August Nelson of Longmont
Boulder District Court Judgment Book, Water Decrees, Vol 2, District 5-6, 1869-1896, pg 135
Head is located in Sec 2, T2N R70W, Boulder County on the NW 1/4 of said section, on the south side of the creek
Natural Stream is Dry Creek that runs from Lykin's Canon, a tributary of the St Vrain
Date of the original appropriation, 1 Apr 1869
Water appropriated is 50 customary inches
Grade, 1/4 in per rod
Length, 1/4 mi
Bottom Width, 1 ft
Top Width, 1 1/2 ft
Depth, 8 in
Acres under irrigation is 170 proposed, 10 actual
First enlargement, 10 May 1872
Appropriation No. 51
Water appropriated is 20 customary inches
Grade, 1/4 in per rod
Width, 6 in wider
Total capacity 70 inches
Second enlargement, 20 May 1874
Appropriation No. 62
Water appropriated is 55 customary inches
Grade, 1/4 in per rod
Bottom Width, 20 in
Top Width, 28 in
Depth, 16 in
Additional capacity 55 inches
Total appropriation 125 customary inches
Total capacity 384 inches

Third enlargement, 1 May 1875
Appropriation No. 67
Water appropriated is 75 customary inches
Grade, 1/4 in per rod
Bottom Width, 2 1/2 ft
Top Width, 3 ft
Depth, 1 1/2 ft
Total appropriation 200 customary inches
Acres under irrigation, 250

Swede Ditch, No. 44
This ditch was first known as the Smead & Pye Ditch, and then the Beaver Ditch, now the Swede Ditch
Water District No. 5
First Judicial District
Jurisdiction, Boulder, Larimer and Weld counties
Owner, Swede Ditch Company of Longmont
Boulder District Court Judgment Book, Water Decrees, Vol 2, District 5-6, 1869-1896, pg 139
Head is located in Sec 20, T3N R70W, Boulder County near the SE 1/4 of the NW 1/4 of said section, near the mouth of the canon on the farm of Chester Smead, on the south side of the creek
Natural stream is St Vrain Creek
General Course is easterly
Date of original appropriation, 1 May 1871
Water appropriated was 575 customary inches
Grade, 1/2 in per rod
Length, 80 rods
Width, 4 ft
Depth, 12 in
Acres under irrigation is not given
First enlargement, 1 Mar 1873
Appropriation No. 53
Additional water appropriated 504 customary inches
Grade, 1/4 in per rod
Length, 7 mi
Bottom Width, 5 ft
Top Width, 6 ft
Depth, 1 1/2 ft
Increased capacity was 612 customary inches
Total appropriation 1080 customary inches
Number of acres under and proposed to be irrigated, 3500

Bear & McCory Ditch, No. 45
Water District No. 5
First Judicial District
Jurisdiction, Boulder, Larimer and Weld counties
Owner, Robert Culver and John Henry Hager of Longmont
Boulder District Court Judgment Book, Water Decrees, Vol 2, District 5-6, 1869-1896, pg 142
Head is located in Sec 1, T2N R70W, Boulder, County in the E 1/4 of said section
Natural Stream is Dry Creek in Lykin's Canon
Date of appropriation, 1 June 1871
Water appropriated is 50 customary inches
Grade, 1/2 in per rod
Length, 40 rods
Bottom Width, 2 ft
Top Width, 3 ft
Depth, 10 in
Capacity, 300 inches
Water claimed, 800 inches
Acres under irrigation, not given
First enlargement, 1 Jan 1875
Appropriation No. 68
Water appropriated is 35 customary inches
Grade, 1/2 in per rod
Bottom Width, 3 ft
Top Width, 4 ft
Depth, 1 ft
Capacity 204 inches
Total capacity of 504 inches
Acres of land under and proposed irrigation, 90 of grass land requiring 1 in of water to irrigate
Total water claimed 800 inches

Highland Ditch, No. 46
Water District No. 5
First Judicial District
Jurisdiction, Boulder, Larimer and Weld counties
Owner, Highland Ditch Company of Longmont
Boulder District Court Judgment Book, Water Decrees, Vol 2, District 5-6, 1869-1896, pg 146
Head is located in Sec 21, T3N R70W, Boulder County at a point just below John Reese's bridge spanning the creek
Natural Stream is St Vrain Creek
General Course is north east
Date of appropriation, 30 Nov 1871
Water appropriated, 2500 customary inches
Grade, 8 ft per mile
Length, 8 or 9 miles
Bottom Width, 12 ft
Top width, 18 ft
Depth, 36 in
Capacity 6480 customary inches
Water claimed 15,000 customary inches

Acres under proposed irrigation, 23,919, under actual irrigation, 13,792 of bluff and hay, requiring 3/4 inches per acre to irrigate
First enlargement, stricken out
Second enlargment, stricken out
Third enlargement, stricken out
Fourth enlargement, 1 June 1876
Appropriation No. 69 1/2
Water appropriated 1000 customary inches
Grade, 8 ft per mile
Total appropriated 3500 customary inches
The fourth enlargment was reduced from 1900 to 1000 customary inches
Fifth enlargement, 1 June 1877
Appropriation No. 71
Water appropriated 1500 customary inches
Grade, 8 ft per mile
Total appropriated 5000 customary inches
Sixth enlargment, 1 June 1878
Appropriation No. 75 1/2
Water appropriatied is 1000 customary inches
Grade, 8 ft per mile
Total appropriated 6000 customary inches
Length, 26 miles
Bottom width, 12 ft
Top Width, 18 ft
Depth, 3 ft

Last Chance Ditch, No. 49
Water District No. 5
First Judicial District
Jurisdiction, Boulder, Larimer and Weld counties
Owner, Last Chance Ditch Company of Plattsville
Boulder District Court Judgment Book, Water Decrees, Vol 2, District 5-6, 1869-1896, pg 150
Head is located in Sec 3, T2N R68W in Weld, Co near the center of the E 1/2 of the NW 1/4 of said section
Natural Stream is St Vrain Creek
General Course is easterly and northeast
Date of appropriation, 15 Mar 1872
Water appropriated is 4230 customary inches
Grade, 3 1/2 feet per mile
Length, 7 1/2 mi
Bottom Width, 9 ft
Top Width, 14 1/2 ft
Depth, 30 in
Acres under proposed irrigation, 3200, under actual irrigation, 1700 of hay land, requiring 4 in of water per acre to irrigate

Spring Creek Ditch, No. 52
Water District No. 5
First Judicial District
Jurisdiction, Boulder, Larimer and Weld counties
Owner, Aaron Peterson of Niwot
Boulder District Court Judgment Book, Water Decrees, Vol 2, District 5-6, 1869-1896, pg 153
Head is located in Sec 22, T1N R70W, Boulder County on the quarter section line of the SW 1/4 of said section
Natural Stream is St Vrain Creek
General Course is easterly
Date of appropriation, 1 June 1872
Water appropriated was 100 customary inches
Grade, 1/2 in per rod
Length, 1/2 mi
Width, 2 ft
Depth, 18 in
Capacity was 432 inches
Acres lying under irrigation, 50 of sandy, alkali land requiring 2 in of water per acre to irrigate

Renner Ditch, No. 60
Water District No. 5
First Judicial District
Jurisdiction, Boulder, Larimer and Weld counties
Owner, Hans Christensen of Longmont
Boulder District Court Judgment Book, Water Decrees, Vol 2, District 5-6, 1869-1896, pg 156
Head located in Sec 9, T2N R70W, Boulder County on the south side of Lykins' Dry Creek on Nels Johnson's land
Natural Stream is Lykins' Dry Creek, a tributary of St Vrain Creek [Left Hand]
General Course is easterly
Date of appropriation, 1 May 1874
Water appropriated was 288 customary inches
Grade, 1/2 in per rod
Length, 3/4 mi
Width, 2 ft
Depth, 12 in
Acres under irrigation, 100
This ditch depends for its supply of water upon waste water from other ditches. The supply is irregular and uncertain, and the amount indefinite.

Richardson Ditch, No. 64
Water District No. 5
First Judicial District
Jurisdiction, Boulder, Larimer and Weld counties
Owner, Swan Magni of Longmont

Boulder District Court Judgment Book, Water Decrees, Vol 2, District 5-6, 1869-1896, pg 159
Head is located in Sec 3, T2N R70W, Boulder County near the center of the NW 1/4 of the SW 1/4 of said section
Natural Stream is Dry Creek in Lykins' Canon
Date of Appropriation, 15 June 1874
Water appropriated was 100 customary inches
Grade, 1/2 in per rod
Length, 1/2 mi
Width, 4 ft
Depth, 14 in
Capacity was 672 customary inches
Acres under irrigation, 240

Ullery Ditch, No. 66
Water District No. 5
First Judicial District
Jurisdiction, Boulder, Larimer and Weld counties
Owner, Swan Anderson of Longmont and Hugo Anderson of Niwot
Boulder District Court Judgment Book, Water Decrees, Vol 2, District 5-6, 1869-1896, pg 162
Head is located in Sec 15, T2N R70W, Boulder County and the SE 1/4 of said section on the north side of Steel Gulch, on Swan Johnson's land
Natural Stream is Steel Gulch
General Course is east
Date of appropriation, 1 July 1874
Water appropriated was 200 customary inches
Length, 1 1/4 mi
Bottom Width, 1 ft
Top Width, 1 1/2 ft
Depth, 8 in
Acres under irrigation, 320, of that 100 acres plowed, 160 acres of meadow, 60 acres of hay requiring 1 inch of water per acre to irrigate

Denio & Taylor Extension Ditch, No. 69
Water District No. 5
First Judicial District
Jurisdiction, Boulder, Larimer and Weld counties
Owner, William H Dickens of Longmont
Boulder District Court Judgment Book, Water Decrees, Vol 2, District 5-6, 1869-1896, pg 165
Head is located in Sec __, T_ R_, about 50 yards south of Denio's Mill in the Town of Longmont
Natural Stream is St Vrain Creek via Denio & Taylor Ditch
Date of Appropriation, 1 June 1875
Water appropriated was 400 customary inches
General Course, south and east
Grade, 3/4 in per rod
Length, 1 mi
Bottom Width, 2 1/2 ft
Top Width, 5 ft
Depth, 24 in
Capacity is 630 customary inches
Acres under irrigation, 200 of bottom, porous, gravel and sand subsoil
This ditch takes its water directly from the Mill Race of said ditch and hence is governed in the amount appropriated by the amount used by said Mill

Titus & Goyn Ditch, No. 72
Water District No. 5
First Judicial District
Jurisdiction, Boulder, Larimer and Weld counties
Owner, Albert Titus of Boulder
Boulder District Court Judgment Book, Water Decrees, Vol 2, District 5-6, 1869-1896, pg 168
Head is located in Sec __, T__ R__, Boulder County on the Groesbeck Place
General Course is south easterly
Natural Stream is Dry Creek, a tributary to St Vrain Creek
Date of appropriation, 1 Apr 1878
Water appropriated 50 customary inches
Grade, 1/2 in per rod
Length, 2 mi
Width, 2 ft
Depth, 12 in
Capacity, 288 customary inches
Acres under irrigation, proposed 300, actual 50, requiring 1 in of water per acre to irrigate

Supply Ditch, No. 75
Water District No. 5
First Judicial District
Jurisdiction, Boulder, Larimer and Weld counties
Owner, Supply Ditch Company of Longmont
Boulder District Court Judgment Book, Water Decrees, Vol 2, District 5-6, 1869-1896, pg 171
Head is located in Sec 20, T3N R70W, Boulder County on the NW 1/4 of said Section on the north bank of the Creek
Natural Stream is St Vrain Creek
General Course is easterly
Date of appropriation, 31 May 1878
Water appropriated was 4000 customary inches
Grade, 3 8/12 ft per mile
Length, 23 mi

Bottom Width, 15 ft
Top Width, 17 1/2 Ft
Depth, 36 in
Capacity, 6480 customary inches
Acres under irrigation, 4000

Taylor Ditch No. 1, No. 78
Water District No. 5
First Judicial District
Jurisdiction, Boulder, Larimer and Weld counties
Owner, Clover Basin Ditch Company of Longmont
Boulder District Court Judgment Book, Water Decrees, Vol 2, District 5-6, 1869-1896, pg 174
Head is located in Sec __, T2N R69W, Boulder County about 20 rods above the head of the Clover Basin Ditch on the farm of Rev'd Mr Lagerman
Natural Stream, Dry Creek
General Course is northeasterly
Date of appropriation, 1 June 1879
Water appropriated, 382 customary inches
Grade, 1 1/2 in per rod
Length, 20 rods
Width, 3 ft
Depth, 20 in
Capacity, 720 customary inches
Acres under irrigation, 655 proposed, 300 actual requiring 1 1/4 inches of water per acre to irrigate
This ditch is a source of supply for the Clover Basin Ditch

Taylor Ditch No. 2, No. 79
Water District No. 5
First Judicial District
Jurisdiction, Boulder, Larimer and Weld counties
Owner, Clover Basin Ditch Company of Longmont
Boulder District Court Judgment Book, Water Decrees, Vol 2, District 5-6, 1869-1896, pg 177
Head is located in Sec __, T2N R69W, Boulder County on the land of Lewis Nelson
Natural Stream is the 2nd Dry Creek, north of Left Hand Creek
General Course is northeasterly
Date of appropriation, 2 June 1879
Water appropriated not to exceed 432 customary inches, and not interfering with vested rights
Grade, 1 1/2 in per rod
Length, 30 rods
Width, 3 ft
Depth, 12 in
Capacity, 432 in
Acres under irrigation, 655 requiring 1 1/2 inches of water per acre to irrigate
This ditch is a source of supply to the Clover Basin Ditch and is owned by the CLover Basin Company

Lagerman Supply Ditch, No. 80
Water District No. 5
First Judicial District
Jurisdiction, Boulder, Larimer and Weld counties
Owner, Frederick Lagerman of Niwot
Boulder District Court Judgment Book, Water Decrees, Vol 2, District 5-6, 1869-1896, pg 180
Head is located in Sec 23, T2N R70W, Boulder County on the NE 1/4 of said section about 682 feet from the north line and about 234 feet from the east line of said section.
Natural stream is Spring Gulch and Left Hand Creek
General Course is northeasterly
Date of appropriation, 14 Nov 1879
Water appropriated is 432 customary inches
Grade 1/4 in per rod
Length, 1000 ft
Width 3 ft
Depth, 12 in
Acres under irrigation is 600

Dickens Private Ditch No. 2, No. 81
Water District No. 5
First Judicial District
Jurisdiction, Boulder, Larimer and Weld counties
Owner, Wm H Dickens of Longmont
Boulder District Court Judgment Book, Water Decrees, Vol 2, District 5-6, 1869-1896, pg 183
Head is located in Longmont, in Boulder County at the SE corner of the Town Site of Longmont, Colo
Natural Stream is Booring Dry Gulch [Dry Creek]
General Course is south
Date of appropriation was 1 Apr 1880
Water appropriated was 450 customary inches
Grade 1/2 in per rod
Length, 1/2 mile
Bottom Width, 2 ft
Top Width, 3 ft
Depth, 15 in
Water claimed, 150 customary inches
Acres under irrigation is 40, is very porous, sandy and gravelly requiring 2 or more inches of water per acre to irrigate

Lykins Gulch Ditch, No. 82
Water District No. 5
First Judicial District
Jurisdiction, Boulder, Larimer and Weld counties
Owner, Thomas S Peck of Longmont
Boulder District Court Judgment Book, Water Decrees, Vol 2, District 5-6, 1869-1896, pg 186
Natural Stream is Lykins' Gulch or Dry Creek No. 1 a tributary of St Vrain Creek
General Course is easterly
Head is located in Sec 1, T2N R70W, in Boulder County on the SW 1/4 of said section on the farm of Robert Culver
Date of appropriation is 15 May 1881
Water appropriated is 150 customary inches
Grade, 1/4 in per rod
Length, 1/2 mile
Width, 2 ft
Depth, 12 in
Capacity was 288 inches
Acres under irrigation is 150, plow land requiring 1 inch of water per acre to irrigate

Bonus Ditch, No 6.
Water District No. 5
First Judicial District
Jurisdiction, Boulder, Larimer and Weld counties
Owner, Freeman Belcher, W L Davis, J K Doolittle, John J Rice and L H Dickson of Longmont
Boulder District Court Judgment Book, Water Decrees, Vol 2, District 5-6, 1869-1896, pg 189
Head is located in Sec 11, T2N R69W, in Boulder County on the south bank of the Creek about 5 rods below the mouth of Left Hand Creek on W H Dickens' farm
Natural Stream is St Vrain Creek
General Course is south easterly
Date of appropriation is 30 Mar 1861
Water appropriated was 648 customary inches
Grade, 1/4 in per rod
Length, 2 1/2 mi
Bottom Width, 4 ft
Top Width, 5 ft
Depth, 12 in
First Enlargement, 30 May 1865
Appropriation No. 22
Water appropriated was 552 customary inches
Grade, 1/4 in per rod
Total appropriation 1200 customary inches
Length, 2 1/2 mi
Width, 5 ft
Depth 20 in
Grade 1/4 in per rod
Capacity 552 inches
Total capacity 1200 inches
Acres under irrigation, 880; 350 acres farming or bluff, 530 acres meadow and pasture, requiring 1 1/2 inches of water per acre to irrigate.

WATER DISTRICT NO. 6

Lower Boulder Ditch, No. 1
Water District No. 6
First Judicial District
Jurisdiction, Boulder, Larimer and Weld counties
Owner, Lower Boulder Ditch Company of Canfield
Boulder District Court Judgment Book, Water Decrees, Vol 2, District 5-6, 1869-1896, pg 192
General Course is easterly, through Secs 16, 15, 14, and 13, T1N R69W, terminating at NE 1/4 Sec 13 T1N R69W
Natural Stream is Boulder Creek
Head is located on the south side of Boulder Creek near west line of Sec 16 T1N R69W
Date of appropriation was 1 Oct 1859
Rate 25 cu ft of water per second
Width, 4 ft
Depth, 18 in
Length, 3 1/2 mi
Enlarged, 1 June 1870
Length, 5 mi
Width, 9 ft
Depth, 2 ft
Rate, 97 cu ft of water per second
Acres under irrigation is proposed at 3000, 1500 actually irrigated at 1 in of water per acre
Appropriation, No. 32

Smith and Goss Ditch, No. 2
Water District No. 6
First Judicial District
Jurisdiction, Boulder, Larimer and Weld counties
Owner, M G Smith and Robert Culver of Boulder
Boulder District Court Judgment Book, Water Decrees, Vol 2, District 5-6, 1869-1896, pg 197
General Course is east
Natural Stream is Boulder Creek
Headgate is located on the north side of said creek about 200 ft below 12th Street bridge in the Town of Boulder
Length, 3/4 mi
Width, 3 ft
Depth, 18 in

Grade, 3 in per rod
Date of appropriation is 15 Nov 1859
Rate, 44.3 cu ft of water per second
Acres under irrigation is 200, requiring about 2 in of water per acre

Howell Ditch, No. 3
Water District No. 6
First Judicial District
Jurisdiction, Boulder, Larimer and Weld counties
Owner, WIlliam R Howell of Canfield
Boulder District Court Judgment Book, Water Decrees, Vol 2, District 5-6, 1869-1896, pg 200
General Course is east, running through Sec 1, T1N R69W
Natural Stream is Boulder Creek
Headgate is located on the south side of said Creek about 50 rods east where west line said Section crosses said stream
Width, 3 ft
Depth, 2 1/2 ft
Length, 300 rods
Grade, 1 in per rod
Date of appropriation is 1 Dec 1859
Rate, 47.55 cu ft of water per second
Acres under irrigation, 200 requiring 1 1/4 inches per acre of water to irrigate

Anderson Ditch, No. 4
Water District No. 6
First Judicial District
Jurisdiction, Boulder, Larimer and Weld counties
Owner, Anderson Ditch Company of Boulder
Boulder District Court Judgment Book, Water Decrees, Vol 2, District 5-6, 1869-1896, pg 202
General Course easterly through Secs 36 & 31, T1N R71 & 70W, terminating on Sec 6, T1S R70W
Natural Stream is Boulder Creek
Headgate is located on the south bank of said creek near the west boundary of Sec 36 T1N R71W
Date of appropriation, 1 Oct 1860
Rate 25 cu ft per second
Width, 4 ft
Depth, 2 ft
Length, 3 mi
Acres under irrigation is 1500
Extension, 1 May 1875
Length, 3 1/2 mi
Width, 4 ft
Depth, 18 in
Grade, 1/2 in to the rod

Godding, Dailey and Plumb Ditch, No. 5
Water District No. 6
First Judicial District
Jurisdiction, Boulder, Larimer and Weld counties
Owner, Dennis Dailey, S J Plumb, Stephen H Carr of Erie and A J Emmons of Longmont and Clinton M Tyler of Boulder
Boulder District Court Judgment Book, Water Decrees, Vol 2, District 5-6, 1869-1896, pg 204
General Course is northeasterly, across the NW 1/4 Sec 31, T2N R68W and connecting hear the south line of Sec 17 T2N R68W
Natural stream is Boulder Creek
Headgate is located on the east bank of said creek, near south line NW 1/4 NW 1/4 Sec 31 T2N R68W
Date of appropriation 1 Mar 1861
Rate 7.24 cu ft per second
Width, 2 ft
Depth, 3 ft
Length, 1 mi
Capacity 23.198 cu ft per second
Acres under irrigation 750 requiring 1 in of water per acre
Extension, 1 Apr 1865
Length, 3 1/2 mi
Width, 5 ft
Depth, 2 ft
Grade, 3 ft per mile
Appropriation No. 26

Houck No. 2 Ditch, No. 6
Water District No. 6
First Judicial District
Jurisdiction, Boulder, Larimer and Weld counties
Owner, Robert Houck of Erie
Boulder District Court Judgment Book, Water Decrees, Vol 2, District 5-6, 1869-1896, pg 207
General Course is northeasterly through Sec 29 and onto Sec 20 T2N R68W
Natural Stream is Boulder Creek
Headgate is located where Idaho Slough leaves said creek
Date of appropriation, 1 Apr 1861
Rate, 7.16 cu ft per second
Width, 2 ft
Depth, 2 ft
Length, 3/4 mi
Grade, 3 ft per mile
Acres under irrigation, 80 requiring 2 in of water per acre

Jones and Donnelly Ditch, No. 7
Water District No. 6
First Judicial District
Jurisdiction, Boulder, Larimer and Weld counties
Owner, W R Howell of Erie and Thomas J Jones of Valmont
Boulder District Court Judgment Book, Water Decrees, Vol 2, District 5-6, 1869-1896, pg 210
General Course is north from 200 yds above the water tank of the C C Railroad and runs through the W 1/2 NW 1/4 and E 1/2 NW 1/4 Sec 27 T1N R70W, terminating on Sec 22 of said township
Natural Stream is South Boulder Creek
Headgate is located about 200 yrds above the CCRR water tank
Date of appropriation, 1 May 1860
Rate, 14.36 cu ft per second
Width, 3 ft
Depth, 2 ft
Length, 1 1/2 mi
Grade, 1/2 in per rod
Acres under irrigation, 320 requiring 2 in of water per acre

Martha M Mathews Ditch, No. 8
Water District No. 6
First Judicial District
Jurisdiction, Boulder, Larimer and Weld counties
Owner, Martha M Mathews of Erie
Boulder District Court Judgment Book, Water Decrees, Vol 2, District 5-6, 1869-1896, pg 212
Date of appropriation, 1 June 1861
General Course is northeasterly
Natural Stream is Boulder Creek
Headgate is located at a point near SWC or SE 1/4 NE 1/4 Sec 11 T1N R69W
Length, 1 mi
Width, 24 in
Depth, 12 in
Grade, 1/4 in per rod
Rate, 4.6 cu in per second
Acres under irrigation, 120 requiring 2 1/2 in per acre

N K Smith and Tyler Ditch, No 9
Water District No. 6
First Judicial District
Jurisdiction, Boulder, Larimer and Weld counties
Owner, Clinton M Tyler of Boulder
Boulder District Court Judgment Book, Water Decrees, Vol 2, District 5-6, 1869-1896, pg 215
Date of appropriation, 1 June 1861
General Course is northeasterly through NE 1/4 NE 1/4 Sec 20 and N 1/2 NW 1/4 and NW 1/4 NE 1/4 Sec 21 T2N R68W
Natural Stream is Boulder Creek
Headgate is located on the east bank of said creek, Sec 20 T2N R68W, Weld Co (changed to headgate Carr & Tyler Ditch)
Width, 4 ft
Depth, 3 ft
Length, 1 mi
Grade, 1/2 in per rod
Rate, 29.04 cu ft per second
Acres under irrigation is 250

Plumb Ditch, No. 10
Water District No. 6
First Judicial District
Jurisdiction, Boulder, Larimer and Weld counties
Owner, S J Plumb of Erie
Boulder District Court Judgment Book, Water Decrees, Vol 2, District 5-6, 1869-1896, pg 217
Date of appropriation, 1 Apr 1862
General Course is NE from east bank of Boulder Creek near the south line of Sec 1 T1N R69W
Natural Stream is Boulder Creek
Headgate is located near the south line of Sec 1 T1N R69W
Width, 3 ft
Depth 2 ft
Length, 3 mi
Grade, 3 ft per mile
Rate, 5.1 cu ft per second
Acres under irrigation is 400 requiring 1 1/4 inches of water per acre

Rural Ditch, No. 12
Water District No. 6
First Judicial District
Jurisdiction, Boulder, Larimer and Weld counties
Owner, Rural Ditch Company of Longmont
Boulder District Court Judgment Book, Water Decrees, Vol 2, District 5-6, 1869-1896, pg 220
Date of appropriation, 10 May 1862
General Course is NE across Secs 20, 21, 16, 15, 10, 3, 2, and 1, T3N, R68W
Natural Stream is Boulder Creek through Idaho Slough
Headgate is located along north line of S 1/2, SE 1/4, Sec 16, T1N, R68W
Original Length, 3 miles
Current Lenth, 7 miles
Width, 4 ft, Enlarged 10 Mar 1863 to 8 ft

Original Depth, 15 in, enlarged 10 Mar 1863 to 3 1/2 ft
Grade, 5/8 in per rod
Rate, 22.75 cu in per second, present rate 198.29 cu ft per second
Acres under irrigation is 1920, 1250 acres irrigated requiring 1 1/2 in per acre
First Enlargement, appropriation No. 15
Date of appropriation, 10 Mar 1863

Green Ditch, No. 13
Water District No. 6
First Judicial District
Jurisdiction, Boulder, Larimer and Weld counties
Owner, Geo C Green, I N Field, E A Barbour and Alex Derwood
Boulder District Court Judgment Book, Water Decrees, Vol 2, District 5-6, 1869-1896, pg 223
Date of appropriation, 15 Sept 1862
General Course is SE
Natural Stream is Boulder Creek
Headgate is located near the center of Sec 22, T1N, R70W
Length, 2 1/2 miles
Width, 5 ft, enlarged on 1 May 1863 to 5 ft, enlarged on 1 May 1864 to __, enlarged on 1 May 1865 to __, enlarged on 1 May 1866 to ___, present width 5 ft
Depth, 24 in
Grade, 1/4 in per rod
Rate, 34.58 cu ft per second
Acres under irrigation is 2000; about 300 acres irrigated
First enlargement, No. 17
Second enlargement, No. 27
Third enlargement, No 29

Farmers Ditch, No. 14
Water District No. 6
First Judicial District
Jurisdiction, Boulder, Larimer and Weld counties
Owner, Farmers Ditch Company of Boulder
Boulder District Court Judgment Book, Water Decrees, Vol 2, District 5-6, 1869-1896, pg 225
Date of appropriation, 1 Oct 1862
General Course is NE for 5 or 6 miles
Natural Stream is Boulder Creek
Headgate is located on the north bank of [Boulder] Creek about 120 rods above the mouth of canon
Length, 6 miles
Width, 7 ft
Depth, 2 ft
Grade, 1/2 in per rod
Rate, 73.29 cu ft per second
Acres under irrigation, 3000

Houck No. 1 Ditch, No. 16
Water District No. 6
First Judicial District
Jurisdiction, Boulder, Larimer and Weld counties
Owner, Robert Houck of Erie
Boulder District Court Judgment Book, Water Decrees, Vol 2, District 5-6, 1869-1896, pg 228
Date of appropriation, 1 Apr 1863
General Course is NE from south side of Boulder Creek through Secs 29, 20, T2N, R68W
Natural Stream is Boulder Creek
Headgate is located on north side of Boulder Creek near SE 1/4, NE 1/4, Sec 30, T2N, R68W
Width, 3 ft
Depth, 2 1/2 ft
Length, 1 mile
Grade, 3 ft to the mile
Rate, 15.97 in per second
Acres under irrigation is 200; 200 acres requiring 2 inches of water per acre

Smith and Emmons Ditch, No. 18
Water District No. 6
First Judicial District
Jurisdiction, Boulder, Larimer and Weld counties
Owner, R N Smith and A J Emmons of Longmont
Boulder District Court Judgment Book, Water Decrees, Vol 2, District 5-6, 1869-1896, pg 231
Date of appropriation, 1 June 1863
General Course is north beginning on Idaho Slough and running through Secs 21, 16 & 4, T2N, R68W
Natural Stream is Boulder Creek
Headgate is located on [Idaho] Slough 64 rods east of west line and 100 rods south of north line, said Sec 21
Width, 6 ft
Depth, 2 ft
Length, 3 1/2 miles
Grade, 8 ft to the mile
Rate, 47.16 cu ft per second
Acres under irrigation, 1000; 750 acres irrigated requiring 1 1/2 in of water per acre

Carr and Tyler Ditch, No. 19
Water District No. 6
First Judicial District
Jurisdiction, Boulder, Larimer and Weld counties
Owner, Clinton M Tyler and Stephen H Carr of Boulder

Boulder District Court Judgment Book, Water Decrees, Vol 2, District 5-6, 1869-1896, pg 233
Date of appropriation, 1 June 1864
General Course is north through Secs 29, 20 and terminates on [Secs] 17, 21, T2N R68W
Natural Stream is Boulder Creek
Headgate is located on north bank of Idaho Slough on NW 1/4, NE 1/4, Sec 29, T2N, R68W
Width, 2 ft 10 in
Depth, 2 ft
Length, 2 miles
Grade, 1 in to the rod
Rate, 33.78 cu ft per second
Acres under irrigation, 500; 400 acres requiring 1/2 to 1 1/4 inches per acre

Butte Mill Ditch, No. 22
Water District No. 6
First Judicial District
Jurisdiction, Boulder, Larimer and Weld counties
Owner, Butte Dutch Irrigating and Milling Company of Boulder
Boulder District Court Judgment Book, Water Decrees, Vol 2, District 5-6, 1869-1896, pg 236
Date of appropriation, 1 Mar 1865
General Course is east and NE
Natural Stream is Boulder Creek
Headgate is located on SE side of North Boulder Creek at a point 16 chains, 30 links W, and 20 chains, 46 links south of the NE Cor W 1/2, NW 1/4, Sec 27, T1N, R70W on Parlin Farm
Length, 3 miles
Width, 5 1/2 ft
Depth, 3 1/2 ft
Grade, 1/2 in per rod
Rate, 110.86 cu ft per second
Acres under irrigation, 3500; 1200 acres having been irrigated

Howell and Beasley Ditch, No. 23
Water District No. 6
First Judicial District
Jurisdiction, Boulder, Larimer and Weld counties
Owner, Wm R Howell, James J Beasley and George W Woy of Canfield
Boulder District Court Judgment Book, Water Decrees, Vol 2, District 5-6, 1869-1896, pg 238
Date of appropriation, 1 Mar 1865
General Course is NE through secs 10, 11, 12, T1N, R69W
Natural Stream is Boulder Creek
Headgate is located on north side Boulder Creek near middle line Sec 10, T1N, R69W
Length, 2 1/2 miles
Width, 4 ft
Depth, 2 ft
Grade, 1/10 ft per chain
Rate, 28.8 cu ft per second
Acres under irrigation, 500; 350 acres irrigated requiring 1 in per acre

Delehant Ditch, No. 23
Water District No. 6
First Judicial District
Jurisdiction, Boulder, Larimer and Weld counties
Owner, Daniel Delahant of Erie
Boulder District Court Judgment Book, Water Decrees, Vol 2, District 5-6, 1869-1896, pg 241
Date of appropriation, 1 May 1865
General Course is NE through Secs 29, 21, T2N, R68W
Natural Stream is Boulder Creek
Headgate is located on south bank of Idaho Slough in Sec 29
Length, 3/4 mile
Width, 3 ft 9 in
Depth, 3 ft
Grade, 1 in to 2 rods
Rate, 37.12 cu ft per second
Acres under irrigation, 260; 120 acres require from 1 1/4 to 2 in per acre

Highland Ditch Southside, No. 28
Water District No. 6
First Judicial District
Jurisdiction, Boulder, Larimer and Weld counties
Owner, T F Gooding, Wm Cole, Andrew Templeton, Peter Groseclose and R N Smith of Longmont
Boulder District Court Judgment Book, Water Decrees, Vol 2, District 5-6, 1869-1896, pg 243
Date of appropriation, 1 June 1865
General Course is NE
Natural Stream is Boulder Creek, through Idaho Slough
Headgate is located on the south bank of Idaho Creek [Slough],SW 1/4, Sec, T2N, R68W
Length, 3 miles, extended on 1 June 1868 to 6 1/4 miles
Width, 7 ft, enlarged on 1 June 1868 to 10 ft
Depth, 30 in
Grade, 1/2 in per rod
Rate, 99.7 cu ft per second, enlarged on 1 June 1868 to 152.2 cu ft per second
Acres under irrigation, 2840; 1140 irrigated requiring 1 1/4 in per acre
First enlargement, No. 30 1/2

Leggett Ditch, No 30
Water District No. 6
First Judicial District
Jurisdiction, Boulder, Larimer and Weld counties
Owner, Jeremiah Leggett, Edgar Sawdey and Wm R Howell of Erie and Ezra K Barker of Boulder
Boulder District Court Judgment Book, Water Decrees, Vol 2, District 5-6, 1869-1896, pg 246
Date of appropriation, 1 May 1868 (half made by 1 June 1862)
General Course is SE through S 1/2, NW 1/4 Sec 17, thence through S 1/2, NE 1/4 Sec 17, S 1/4 NW 1/4 Sec 16, N 1/2, NE 1/4, Sec 16, NW Cor Sec 15, S 1/2, SW 1/4, Sec 10 to Boulder Creek
Natural Stream is Boulder Creek
Headgate is located on east bank Boulder Creek, on NE 1/2, Sec 18, T1N, R69W
Length, 3 miles
Width, 3 1/2 ft
Depth, 2 ft
Grade, 1/2 in per rod
Rate, 31.35 cu ft per second
Acres under irrigation, 900; 800 acres irrigated requiring 1 1/4 in per acre

Taylor Ditch, No. 31
Water District No. 6
First Judicial District
Jurisdiction, Boulder, Larimer and Weld counties
Owner, Mrs Daniel Smith, James H Taylor and Florence Taylor of Longmont
Boulder District Court Judgment Book, Water Decrees, Vol 2, District 5-6, 1869-1896, pg 249
Date of appropriation, 1 Apr 1870
General Course is east or very nearly east
Natural Stream is Boulder Creek
Headgate is located at a point 40 rods north of south line of SE 1/4 Sec 10, about 300 ft from the east line, T2N, R69W
Length, 1/2 mile
Width, 24 in
Grade, 1/4 in per rod
Rate, 10.71 cu ft per second
Acres under irrigation 200, requiring 2 in per acre

Boulder and Weld County Ditch, No. 33
Water District No. 6
First Judicial District
Jurisdiction, Boulder, Larimer and Weld counties
Owner, [no owner listed, but the Shelton, Geo Green and Graham farms are listed]
Boulder District Court Judgment Book, Water Decrees, Vol 2, District 5-6, 1869-1896, pg 251
Date of appropriation, 1 May 1871
General Course is east from a point on the south side of Boulder Creek just below the Laramie Crossing to the head of the Slough to the SE Cor Geo Green's farm, thence east near the SE [cor] of Graham's field near cor Sec 7, T1N, R68W in Weld Co
Natural Stream is Boulder Creek
Headgate is located on the Shelton farm in Boulder County, east side of Boulder Creek
Length, 5 miles
Width, 10 ft
Depth, 24 in
Grade, 3 ft to the mile
Rate, 59.4 cu ft per second
Acres under irrigation, 2500 requiring 1 in per acre

Town of Boulder Ditch and Reservoir, No. 37
Water District No. 6
First Judicial District
Jurisdiction, Boulder, Larimer and Weld counties
Owner, City of Boulder
Boulder District Court Judgment Book, Water Decrees, Vol 2, District 5-6, 1869-1896, pg 254
Date of appropriation, 17 June 1875
Natural Stream is Boulder Creek
Headgate and wing dame runs NE through Sec 35, 26, 25, 36 and 25, T1N, R71W
Reservoir situated in the SW 1/4, SW 1/4, Sec 25, T1N, R71W
Length, 1 mile 2/10
Width, 3 ft bottom, 45 degree walls
Depth, 1 ft, enlarged 30 Mar 1876 to 16 1/2 in
Grade, 5 28/100 ft per mile
Reservoir capacity, 1 millio gallons
Rate, 6 17/90 cu in [ft] per second

Boulder & White Rock Ditch, No. 35
Water District No. 6
First Judicial District
Jurisdiction, Boulder, Larimer and Weld counties
Owner, Boulder & White Rock Ditch Company
Boulder District Court Judgment Book, Water Decrees, Vol 2, District 5-6, 1869-1896, pg 267
Date of appropriation, 1 Nov 1873
General Course is north and NE beginning near 12th Street in the Town of Boulder and terminates in Sec 24, T2N, R69W as to one branch, and the other in Sec 10, T1N, R69W
Natural Stream is Boulder Creek

Headgate is located on the north side of [Boulder] Creek
Length, 13 1/2 miles
Width, 17 1/4 ft
Depth, 2 1/2 ft
Grade, 46.06 ft to mile for the first 700 yds, then 4 ft 60/100 per miles
Acres under irrigation, 12000; 7500 acres require 1 in per acre

Dry Creek Ditch, No 11
Water District No. 6
First Judicial District
Jurisdiction, Boulder, Larimer and Weld counties
Owner, G Berkley and M G Smith [there are also claims by David H Nichols, Mary S Stoddard, Elizabeth Harden, Robert Culver, G W Rust and Perry White]
Boulder District Court Judgment Book, Water Decrees, Vol 2, District 5-6, 1869-1896, pg 268
Date of appropriation, 1 June 1862
General Course is east
Natural Stream is Boulder Creek
Headgate is located near 12th Street Bridge in Boulder, same as the headgate of Boulder and White Rock Ditch
Length, 2 miles
Width, 8 ft
Depth, 24 in
Grade, 1 1/2 in per rod
Rate, 148.49 cu ft per second
Acres under irrigation, 300; 80 acres irrigated by Berkley, 0 acres by Smith; 160 by Nichols requiring 2 in per acre, 80 acres by Mary Stoddard et al, requiring 2 in per acre, 20 acres by Wm Breach, requiring 2 1/2 in per acre

Hardin Ditch, No. 11
Water District No. 6
First Judicial District
Jurisdiction, Boulder, Larimer and Weld counties
Owner, Sylvanus Wellman of Boulder
Boulder District Court Judgment Book, Water Decrees, Vol 2, District 5-6, 1869-1896, pg 274
Date of appropriation, 1 June 1862
General Course is south and E
Natural Stream if Boulder Creek
Headage is located on the south side of Dry Creek in Block 9, Culver's Subdivision of S 1/2, SE 1/4, Sec 30, T1N, R70W
Length, 1 3/4 miles
Width, 24 in
Depth, 18 in
Grade, 2 in per rod
Acres under irrigation, 480

Wellman, Nichols and Hahn Ditch, No. 11
Water District No. 6
First Judicial District
Jurisdiction, Boulder, Larimer and Weld counties
Owner, D H Nichols and Sylvanus Wellman of Boulder and S B Hahn of Central City
Boulder District Court Judgment Book, Water Decrees, Vol 2, District 5-6, 1869-1896, pg 276
Date of appropriation, 1 June 1862
General Course is E, beginning on the south bank of Dry Creek, which receives its water from Boulder Creek running through Secs 29, NW 1/4 Sec 28, T1N, R70W
Natural Stream is Boulder Creek
Headgate is located on south bank of Dry Creek near center Sec 29
Length, 1 mile
Width, 24 in
Depth, 18 in
Grade, 1/2 in per rod
Rate, 10.77 cu ft per second
Acres under irrigation, 200

McCarty Ditch, No. 11
Water District No. 6
First Judicial District
Jurisdiction, Boulder, Larimer and Weld counties
Owner, Mary S Stoddard, Robert Culver, heirs of Elizabeth Harden, George W Rust and Perry White of Boulder
Boulder District Court Judgment Book, Water Decrees, Vol 2, District 5-6, 1869-1896, pg 277
Date of appropriation, 1 June 1862
General Course is east
Natural Stream is Dry Creek (now called Boulder & White Rock Ditch)
Headgate is located on Front Street where Boulder & White Rock Ditch crosses Boulder Creek
Length, 1 1/2 miles
Width, 2 1/2 ft
Depth, 5 in
Grade, 1 1/2 in per rod
Rate, 4.68 cu ft per second

North Boulder Farmers Ditch, No. 11
Water District No. 6
First Judicial District
Jurisdiction, Boulder, Larimer and Weld counties
Owner, North Boulder Farmers Ditch Company

Boulder District Court Judgment Book, Water Decrees, Vol 2, District 5-6, 1869-1896, pg 279
Date of appropriation, 1 June 1862
General Course is NE
Natural Stream is Boulder Creek
Headgate is located the same as Boulder & White Rock Ditch a few rods below 12th Street Bridge in Boulder
Length, 6 miles
Width, 24 in, enlarged on 1 June 1863 to 5 ft, enlarged on 15 June 1864 to 8 ft
Depth, 18 in, enlarged 1 June 1863 to 2 1/2 ft
Grade, 1/2 in per rod
Acres under irrigation 1400

Boulder and Left Hand Ditch, No. 36
Water District No. 6
First Judicial District
Jurisdiction, Boulder, Larimer and Weld counties
Owner, Boulder and Left Hand Ditch Company of Longmont [Code Elsberry and Charles P Hamlin are listed as original builders. William Breach, D H Nichols, M G Smith, G Berkley, Sylvanus Wellman, S B Hahn, Robert Culver, Mary S Stoddard, George W Rust, Perry White, the heirs of Elizabeth Harden, (no first name) Hahn are listed as claimants]
Boulder District Court Judgment Book, Water Decrees, Vol 2, District 5-6, 1869-1896, pg 280
Date of appropriation, 1 Dec 1873, enlarged 1 Apr 1876
General Course is NE from the town of Boulder, via White Rock Mills through T1&2N, R69W
Natural Stream is Boulder Creek
Headgate is located where a slough intersects Boulder Creek near the Town of Boulder
Length, 14 miles
Width, 14 ft, enlarged on 1 Apr 1876 to 14 ft
Depth, 24 in, enlarged on 1 Apr 1876 to 3 ft
Grade, 4 ft 4 in per mile
Rate, 163.8 cu ft per second
Acres under irrigation, 4000; 2000 acres requiring 1 in per acre
First Enlargement, No. 38

Wellman Ditch, No. 39
Water District No. 6
First Judicial District
Jurisdiction, Boulder, Larimer and Weld counties
Owner, Wellman Ditch Company of Boulder
Boulder District Court Judgment Book, Water Decrees, Vol 2, District 5-6, 1869-1896, pg 283
Date of appropriation, 1 May 1878
General Course is east through SE 1/4, NW 1/4; Sw 1/4 NE 1/4; NE 1/4 SE 1/4, Sec 32, and NW 1/4 SW 1/4; SE 1/4 NW 1/4, S 1/2, NE 1/4 Sec 33, 34, T1N, R70W to Boulder Creek
Natural Stream is Boulder Creek
Headgate is located on the NW Cor SE 1/4, NW 1/4, Sec 32, T1N, R70W
Length, 3 miles
Width, 3 ft
Depth, 18 in
Grade, 1/4 in per rod
Rate, 12.74 cu ft per second
Acres under irrigation, 1200

Mathews Ditch, No. 40
Water District No. 6
First Judicial District
Jurisdiction, Boulder, Larimer and Weld counties
Owner, Milton Mathews, George W Mathews, Newton Mathews and Sarah Mathews of Erie
Boulder District Court Judgment Book, Water Decrees, Vol 2, District 5-6, 1869-1896, pg 286
Date of appropriation, 13 Feb 1879
General Course is NE
Natural Stream is Boulder Creek
Headgate is located on a point near SW Cor, SW 1/4, NE 1/4, Sec 16, T1N, R69W
Length, 3 miles
Width, 8 ft
Depth, 24 in
Grade, 1/4 in per rod
Rate, 60.6 cu ft per second
Acres under irrigation, 4000; 140 acres requiring 2 1/2 inches per acre

Revolution Ditch, No. 41
Water District No. 6
First Judicial District
Jurisdiction, Boulder, Larimer and Weld counties
Owner, Revolution Ditch Company of Longmont
Boulder District Court Judgment Book, Water Decrees, Vol 2, District 5-6, 1869-1896, pg 289
Date of appropriation, 7 Dec 1881
General Course is east & NE, through Secs 17, 16, 9, 10, 11, & 2, T1N, R69W, and across Sec 35, 26, 27, 22 & 23, T2N, R69W and terminates in Sec 24 near the County line
Natural Stream is Boulder Creek
Headgate is located at a point 38 rods north of center line of Sec 18, abt 22 rods west of east line of Sec 18, T1N, R69W on north side of Boulder Creek
Length, 11 miles

Width, 10 ft
Depth, 36 in
Grade, 3 ft 8 in per mile
Rate, 99.97 cu ft per second
Acres under irrigation, 3500

McGinn Ditch, No. 1
Water District No. 6
First Judicial District
Jurisdiction, Boulder, Larimer and Weld counties
Owner, McGinn Ditch Company of Boulder
Boulder District Court Judgment Book, Water Decrees, Vol 2, District 5-6, 1869-1896, pg 292
Date of appropriation, 1 May 1860
General Course is NE through Secs 10, 3 & 2, T1S, R70W
Natural Stream is South Boulder Creek
Headgate is located NW 1/4, Sec 10, T1S, R70W, on Doran Lands on the east side of the Creek
Length, 3 miles
Width, 18 in, enlarged 1 May 1864 to 18 in, enlarged on 1 June 1865 to 3 3/4 ft
Depth, 9 in, enlarged on 1 May 1864 to 9 in, enlarged on 1 June 1865 to 12 in
Grade, 1/2 in per rod
Rate, 14.06 cu ft per second
Acres under irrigation, 2000; 510 irrigated
First enlargement, No. 10, 1 May 1864
Second enlargement, No. 15, 1 June 1865

Shearer Ditch, No 2
Water District No. 6
First Judicial District
Jurisdiction, Boulder, Larimer and Weld counties
Owner, Andrew Dunn and Michael Shanahan of Boulder
Boulder District Court Judgment Book, Water Decrees, Vol 2, District 5-6, 1869-1896, pg 295
Date of appropriation, 1 June 1860
General Course is NE from SE bank of [South Boulder] Creek on Sec 16, T1S, R70W
Natural Stream is South Boulder Creek
Headgate is located on P Dunn's farm on said Sec
Length, 1 mile
Width, 3 ft
Depth, 2 ft
Grade, is 1/2 in per rod
Rate, 26.08 cu ft per second
Number of acres under irrigation, 300; 100 acres requiring 2 in per acre

Howard Ditch, No. 3
Water District No. 6
First Judicial District
Jurisdiction, Boulder, Larimer and Weld counties
Owner, A G Burke, N R Howard, Geo F Chase and D K Sternberg of Boulder
Boulder District Court Judgment Book, Water Decrees, Vol 2, District 5-6, 1869-1896, pg 297
Date of appropriation, 1 Apr 1860
General Course is north running through Stotts farm, Nephi Howard farm, and the farms of G F Chase, and D K Sternberg
Natural Stream is South Boulder Creek
Headgate is located on west bank [South Boulder] Creek on the Stotts place
Length, 3 1/2 miles
Width, 3 ft
Depth, 2 ft
Grade, 1 in per rod
Rate, 36 cu ft per second
Acres under irrigation, 1000; land is also under Dry Creek No. 2 Ditch, estimated to require from 1 to 2 in per acre

East Boulder Ditch, No. 4
Water District No. 6
First Judicial District
Jurisdiction, Boulder, Larimer and Weld counties
Owner, East Boulder Ditch Company of Boulder
Boulder District Court Judgment Book, Water Decrees, Vol 2, District 5-6, 1869-1896, pg 300
Date of appropriation, 1 Apr 1862
General Course is NE
Natural Stream is South Boulder Creek
Headgate is located on the south bank of South Boulder Creek on N M Howard farm
Length, 4 miles
Width, 6 ft, enlarged on 1 June 1872 to 7 ft
Depth, 3 ft
Grade, 1/2 in per rod
Rate, 127.2 cu ft per second
Acres under irrigation 2000; 1410 acres requiring 2 in per acre
First enlargement, No. 27, 1 June 1872

South Boulder and Bear Creek Ditch, No. 5
Water District No. 6
First Judicial District
Jurisdiction, Boulder, Larimer and Weld counties
Owner, South Boulder and Bear Creek Ditch Company of Boulder

Boulder District Court Judgment Book, Water Decrees, Vol 2, District 5-6, 1869-1896, pg 302
Date of appropriation, 25 May 1862
General Course is NE through Sec 16, NW through Secs 9, 5, T1S, R70W, NE through Sec 32, T1N, R70W
Natural Stream is South Boulder Creek
Headgate is located on north side of [South Boulder] Creek, near NE Cor Sec 20, T1S, R70W
Length, 4 miles
Width, 48 in, enlarged 9 May 1865 to 6 ft, enlarged 15 May 1868 to 7 ft, enlarged 15 May 1871 to 10 ft
Depth, 12 in, enlarged 15 May 1868 to 18 in; enlarged on 15 May 1871 to 24 in
Grade, 1/2 of 1/10 in per rod, now 1 6/100 ft to 300 ft
Rate, 129.1 cu ft per second
Acres under irrigation, 2000; 1100 acres irrigated
First enlargement, No. 8
Second enlargement, No. 20
Third enlargement, No. 23

Cottonwood No. 2 Ditch, No. 6
Water District No. 6
First Judicial District
Jurisdiction, Boulder, Larimer and Weld counties
Owner, Cottonwood Ditch Company of Valmont
Boulder District Court Judgment Book, Water Decrees, Vol 2, District 5-6, 1869-1896, pg 306
Date of appropriation, 15 Apr 1863
General Course is NE
Natural Stream is South Boulder Creek
Headgate is loacted 20 rods south [of] base line on the Hanna farm
Length, 3 miles
Width, 5 ft
Depth, 18 in
Grade, 1/2 in per rod
Rate, 33.697 cu ft persecond
Acres under irrigation, 1000; 500 acres require 1 in per acre

Dry Creek Ditch, No. 7
Water District No. 6
First Judicial District
Jurisdiction, Boulder, Larimer and Weld counties
Owner, William A Davidson of Valmont
Boulder District Court Judgment Book, Water Decrees, Vol 2, District 5-6, 1869-1896, pg 309
Date of appropriation, 1 May 1863
General Course is NE
Natural Stream is South Boulder Creek
Headgate is located on south side of [South Boulder] Creek on the farm owned by J B Viele
Lenth, 6 miles
Width, 5 ft
Depth, 20 in
Grade, 8 ft per mile
Rate, 29.95 cu ft per second
Acres under irrigation, 700; 200 requiring 1 in per acre

Dry Creek No. 2 Ditch, No. 9
Water District No. 6
First Judicial District
Jurisdiction, Boulder, Larimer and Weld counties
Owner, N R Howard, A G Burke, Geo F Chase, Andrew Reed, J C Peabody, J Hogan, D K Sternberg and Henry Neikirk of Boulder
Boulder District Court Judgment Book, Water Decrees, Vol 2, District 5-6, 1869-1896, pg 311
Date of appropriation, 1 May 1864
General Course is north on the west side of South Boulder Creek
Natural Stream is South Boulder Creek
Headgate is located 1/2 mile west [of] Marshall Coal Bank
Lenth, 6 miles
Width, 5 ft
Depth, 24 in
Grade, 1 in per rod
Rate, 69 cu ft per second
Acres under irrigation, 2000; 1000 also under the Howard Ditch; 2000 from both ditches requiring 1 1/2 in per acre

Andrews and Farwell Ditch, No. 11
Water District No. 6
First Judicial District
Jurisdiction, Boulder, Larimer and Weld counties
Owner, Henry C Wilson, Charles Rinkis and Jas A King of Valmont, and Thomas Field of Denver
Boulder District Court Judgment Book, Water Decrees, Vol 2, District 5-6, 1869-1896, pg 314
Date of appropriation, 1 June 1864
General Course is NE from the west bank of Dry Creek Ditch
Natural Stream is South Boulder Creek
Headgate is located near the house of Mrs Beal on the Pease farm
Length, 1 1/2 miles
Width, 18 in, enlarged 1 Apr 1871 to 3 ft
Depth, 6 in, enlarged 1 Apr 1871 to 12 in
Grade, 1/4 in per rod

Rate, 1.35 cu ft per second, after enlargement 7.61 cu ft per second
Acres under irrigation, 200; 140 acres requiring 2 in per acre
First Enlargement, No 25

Enterprise Ditch, No. 12
Water District No. 6
First Judicial District
Jurisdiction, Boulder, Larimer and Weld counties
Owner, Enterprise Irrigating Ditch Company of Boulder [landowners Viele, Howard, Hake, DeBacker, Barker, Barter, Petty, Staples, Duffy, Jackson and D Solander]
Boulder District Court Judgment Book, Water Decrees, Vol 2, District 5-6, 1869-1896, pg 317
Date of appropriation, 1 Feb 1865
General Course is NE through the farms of Viele, Howard, Hake, DeBacker, Barker, Barter, Petty, Staples, Duffy, Jackson, and NW corner of D Solander's farm
Natural Stream is South Boulder Creek
Headgate is located on the west side of Dry Creek about 120 rods from the head at [South Boulder] Creek in T1S, R70W
Length, 4 miles
Width, 6 ft, enlarged on 1 May 1866 to 7 ft, present width 9 ft
Depth, 18 in
Grade, 1/3 in per rod
Rate, 34.08 cu ft per second, enlarged on 1 May 1866 to 40.76 cu ft [per second], present rate 54.25 cu ft per second
Acres under irrigation, 1200; 900 acres requiring 1 1/4 in per acre
First Enlargement, No. 18

Leyner Ditch, No. 13
Water District No. 6
First Judicial District
Jurisdiction, Boulder, Larimer and Weld counties
Owner, Leyner Ditch Company of Boulder
Boulder District Court Judgment Book, Water Decrees, Vol 2, District 5-6, 1869-1896, pg 320
Date of appropriation, 1 Apr 1865
General Course is NE through Secs 20, 21, 22, 23 & 13, T1N, R69W
Natural Stream is South Boulder Creek
Headgate is located on east bank of Dry Creek Ditch, which is supplied from [South Boulder] Creek
Length, 5 1/2 [miles]
Width, 7 1/2 ft
Depth, 3 ft
Grade, 3/4 in per rod
Rate, 164 cu ft per second
Acres under irrigation, 2000; 600 acres requiring 2 in per acre

Marshallville Ditch, No. 14
Water District No. 6
First Judicial District
Jurisdiction, Boulder, Larimer and Weld counties
Owner, Marshallville Ditch Company of Boulder
Boulder District Court Judgment Book, Water Decrees, Vol 2, District 5-6, 1869-1896, pg 322
Date of appropriation, 1 June 1865
General Course is east along NW side of Goodhue Ditch and into N 1/2, Sec 34, T1N, R59W, terminating near NE Cor Sec 34, T1N, R69W
Natural Stream is South Boulder Creek
Headgate is located around E 1/4, SW 1/4, Sec 16, T1S, R70W
Length, 2 mi, enlarged on 30 June 1878 to 7 miles
Width, 3 ft, enlarged 30 June 1878 to 6 1/2 ft
Depth, 18 in, enlarged 30 June 1878 to 16 in [??]
Grade, 1/3 in per rod
Rate, 14.76 cu ft per second, present rate 31.92 cu ft per second
Acres under irrigation, 1200; 450 acres requiring 1 in per acre
First Enlargement, No. 33

Central Ditch, No. 16
Water District No. 6
First Judicial District
Jurisdiction, Boulder, Larimer and Weld counties
Owner, John T Mitchell and Levi Hake of Boulder
Boulder District Court Judgment Book, Water Decrees, Vol 2, District 5-6, 1869-1896, pg 325
Date of appropriation, 15 May 1866
General Course is NE
Natural Stream is South Bulder [Creek]
Headgate is located 150 yds SW of NW Cor, SW 1/4, SE 1/4, Sec 3, T1S, R70W
Length, 3/4 mile
Width, 2 1/2 ft
Depth, 18 in
Grade, 1/2 in per rod
Rate, 14.36 cu ft per second
Acres under irrigation, 100; requiring 250 in of water

Cottonwood No. 1 Ditch, No. 17
Water District No. 6
First Judicial District
Jurisdiction, Boulder, Larimer and Weld counties
Owner, Cottonwood Ditch Company of Canfield
Boulder District Court Judgment Book, Water Decrees, Vol 2, District 5-6, 1869-1896, pg 328
Date of appropriation, 1 Apr 1866
General Course is NE running through Secs 19, 20 & 21, T1N, R69W
Headgate is located on Dry Creek Ditch, 1/4 mile west of center, Sec 30, T1N, R69W
Length, 6 miles
Width, 4 ft, enlarged on 15 Oct 1870 to 6 ft
Depth, 16 in, enlarged 15 Oct 1870 to 22 in
Grade, 1/4 in per rod
Rate, 15.58 cu ft per second, present capacity is 36.72 cu ft per second
Acres under irrigation, 2500; 1400 acres requiring 1 in per acre
First Enlargement, No. 22

South Ditch, No. 19
Water District No. 6
First Judicial District
Jurisdiction, Boulder, Larimer and Weld counties
Owner, John T Mitchell and Levi Hake of Boulder
Boulder District Court Judgment Book, Water Decrees, Vol 2, District 5-6, 1869-1896, pg 331
Date of appropriation, 1 June 1866
General Course is east NE
Natural Stream is South Boulder Creek
Headgate is located 100 yds SE of NW Cor, SW 1/4, SE 1/4, Sec 3, T1S, R70W, on SE bank from Dry Creek
Length, 1 mile
Width, 3 1/2 ft
Depth, 12 in
Grade, 1/4 in per rod
Rate, 9.16 cu ft per second
Number of acres under irrigation, 125; requiring 250 inches of water

South Boulder Canyon Ditch, No. 21
Water District No. 6
First Judicial District
Jurisdiction, Boulder, Larimer and Weld counties
Owner, South Boulder Canyon Ditch Company of Boulder
Boulder District Court Judgment Book, Water Decrees, Vol 2, District 5-6, 1869-1896, pg 333
Date of appropriation, 15 May 1870
General Course is NE through Secs 2, 9, & 10, T1N, R70W
Natural Stream is South Boulder Creek
Headgate is located near SE Cor, Sec 9, T1S, R70W, on east side of [South Boulder] Creek
Length, 5 miles, extended on 15 May 1871 to 10 miles
Width, 5 ft, enlarged on 15 May 1871 to 10 ft
Depth, 15 in, enlarged on 15 May 1871 to 3 ft
Grade, 1/2 in per rod
Rate, 192 cu ft per second
Number of acres under irrigation; 4000; 1100 requiring 1 in per acre
First Enlargement, No. 24

Davidson Ditch, No. 26
Water District No. 6
First Judicial District
Jurisdiction, Boulder, Larimer and Weld counties
Owner, Davidson Ditch Company of Valmont
Boulder District Court Judgment Book, Water Decrees, Vol 2, District 5-6, 1869-1896, pg 336
Date of appropriation, 15 Apr 1872
General Course is east through SW 1/4, Sec 12, T1S, R70W
Natural Stream is South Boulder Ditch
Headgate is located on NW 1/4, Sec 29, T1S, R70W
Length, 10 miles, 4108 ft
Width, 8 ft, enlarged 10 May 1875 to 8 1/2 ft
Depth, 3 ft
Grade, 8 ft per miles
Rate, 116.3 cu ft per second, enlarged on 10 May 1875 to 125.05 cu ft per second
Number of acres under irrigation, 4500; 1000 acres irrigated
First Enlargement, No. 32

South Boulder and Coal Creek Ditch, No. 28
Water District No. 6
First Judicial District
Jurisdiction, Boulder, Larimer and Weld counties
Owner, South Boulder and Coal Creek Ditch Company of Louisville
Boulder District Court Judgment Book, Water Decrees, Vol 2, District 5-6, 1869-1896, pg 339
Date of appropriation, 1 June 1872
General Course is north of east through Secs 30, 29, 21, 22, & 23, T1S, R70W terminating in Sec 14, T1S, R70W
Natural Stream is South Boulder Creek
Headgate is located on south bank of [South Boulder] Creek at mouth of South Boulder Canyon

Length, 8 1/2 miles
Width, 7 ft
Depth, 18 in
Grade, 1/2 in per rod
Rate, 53.55 cu ft per second
Acres under irrigation, 3500; 860 acres requires 1 1/2 in per acre

Goodhue Ditch and Reservoir, No. 29
Water District No. 6
First Judicial District
Jurisdiction, Boulder, Larimer and Weld counties
Owner, Abner C Goodhue of Louisville
Boulder District Court Judgment Book, Water Decrees, Vol 2, District 5-6, 1869-1896, pg 342
Date of appropriation, 1 June 1873
General Course is east
Natural Stream is South Boulder Creek
Headgate is located near SE 1/4, Sec 21, T1S, R69W
Length, 1/4 mile
Width, 4 ft
Depth, 12 in
Grade, 2 in per rod
Rate, 30.31 cu ft per second
Number of acres under irrigation, 500; 10 acres requiring 1 in per acre

South Boulder and Rock Creek Ditch, No. 30
Water District No. 6
First Judicial District
Jurisdiction, Boulder, Larimer and Weld counties
Owner, South Boulder and Rock Creek Ditch Company of Louisville
Boulder District Court Judgment Book, Water Decrees, Vol 2, District 5-6, 1869-1896, pg 344
Date of appropriation, 1 June 1873
General Course is east and NE
Natural Stream is South Boulder Creek
Headgate is located on east bank of South Boulder Creek, on SE 1/4, SE 1/4, Sec 20, T1S, R70W
Length, 19 miles
Width, 9 ft
Depth, 24 in
Grade, 6 ft per mile
Rate, 65.93 cu ft per second
Number of acres under irrigation, 4000; 1900 acres requiring 1 in per acre

Autrey and Eggleston Ditch, No. 1
Water District No. 6
First Judicial District
Jurisdiction, Boulder, Larimer and Weld counties
Owner, George Autrey and George W Eggleston of Langford
Boulder District Court Judgment Book, Water Decrees, Vol 2, District 5-6, 1869-1896, pg 348
Date of appropriation, 1 June 1860
General Course is NE
Natural Stream is Coal Creek
Headgate is located on north side of [Coal] Creek, NE 1/2, Sec 27, T1S, R70W
Length, 1 mile
Width, 2 1/2 ft
Depth, 8 in
Grade, 1/2 in per rod
Rate, 4.16 cu ft per second
Acres under irrigation, 80

William C Hake Ditch, No. 2
Water District No. 6
First Judicial District
Jurisdiction, Boulder, Larimer and Weld counties
Owner, William C Hake of Louisville
Boulder District Court Judgment Book, Water Decrees, Vol 2, District 5-6, 1869-1896, pg 350
Date of appropriation, 1 June 1861
General Course is NE in SW 1/4, SW 1/4, Sec 24, T1S, R70W
Natural Stream is Coal Creek
Headgate is located on north side of [Coal] Creek in Sec [24]
Length, 1/2 mile
Width, 10 in
Depth, 12 in
Grade, 3/4 in per rod
Rate, 2.94 cu ft per second
Acres under irrigation, 400

Eggleston No. 2 Ditch, No. 3
Water District No. 6
First Judicial District
Jurisdiction, Boulder, Larimer and Weld counties
Owner, Geo W Eggleston of Langford
Boulder District Court Judgment Book, Water Decrees, Vol 2, District 5-6, 1869-1896, pg 353
Date of appropriation, 1 May 1862
General Course is NE
Natural Stream is Coal Creek
Headgate is located on north side of Coal Creek, at a point 10 rods E, SW Cor, SW 1/4, NW 1/4, Sec 26, T1S, R70W
Length, 160 rods
Width, 24 in

Depth, 9 in
Grade, 1/2 in per rod
Rate, 4.65 cu ft per second
Acres under irrigation, 40

McKenzie Ditch, No. 4
Water District No. 6
First Judicial District
Jurisdiction, Boulder, Larimer and Weld counties
Owner, William McKenzie of Boulder
Boulder District Court Judgment Book, Water Decrees, Vol 2, District 5-6, 1869-1896, pg 355
Date of appropriation, 1 June 1866
General Course is north of east
Natural Stream is Coal Creek
Headgate is located on south Side of [Coal] Creek, near center of NW 1/4, NW 1/2, Sec 34, T1S, R70W
Length, 1/2 mile
Width, 3 ft
Depth, 18 in
Grade, 1/2 in per rod
Rate, 18 ct ft per second
Acres under irrigation, 70

Eggleston No. 1 Ditch, No. 5
Water District No. 6
First Judicial District
Jurisdiction, Boulder, Larimer and Weld counties
Owner, Geo W Eggleston of Langford
Boulder District Court Judgment Book, Water Decrees, Vol 2, District 5-6, 1869-1896, pg 358
Date of appropriation, 1 Oct 1869
General Course is east and SE
Natural Stream is Coal Creek
Headgate is located on south side of Coal Creek on E 1/2, Sec 27, T1S, R70W
Length, 120 rods
Width, 24 in
Depth, 12 in
Grade, 1/2 in per rod
Rate, 6.58 cu ft per second
Acres under irrigation, 60

Last Chance Ditch, No. 6
Water District No. 6
First Judicial District
Jurisdiction, Boulder, Larimer and Weld counties
Owner, John W Brown of Golden
Boulder District Court Judgment Book, Water Decrees, Vol 2, District 5-6, 1869-1896, pg 360
Date of appropriation, 1 May 1870
General Course is east for 7 miles
Natural Stream is Coal Creek
Length, 7 miles
Width, 3 ft
Depth, 12 in
Grade, 1/2 in per rod
Rate, 10.78 cu ft per second
Acres under irrigation, 100

Church Ditch, No. 7
Water District No. 6
First Judicial District
Jurisdiction, Boulder, Larimer and Weld counties
Owner, George H Church of Denver
Boulder District Court Judgment Book, Water Decrees, Vol 2, District 5-6, 1869-1896, pg 363
Date of appropriation, 20 Sept 1870
General Course is east
Natural Stream is Coal Creek
Headgate is located on the south Side of [Coal] Creek, 1/2 mi below the mouth of canyon in Jefferson County
Length, 11 miles
Width, 3 ft
Depth, 18 in
Grade, 1/2 in per rod
Rate, 18.11 cu ft per second
Acres under irrigation, 150

Kinnear Ditch and Reservoir, No. 8
Water District No. 6
First Judicial District
Jurisdiction, Boulder, Larimer and Weld counties
Owner, John S Kinnear of Golden
Boulder District Court Judgment Book, Water Decrees, Vol 2, District 5-6, 1869-1896, pg 365
Date of appropriation, 20 May 1872
General Course is east trending south after 1 mile
Natural Stream is Coal Creek
Headgate is located on south side [Coal] Creek, 1/4 mile below mouth of canyon in Jefferson County
Length, 8 miles
Width, 4 1/2 ft
Depth, 20 in
Grade, 8 ft per mile
Rate, 26.476 cu ft per second
Acres under irrigation, 600

Four Mile Canyon Ditch, No. 1
Water District No. 6
First Judicial District
Jurisdiction, Boulder, Larimer and Weld counties
Owner, Clinton M Tyler of Boulder

Boulder District Court Judgment Book, Water Decrees, Vol 2, District 5-6, 1869-1896, pg pg 368
Date of appropriation, 1 Apr 1875
General Course is SE across the NE Cor, Sec 13, terminates on Sec 18, T1N, R70W
Natural Stream is Four Mile Canyon Creek
Headgate is located at the base of the mountains on souith bank of Four Mile Canyon Creek
Length, 3/4 mile
Width, 5 ft
Depth, 20 in
Grade, 2 in per rod
Rate, 76.56 cu ft per second
Acres under irrigation, 600

Forbes Ditch, No. 2
Water District No. 6
First Judicial District
Jurisdiction, Boulder, Larimer and Weld counties
Owner, Clinton M Tyler of Boulder
Boulder District Court Judgment Book, Water Decrees, Vol 2, District 5-6, 1869-1896, pg 370
Date of appropriation, 1 Apr 1878
General Course is SE along base of the mountains terminated on Sec 13, T1N, R71W
Natural Stream is Four Mile Canyon Creek
Headgate is located on right bank of [Four Mile Canyon] Creek, on SE 1/4, Sec 12, T1N, R71W
Length, 1/2 mile
Width, 4 1/2 ft
Depth, 2 ft
Grade, 1 in per rod
Rate, 60.66 cu ft per second
Acres under irrigation, 400; requiring 2 in per acre

Six Mile Bottom Ditch, No. 1
Water District No. 6
First Judicial District
Jurisdiction, Boulder, Larimer and Weld counties
Owner, [not listed]
Boulder District Court Judgment Book, Water Decrees, Vol 2, District 5-6, 1869-1896, pg 373
Date of appropriation, 1 Apr 1875
General Course is SE, terminating at the east line, Sec 32, T2N, R70W
Natural Stream is Jains' Gulch a tributary of Left Hand Creek
Headgate is located on the right bank of [Jains'] Gulch
Length, 3/4 mile
Width, 4 ft
Depth, 30 in
Grade, 1/2 in per rod
Rate, 48.8 cu ft per second
Acres under irrigation, 900

North Branch Six Mile Bottom Ditch, No. 2
Water District No. 6
First Judicial District
Jurisdiction, Boulder, Larimer and Weld counties
Owner, Clinton M Tyler of Boulder
Boulder District Court Judgment Book, Water Decrees, Vol 2, District 5-6, 1869-1896, pg 375
Date of appropriation, 1 Apr 1875
General Course is east from left bank of Jains' Gulch terminating on the east line, Sec 32, T1N, R70W
Natural Stream is Jains' Gulch a tributary of Left Hand Creek
Headgate is located on east bank Jains' Gulch, near NW 1/4, Sec 32, T1N, R70W
Length, 3/4 mile
Width, 5 ft
Depth, 24 in
Grade, 1/2 in per rod
Rate, 48.8 cu ft per second
Acres under irrigation, 550

Sternberg Ditch, No. 34
Water District No. 6
First Judicial District
Jurisdiction, Boulder, Larimer and Weld counties
Owner, Jay Sternberg of Boulder
Boulder District Court Judgment Book, Water Decrees, Vol 2, District 5-6, 1869-1896, pg 378
Date of appropriation, 28 Nov 1872
General Course is NE and runs through N 1/2, NE 1/4 and S 1/2, NE 1/4, Sec 31, T1N, R70W
Natural Stream is Boulder Creek
Headgate is located on south bank of [Boulder] Creek near SW Cor, N 1/2, NE 1/4, Sec 31, T1N, R70W
Length, 1/2 mile
Width, 8 ft, enlarged on 1 July 1875 to 10 ft
Depth, 3 ft
Grade, 1/2 in per 5 rods
Rate, 67 cu ft per second, present 87 cu ft per second
Acres under irrigation, 1000

Colorado State Mills Ditch
Water District No. 6
First Judicial District
Jurisdiction, Boulder, Larimer and Weld counties
Owner, Mrs Ella B Young
Boulder District Court Judgment Book, Water Decrees, Vol 2, District 5-6, 1869-1896, pg 379

Date of appropriation, 1 Apr 1860
General Course is NE beginning on the NW 1/4, Sec 36, T1N, R71W
Natural Stream is Boulder Creek
Headgate is located in Boulder Canyon, west from the Mill 1200 ft
Length, 1/2 mile
Width, 7 ft
Depth, 24 in
Grade, 13 ft per mile
Rate, 74 ct ft per second
Used for milling purposes only

WATER DISTRICT NO. 5

Highland Ditch, No. 46 Amended
Water District No. 5
First Judicial District
Jurisdiction, Boulder, Larimer and Weld counties
Owner, John Rees [landowner]
Boulder District Court Judgment Book, Water Decrees, Vol 2, District 5-6, 1869-1896, pg 381
Date of appropriation, 30 Nov 1871
General Course is NE
Natural Stream is St Vrain Creek
Headgate is located on north side of [St Vrain] Creek in Sec 21, T3N, R70W, at a point immediately below John Rees' bridge across the creek
Length,
Width,
Depth,
Grade, 8 ft per mile
Rate, 6480 customary inches
Second appropriation, 1 June 1878, 980 [customary] inches

Cochran Ditch, No. 1
Water District No. 5
First Judicial District
Jurisdiction, Boulder, Larimer and Weld counties
Owner, Henry Hornbaker and Sylvanus Budd of Niwot
Boulder District Court Judgment Book, Water Decrees, Vol 2, District 5-6, 1869-1896, pg pg 383
Date of appropriation, 1 Sept 1860
General Course is NE
Natural Stream is Left Hand Creek
Headgate is located in Sec 27, T2N, R70W
Length, 1 1/2 miles
Width, 1 ft, enlarged on 15 June 1866 to 4 ft
Depth, 3 in, enlarged on 15 June 1866 to 24 in
Grade, 1/4 in per rod
Rate, 36 customary in
Water claimed, 200 in, capacity increased to 1116 inches, total 1152 inches
Acres under irrigation, 400, requires 1 1/2 in per acre
First Enlargement, No. 15

Hornbaker Ditch, No. 2
Water District No. 5
First Judicial District
Jurisdiction, Boulder, Larimer and Weld counties
Owner, H H Hornbaker, J F Gould, P M Hinman, Sylvanus Budd and Rudolf Greub of Niwot
Boulder District Court Judgment Book, Water Decrees, Vol 2, District 5-6, 1869-1896, pg 386
Date of appropriation, 15 May 1861
General Course is south of E
Natural Stream is Left Hand Creek
Headgate is located in Sec 26, T2N, R70W
Length, 3/4 miles, enlarged on 15 June 1865 to 1 1/2 miles
Width, 2 ft, enlarged on 15 June 1865 to 4 ft
Depth, 10 in, enlarged on 15 June 1865 to 2 1/2 ft
Grade, 1/2 in per rod
Rate, 240 customary in, increased capacity 1200 in
Water claimed, 300 in, after enlargement 840 in
Acres under irrigation, [not given], except that of Rudolf Greub requiring 100 in; 600 acres after enlargement
First Enlargement, 15 July 1865, No. 9
Second Enlargment, 1 June 1865, No. 12

Williamson and Cavey Ditch, No. 3
Water District No. 5
First Judicial District
Jurisdiction, Boulder, Larimer and Weld counties
Owner, Samuel Williamson, Nicholas Bader estate, Henry H Birch, Jerome F Gould, of Niwot, Webb of Boulder and Thomas Cavey of Longmont
Boulder District Court Judgment Book, Water Decrees, Vol 2, District 5-6, 1869-1896, pg 389
Date of appropriation, 31 May 1862
General Course is NE
Natural Stream is Left Hand Creek
Headgate is located [not given]
Length,
Width, 2 ft, enlarged on 1 May 1863 to 3 ft, enlarged on 10 May 1865 to 6 ft
Depth, 12 in, enlarged on 1 May 1863 to 1 1/2 ft
Grade, 1/2 in per rod
Capacity, 288 customary in, increased to 360 customary in, total 648 customary inches, increased to 1188 in
Claim, 300 in, enlarged to 360 in, enlarged to 1500 customary in

Acres under irrigation, [not given], enlarged to 1000 acres, requiring 1 1/2 in per acre
First Enlargement, 1 May 1863, No. 4
Second Enlargment, 10 May 1865, No. 10

Holland Ditch, No. 4 (formerly Arbuthnot No. 1)
Water District No. 5
First Judicial District
Jurisdiction, Boulder, Larimer and Weld counties
Owner, Chris Nelson, Wm Arbuthnot, A P Lawson, Mrs M A Grill, Barnett Dodd, M E Bader estate, J Hugo Anderson, Henry H Birch, Sam Williamson, Granville Holland and Fred Bond of Niwot
Boulder District Court Judgment Book, Water Decrees, Vol 2, District 5-6, 1869-1896, pg 394
Date of appropriation, 1 May 1863
General Course is NE
Natural Stream is Left Hand Creek
Headgate is located in Sec 28, T2N, R70W on the north side of the Creek in a SW direction to the Haystack Mountain
Length, [not given], second enlargement to 3 miles on 25 Nov 1873
Width, 1 ft enlarged to 2 ft on 15 May 1866
Depth, 12 in, enlarged to 2 ft on 15 May 1866, enlarged on 25 Nov 1873 to 5 ft wide on the bottom, 7 ft wide on the top
Grade, 1 in to the rod
Capacity, 120 inches, enlarged to 288 customary inches, enlarged to 2304 cutomary inches on 25 Nov 1873, total 2592 customary inches
Acres under irrigation, 80; acres after enlargement 2000, actual 1500, requiring 1 in per acre
Soil is meadow and farm
First Enlargement, 1 May 1866, No. 14
Second Enlargement, 21 Oct 1873, No. 26

Bader No. 2 Ditch, No. 5
Water District No. 5
First Judicial District
Jurisdiction, Boulder, Larimer and Weld counties
Owner, John G Bader and William Arbuthnot of Boulder
Boulder District Court Judgment Book, Water Decrees, Vol 2, District 5-6, 1869-1896, pg 398
Date of appropriation, 31 May 1863
General Course
Natural Stream is Left Hand Creek
Headgate is located
Length, enlarged to 2 miles on 15 Mar 1870
Width, 1 ft, enlarged to 2 9/12 ft on 15 Mar 1870
Depth, 12 in
Grade, 3/4 in per rod, enlarged to 1 in per rod, on 15 Mar 1870
Capacity, 144 customary inches, enlarged to 252 inches o 15 Mar 1870, total 396 in
Acres under irrigation [not given], enlarged to 300 acres on 15 Mar 1870
First Enlargement, 15 Mar 1870, No. 19

Farmers Ditch, No. 6
Water District No. 5
First Judicial District
Jurisdiction, Boulder, Larimer and Weld counties
Owner, Farmers Ditch Company, William Arbuthnot, Richard Goyn and P M Hinman of Longmont
Boulder District Court Judgment Book, Water Decrees, Vol 2, District 5-6, 1869-1896, pg 401
Date of appropriation, 1 June 1863
General Course is SE
Natural Stream is Left Hand Creek
Headgate is located Sec 28, T2N, R70W, about 3 miles below the mountains
Length, 1 mile, enlarged to 4 1/2 miles on 15 Oct 1866
Width, 1 ft, enlarged to 2 ft on 1 July 1865, enlarged to 4 ft on 15 Oct 1866
Depth, 12 in, enlarged to ft on bottom, 6 ft on top on 15 Oct 1866, enlarged to 6 ft on bottom, 8 ft on top on 16 Nov 1870
Grade, 1 in per rod, enlarged to 1 1/2 in per rod on 15 Oct 1866
Capacity, 120 inches, enlarged to 144 in on 1 July 1865, total 288 inches, total 720 customary inches, increased to 1296 on 16 Nov 1870, total 2016 inches
Acres under irrigation [not given], enlarged to 80 acres on 1 July 1865, requiring 2 in per acre, enlarged to 1240 on 16 Nov 1870
First Enlargement, 15 June 1865, No. 13
Second Enlargement, 15 Oct 1866 [not recognized]
Second Enlargement, 1 Nov 1870, No. 21

Baum and Goyn Ditch, No. 7
Water District No. 5
First Judicial District
Jurisdiction, Boulder, Larimer and Weld counties
Owner, Frederick Baum and Richard Goyn of Niwot
Boulder District Court Judgment Book, Water Decrees, Vol 2, District 5-6, 1869-1896, pg 406
Date of appropriation, 26 Sept 1863
General Course is east
Natural Stream is Left Hand Creek
Headgate is located in Sec 27, T2N, R70W on the south side of the creek

Length, 1 1/4 miles, enlarged to 2 miles on 1 May 1867
Width, 2 ft, enlarged to 3 ft on 1 May 1867
Depth, 18 in, enlarged to 2 ft on 1 May 1867
Grade, 1/2 in per rod
Capacity, 432 inches, claimed 200 inches, enlarged by 432 customary inches, 864 inches total, claim enlarged to 500 inches
Acres under irrigation, 450; requiring 2 in per acre
Soil is sandy and porous
First Enlargement, 1 May 1867, No. 17

Bader No. 1 Ditch, No. 8
Water District No. 5
First Judicial District
Jurisdiction, Boulder, Larimer and Weld counties
Owner, George G Bader of Altona, Merritt L Hinman and William Arbuthnot of Niwot
Boulder District Court Judgment Book, Water Decrees, Vol 2, District 5-6, 1869-1896, pg 409
Date of appropriation, 31 May 1864
General Course
Natural Stream is Left Hand Creek
Headgate is located
Length, 4 miles
Width, 2 ft
Depth, 12 in
Grade, 1 in per rod
Capacity, 288 customary inches
Acres under irrigation, 265

Altona Ditch, No. 11 (formerly Noblit Ditch)
Water District No. 5
First Judicial District
Jurisdiction, Boulder, Larimer and Weld counties
Owner, Altona Ditch Company of Altona
Boulder District Court Judgment Book, Water Decrees, Vol 2, District 5-6, 1869-1896, pg 411
Date of appropriation, 31 May 1865
General Course is SE
Natural Stream is Left Hand Creek
Headgate is located in Sec 13, T2N, R71W
Length, 1 mile, enlarged to 3 miles on 15 Nov 1874
Width, 16 in, enlarged to 3 ft on the bottom, 5 ft on the top on 15 Nov 1874
Depth 8 in, enlarged to 2 ft on 15 Nov 1874
Grade, 3/8 in per rod, enlarged to 1/2 in per rod on 15 Nov 1874
Capacity, 128 customary inches, claimed 200 inches, enlarged to 1024 customary inches on 15 Nov 1874, total 1125 customary inches, actual appropriation 500 inches
Acres under irrigation, [not given], enlarged to 1500 acres on 15 Nov 1874, 500 acres requiring 1 in per acre
First Enlargement, 15 Apr 1875, No. 29

Table Mountain Ditch, No. 15 [16]
Water District No. 5
First Judicial District
Jurisdiction, Boulder, Larimer and Weld counties
Owner, Table Mountain Ditch Company of Niwot
Boulder District Court Judgment Book, Water Decrees, Vol 2, District 5-6, 1869-1896, pg 414
Date of appropriation, 25 June 1866
General Course is east and NE
Natural Stream is Left Hand Creek
Headgate is located Sec 19, T2N, R70W
Length, 1 1/2 miles, originally built for 3/4 mile, then adopted the line of an old ditch for 3/4 mile
Width, 3 ft, enlarged to 4 ft on 1 May 1869, enlarged to 5 ft on 15 Apr 1874
Depth, 18 in, enlarged to 2 ft on 1 May 1869, enlarged to 3 ft on 15 Apr 1874
Grade, [not given], enlarged to 1 in per rod on 1 May 1869
Capacity, 648 customary inches, claimed 432 inches, enlarged to 504 inches, total 1152 customary inches, claimed 864 inches, enlarged to 1008 inches, total 2160 inches
Acres under irrigation, [not given], [1869 not given], enlarged to 2250 on 15 Apr 1874, actual acreage irrigated 1100 acres, water claimed 2000 inches
First Enlargement, 1 Apr 1869,
Second Enlargement, 15 Apr 1874, No. 27

Way Ditch, No. 18
Water Dist No. 5
First Judicial District
Jurisdiction, Boulder, Larimer and Weld counties
Owner, Enoch Way of Niwot
Boulder District Court Judgment Book, Water Decrees, Vol 2, District 5-6, 1869-1896, pg 418
Date of appropriation, 1 May 1868
General Course is east
Natural Stream is Left Hand Creek
Headgate is located, Sec 24, T2N, R70W on the north bank
Length, 1 mile
Width, 3 ft
Depth, 12 in
Grade, 1/4 in to the rod
Capacity, 432 customary inches, 500 inches claimed

Acres under irrigation, 240 acres requiring 1 1/2 inches to irrigate, 3000 inches appropriated

Toll Gate Ditch, No. 20
Water District No. 5
First Judicial District
Jurisdiction, Boulder, Larimer and Weld counties
Owner, Toll Gate Ditch Company of Altona
Boulder District Court Judgment Book, Water Decrees, Vol 2, District 5-6, 1869-1896, pg 421
Date of appropriation, 1 Apr 1870
General Course is NE
Natural Stream is Left Hand Creek
Headgate is located, Sec __, T2N, R70W, above the mouth of Left Hand Canyon, north side of the creek
Length, 1 1/2 miles
Width, 22 in, enlarged on 5 May 1871 to 2 1/2 feet, enlarged on 1 May 1874 to 4 ft
Depth, 8 in, enlarged on 5 May 1871 to 10 in, enlarged on 1 May 1874 to 1 ft, enlarged on 3 May 1879 to 4 ft
Grade, 1/2 in to the rod
Capacity, 176 customary inches, 132 inches appropriated, enlarged on 5 May 1871 by 124 inches, total 300 inches, 300 inches claimed; enlarged on 1 May 1874 to 288 inches
Acres under irrigation, on 3 May 1879 is 1450 acres, requiring 1 1/2 inches to irrigate, 470 acres actually irrigated, claimed 900 inches, actually appropriated 480 inches
First Enlargement, 5 May 1871, No. 27
Second Enlargement, 1 May 1874, No. 31
Third Enlargement, 3 May 1879, No. [not given]

Star Ditch, No. 22
Water District No. 5
First Judicial District
Jurisdiction, Boulder, Larimer and Weld counties
Owner, Star Ditch Company of Longmont
Boulder District Court Judgment Book, Water Decrees, Vol 2, District 5-6, 1869-1896, pg 425
Date of appropriation, 1 Apr 1871
General Course is SE
Natural Stream is LEft Hand Creek
Headgate is located, Sec 28, T2N, R70W
Length, 4 1/2 miles
Width, 4 ft
Depth, 18 in
Grade, 1/2 in per rod
Capacity, 864 customary inches, 2000 inches claimed
Acres under irrigation, 2000 acres requiring 1 inch to irrigate

Johnson Ditch, No. 25
Water District No. 5
First Judicial District
Jurisdiction, Boulder, Larimer and Weld counties
Owner, R F Balker, Richard Goyn, Anna Johnson and C A Johnson of Niwot
Boulder District Court Judgment Book, Water Decrees, Vol 2, District 5-6, 1869-1896, pg 427
Date of appropriation, 1 Apr 1873
General Course is E
Natural Stream is Left Hand Creek
Headgate is located, Sec 29, T2N, R70W
Length, 2 mi
Width, 3 ft
Depth, 12 in
Grade, 1/2 in per rod
Capacity, 432 customary inches, appropriated 360 inches
Acres under irrigation, 540 acres requiring 1 in to irrigate

Lake Ditch, No. 27
Water District No. 5
First Judicial District
Jurisdiction, Boulder, Larimer and Weld counties
Owner, Lake Ditch Company of Altona
Boulder District Court Judgment Book, Water Decrees, Vol 2, District 5-6, 1869-1896, pg 430
Date of appropriation, 15 Apr 1874
General Course is NE
Natural Stream is Left Hand Creek
Headgate is located, Sec [not given], T2N, R71W
Length, 358 rods, enlarged on 15 Apr 1879 to 3 1/2 miles
Width, 1 1/2 ft, enlarged on 15 Apr 1879 to 4 ft bottom, 6 ft top
Depth, 12 in, enlarged on 15 Apr 1879 to 14 in
Grade, 1/4 in to the rod
Capacity, 216 inches, claimed 288 inches, known use 80 inches, enlarged on 15 Apr 1879 to 582 inches, total 798 inches, actual use only 200 inches
Acres under irrigation, 2340 acres requiring 1 1/2 inches to irrigate, actual irrigation of 225 acres
First Enlargement, No. 30, 15 Apr 1879

Bacon (North Side) Ditch, No. 86
Water District No. 5
First Judicial District
Jurisdiction, Boulder, Larimer and Weld counties
Owner, J W Bacon of Longmont
Boulder District Court Judgment Book, Water Decrees, Vol 2, District 5-6, 1869-1896, pg 433
Date of appropriation, 20 May 1881

General Course is SE
Natural Stream is Big Hollow, a tributary of the St Vrain
Headgate is located, Sec 2, T3N, R68W, near the west line of the E 1/4 of Sec 2 in Weld County
Length, 3 miles
Width, 3 1/2 ft
Depth, 15 in
Grade, 6 ft to the mile
Capacity, 140 customary inches
Acres under irrigation, 60 acres, actually irrigated 45 (25 acres meadow, 20 acres bluff), requiring 4 & 2 inches per acre to irrigate

Knoth, Streeter & Lake Ditch
Water District No. 5
First Judicial District
Jurisdiction, Boulder, Larimer and Weld counties
Owner, Conrad W Knoth, Rienzi Streeter, Charles Lake of Longmont
Boulder District Court Judgment Book, Water Decrees, Vol 2, District 5-6, 1869-1896, pg 435
Date of appropriation, 15 Mar 1873
General Course is SE
Natural Stream is St Vrain Creek through the Oligarchy Ditch
Headgate is located, Sec 29, T3N, R69W, near the NE corner of Sec 29
Length, 2 miles
Width, 3 ft
Depth, 18 in
Grade, "considerable fall grade"
Capacity, 648 customary inches, claimed 150 inches
Acres under irrigation, 120 acres requiring 2 in to irrigate

Oligarchy Extension Ditch
Water District No. 5
First Judicial District
Jurisdiction, Boulder, Larimer and Weld counties
Owner, Oligarchy Extension Irrigating Ditch Company
Boulder District Court Judgment Book, Water Decrees, Vol 2, District 5-6, 1869-1896, pg 437
Date of appropriation, 1 Apr 1871
General Course is E
Natural Stream is St Vrain Creek
Headgate is located, Sec 30, T3N, R69W at the eastern terminus of the Oligarchy Ditch
Length, 8 mi
Width, 5 ft bottom, 8 ft top, enlarged on 1 May 1873 to 12 ft bottom 13 ft top
Depth, 12 in, enlarged on 1 May 1873 to 30 in
Grade, 1/2 in to the rod
Capacity, 936 customary inches, increased on 1 May 1873 to 3564 inches, total 4500 inches
Acres under irrigation, after enlargement was 3000 to 4000 acres
First Enlargement, 1 May 1873

Taylor Private Ditch
Water District No. 5
First Judicial District
Jurisdiction, Boulder, Larimer and Weld counties
Owner, David C Taylor of Longmont
Boulder District Court Judgment Book, Water Decrees, Vol 2, District 5-6, 1869-1896, pg 439
Date of appropriation, 10 May 1872
General Course is SE
Natural Stream is St Vrain Creek through the Peck Lateral Ditch
Headgate is located, Sec 36, T3N, $70W on the line of the Pella Ditch about 80 rods east of the Larimer Rd
Length, 285 rods
Width, 2 1/2 ft
Depth, 8 in
Grade, 1/4 in to the rod
Capacity, 240 customary inches, appropriated 50 customary inches
Acres under irrigation, 50 acres requiring 1 inch to irrigate

Crocker Ditch, No. 23
Water District No. 5
First Judicial District
Jurisdiction, Boulder, Larimer and Weld counties
Owner, John G Bader and H H Crocker of Altona, and Clinton M Tyler of Boulder
Boulder District Court Judgment Book, Water Decrees, Vol 2, District 5-6, 1869-1896, pg 440
Date of appropriation, 1 May 1871
General Course is SE
Natural Stream is Left Hand Creek
Headgate is located, Sec 18, T2N, R70W on Left Hand Creek near the foot of the mountains
Length, 2 mi, enlarged on 1 June 1872 to 4 mi
Width, 1 1/2 ft, enlarged on 1 June 1872 to 3 ft
Depth, 7 in, enalrged on 1 June 1872 to 1 ft
Grade, 2 in to the rod
Capacity, 126 customary inches, appropriated 108 customary inches, incred on 1 June 1872 to 306 customary inches, total 432 inches
Acres under irrigation, 1800 acres requiring 1 1/2 inches to irrigate
First Enlargement, 1 June 1872, No. 24

Neikirk Ditch
Water District No. 5
First Judicial District
Jurisdiction, Boulder, Larimer and Weld counties
Owner, Henry Neikirk of Boulder
Boulder District Court Judgment Book, Water Decrees, Vol 2, District 5-6, 1869-1896, pg 444
Date of appropriation, 1 May 1875 [1877]
General Course is south
Natural Stream is St Vrain Creek through the Highland Ditch
Headgate is located, Sec 11, T3N, R69W on teh SW 1/4 of Sec 1 on the line of the Highland Ditch, through which it takes its water
Length, 3/4 mi
Width, 2 ft bottom, 2 1/2 ft top
Depth, 12 in
Grade, 1/2 in to the rod
Capacity, 324 customary inches, claimed 125 customary inches
Acres under irrigation, 220 acres requiring 1 in to irrigate

Knoth Private Ditch No. 1
Water District No. 5
First Judicial District
Jurisdiction, Boulder, Larimer and Weld counties
Owner, Conrad W Knoth of Longmont
Boulder District Court Judgment Book, Water Decrees, Vol 2, District 5-6, 1869-1896, pg 445
Date of appropriation, 10 Mar 1879
General Course is SE
Natural Stream is St Vrain Creek by the Supply Ditch
Headgate is located, Sec 13, T4N, R70W in the SW corner of the NE 1/4 of Sec 13
Length, 2 mi
Width, 4 ft
Depth, 18 in
Grade, 3 ft per mile
Capacity, 864 customary inches, claimed 320 inches
Acres under irrigation, 320 acres requiring 1 inch to irrigate

Knoth Private Ditch No. 2
Water District No. 5
First Judicial District
Jurisdiction, Boulder, Larimer and Weld counties
Owner, Conrad W Knoth of Longmont
Boulder District Court Judgment Book, Water Decrees, Vol 2, District 5-6, 1869-1896, pg 447
Date of appropriation, 1 May 1879
General Course is east
Natural Stream is St Vrain Creek through the Supply Ditch
Headgate is located, Sec 12, T4N, R70W near the NE corner of the SE 1/4 of Sec 12
Length, 160 rods
Width, 1 1/2 ft
Depth, 10 in
Grade, 3 feet to the mile
Capacity, 180 customary inches, claimed 160 inches
Acres under irrigation, 130 acres requiring 1 1/2 inches to irrigate

Davis (Individual) Ditch
Water District No. 5
First Judicial District
Jurisdiction, Boulder, Larimer and Weld counties
Owner, George F Davis of Longmont
Boulder District Court Judgment Book, Water Decrees, Vol 2, District 5-6, 1869-1896, pg 448
Date of appropriation, 17 May 1874
General Course is S
Natural Stream is St Vrain Creek through the Highland and Davis Lateral Ditches
Headgate is located, Sec 24, T3N, R69W on the north line of the NW Corner of Sec 24
Length, 1/2 mi
Width, 20 in bottom, 3 ft top
Depth, 18 in
Grade, 1/2 in to the rod
Capacity, 50 customary inches
Acres under irrigation, 155 acres requring 1 in to irrigate

Bond's Private Ditch
Water District No. 5
First Judicial District
Jurisdiction, Boulder, Larimer and Weld counties
Owner, Isaac L Bond and George S Bond of Longmont
Boulder District Court Judgment Book, Water Decrees, Vol 2, District 5-6, 1869-1896, pg 449
Date of appropriation,
General Course is
Natural Stream is St Vrain Creek through the Highland and other ditches
Headgate is located, Sec 24, T3N, R69W, in the corner of Sec 24
Length, 1 1/2 mi
Width, 2 ft bottom, 2 1/2 ft top
Depth, 12 in
Grade, 1/2 inch to the rod

Capacity, 324 customary inches, claimed 24 inches
Acres under irrigation, 395 acres

Terry Ditch No. 1
Water District No. 5
First Judicial District
Jurisdiction, Boulder, Larimer and Weld counties
Owner, Seth Terry of Longmont
Boulder District Court Judgment Book, Water Decrees, Vol 2, District 5-6, 1869-1896, pg 451
Date of appropriation, 10 May 1873
General Course is SE
Natural Stream is St Vrain Creek through the Highland & Supply Ditches
Headgate is located, Sec 6, T3N, R69W on the E 1/4 of Sec 6
Length, 1 1/2 mi
Width, 2 ft bottom, 4 ft top
Depth, 24 in
Grade, 2 ft per mile
Capacity, 864 customary inches, claimed 40 inches
Acres under irrigation, 120 acres, actual 100 acres requiring 1 in to irrigate

Terry Ditch No. 2
Water District No. 5
First Judicial District
Jurisdiction, Boulder, Larimer and Weld counties
Owner, Seth Terry of Longmont
Boulder District Court Judgment Book, Water Decrees, Vol 2, District 5-6, 1869-1896, pg 452
Date of appropriation, 1 May 1877
General Course is east
Natural Stream is St Vrain Creek through the Highland Ditch
Headgate is located, Sec 18, T3N, R69W about the centre of the north line of the E 1/4 of Sec 18
Length, 1 1/4 mi
Width, 2 ft
Depth, 24 in
Grade, 15 ft per mile
Capacity, 576 inches, claimed 50 inches
Acres under irrigation, 80 acres, requiring 3/4 inch to irrigate

Terry Ditch No. 3
Water District No. 5
First Judicial District
Jurisdiction, Boulder, Larimer and Weld counties
Owner, Seth Terry of Longmont
Boulder District Court Judgment Book, Water Decrees, Vol 2, District 5-6, 1869-1896, pg 453
Date of appropriation, 1 May 1878
General Course is east
Natural Stream is St Vrain Creek through the Highland Ditch
Headgate is located, Sec 18, T3N, R69W near the center of the south line of the SE 1/4 of Sec 18
Length, 1 1/4 miles
Width, 2 ft
Depth, 24 in
Grade, 15 ft to the mile
Capacity, 576 customary inches, claimed 50 inches
Acres under irrigation, 80 acres requiring 3/4 inch to irrigate

Fred Sigley Ditch
Water District No. 5
First Judicial District
Jurisdiction, Boulder, Larimer and Weld counties
Owner, Fred C Sigley of Longmont
Boulder District Court Judgment Book, Water Decrees, Vol 2, District 5-6, 1869-1896, pg 455
Date of appropriation, 15 May 1878
General Course is S
Natural Stream is St Vrain Creek through the Highland Ditch
Headgate is located, Sec 13, T3N, R69W, at a point on the Highland Ditch near the NW Corner of the SW 1/4 of Sec 13
Length, 1/2 mile
Width, 2 ft bottom, 4 ft top
Depth, 24 in
Grade, 1/4 in to the rod
Capacity, 864 inches, claimed 100 inches
Acres under irrigation, 150 acres, actual 113 acres

Sigley Lateral No. 1 East Ditch
Water District No. 5
First Judicial District
Jurisdiction, Boulder, Larimer and Weld counties
Owner, W B Sigley of Longmont
Boulder District Court Judgment Book, Water Decrees, Vol 2, District 5-6, 1869-1896, pg 456
Date of appropriation, 1 Apr 1874
General Course is south
Natural Stream is St Vrain Creek through the Highland and Supply Ditches
Headgate is located, Sec 13, T3N, R69W, on the county line between Boulder and Weld Counties on the SE 1/4 of Sec 13
Length, 60 rods
Width, 2 1/2 ft bottom, 3 ft top

Depth, 18 in
Grade, 3 in to the rod for the first few rods, much less the rest of the way
Capacity, 594 inches, claimed 40 inches
Acres under irrigation, 28 acres

Robert Stephens Claim
Water District No. 5
First Judicial District
Jurisdiction, Boulder, Larimer and Weld counties
Owner, Robert Stephens of Longmont
Boulder District Court Judgment Book, Water Decrees, Vol 2, District 5-6, 1869-1896, pg 457
Date of appropriation, 10 June 1874
General Course is
Natural Stream is St Vrain through the Highland Ditch
Headgate is located, [not given]
Length,
Width,
Depth,
Grade,
Capacity, 10 June 1874 claim 90 inches, 10 June 1875 claim 90 inches, 10 June 1876 claim 110 inches, 10 June 1877 claim 110 inches
Acres under irrigation, 240 acres, actual 180 acres requiring 1 inch to irrigate

Left Hand Reservoir, No. 3
Water District No. 5
First Judicial District
Jurisdiction, Boulder, Larimer and Weld counties
Owner, P M Hinman, Richard Goyn and H H Hornbaker of Niwot
Boulder District Court Judgment Book, Water Decrees, Vol 2, District 5-6, 1869-1896, pg 460
Date of appropriation, 15 Apr 1877
General Course is
Natural Stream is Left Hand Creek through the Farmers, Baum and Goyn Ditches
Reservoir is located, Sec 25, 26, 36, 36, T2N, R70W
Length, 1/2 mile
Width, 40 rods
Depth, 144 in
Grade,
Capacity, 36,130, 396, 400 cu inches
Acres under irrigation, 1000 acres, actual 40 acres

Lagerman Reservoir, No. 4
Water District No. 5
First Judicial District
Jurisdiction, Boulder, Larimer and Weld counties
Owner, Frederick Lagerman
Boulder District Court Judgment Book, Water Decrees, Vol 2, District 5-6, 1869-1896, pg 462
Date of appropriation, 3 Sept 1878
General Course is
Natural Stream is Left Hand Creek vis Table Mountain Ditch and laterals, sloughs and a dry creek called Spring Gulch
Reservoir is located, E 1/2 of the SE 1/4 of Sec 14 and the W 1/2 of the SW 1/4 of Sec 13 T2N, R70W
Length,
Width,
Depth,
Grade,
Capacity, 23,357,000 cu ft
Acres under irrigation, 600 acres, requiring 1 foot per 1 square foot of land

Divide Reservoir, No. 5
Water District No. 5
First Judicial District
Jurisdiction, Boulder, Larimer and Weld counties
Owner, Henry Neikirk of Boulder
Boulder District Court Judgment Book, Water Decrees, Vol 2, District 5-6, 1869-1896, pg 465
Date of appropriation, 1 Mar 1879
General Course is
Natural Stream is St Vrain Creek by the Highland and Supply ditches
Reservoir is located, Sec 10, T3N, R69W, W 1/2 of Sec 11 and E 1/2 Sec 10, a natural basin or depression with a dyke or dam thrown around the lower side
Length,
Width,
Depth,
Grade,
Capacity, 23,462,180 cu ft, appropriated 39,204,000 cu ft
Acres under irrigation, 10,000 acres

Pleasant Valley Reservoir, No. 1
Water District No. 5
First Judicial District
Jurisdiction, Boulder, Larimer and Weld counties
Owner, Pleasant Valley Reservoir, Fish & Ditch Company of Longmont
Boulder District Court Judgment Book, Water Decrees, Vol 2, District 5-6, 1869-1896, pg 467
Date of appropriation, 1 June 1871
General Course is
Natural Stream is St Vrain Creek by the Rough & Ready Ditch
Reservoir is located, Secs 16 & 19, T3N, R69W

Length, 1 mi
Width, 1/2 mi
Depth, 8 ft
Grade,
Capacity, 70,054,400 cu ft, in a natural basin north and south, a little over a mile long, by about 1/2 mile wide
Acres under irrigation, 200 acres, enlarged to 3000

Highland Lake Reservoir No. 2
Water District No. 5
First Judicial District
Jurisdiction, Boulder, Larimer and Weld counties
Owner, Lorin C Mead, of Longmont and Clarkson A Pound of Longmont
Boulder District Court Judgment Book, Water Decrees, Vol 2, District 5-6, 1869-1896, pg 470
Date of appropriation, 31 May 1874
General Course is [NA]
Natural Stream is St Vrain Creek from the Highland Ditch
Reservoir is located, Secs 4,5,8 & 9, T3N, R68W
Length,
Width,
Depth, 240 in
Grade,
Capacity, [claimed] 7,812,078,796 cu in
Acres under irrigation, 300 acres

Highland Reservoir No. 1, No. 6
Water District No. 5
First Judicial District
Jurisdiction, Boulder, Larimer and Weld counties
Owner, Highland Reservoir and Ditch Company, of Longmont
Boulder District Court Judgment Book, Water Decrees, Vol 2, District 5-6, 1869-1896, pg 472
Date of appropriation, 15 Nov 1879
General Course is
Natural Stream is St Vrain Creek by the Highland Ditch
Reservoir is located, Sec 22, T3N, R68W, originally known as the Howlet Lake
Length,
Width,
Depth,
Grade,
Capacity, 33,889,104 cu ft
Acres under irrigation,

Knoth Reservoir No. 7
Water District No. 5
First Judicial District
Jurisdiction, Boulder, Larimer and Weld counties
Owner, Conrad W Knoth, of Longmont
Boulder District Court Judgment Book, Water Decrees, Vol 2, District 5-6, 1869-1896, pg 474
Date of appropriation, 25 Apr 1880
General Course is
Natural Stream is St Vrain Creek by the Supply Ditch and Knoth's Private Ditch No. 2
Reservoir is located, Sec 7, T3N, R69W, SW 1/4 of Section 7
Length, 50 rods
Width, 20 rods
Depth, 72 in
Grade,
Capacity, 1,633,500 cu ft
Acres under irrigation, 80 acres, requiring 1 in to irrigate

Highland Reservoir No. 2, No. 8
Water District No. 5
First Judicial District
Jurisdiction, Boulder, Larimer and Weld counties
Owner, Highland Reservoir and Ditch Company
Boulder District Court Judgment Book, Water Decrees, Vol 2, District 5-6, 1869-1896, pg 476
Date of appropriation, 15 Nov 1881
General Course is
Natural Stream is St Vrain Creek
Reservoir is located, Secs 5 & 6, T3N, R69W, SW 1/4 of the NW 1/4 of the SE 1/4 of Sec 5 and part of the SE 1/4 of Sec 6
Length,
Width,
Depth,
Grade,
Capacity, 71,855,680 cu ft
Acres under irrigation, 1500 acres

Highland Reservoir No. 3, No 8
Water District No. 5
First Judicial District
Jurisdiction, Boulder, Larimer and Weld counties
Owner, Highland Reservoir and Ditch Company
Boulder District Court Judgment Book, Water Decrees, Vol 2, District 5-6, 1869-1896, pg 479
Date of appropriation, 15 Nov 1881
General Course is [NA]
Natural Stream is St Vrain Creek
Reservoir is located, Sec 27, T3N, R68W, S 1/2 of Sec 27

Length,
Width,
Depth,
Grade,
Capacity, 33,889,10[0] cu ft, claimed 29,007,436,000 cu in
Acres under irrigation,

Titus & Goyn Ditch, No. 72
Water District No. 5
First Judicial District
Jurisdiction, Boulder, Larimer and Weld counties
Owner, Albert Titus of Boulder
Boulder District Court Judgment Book, Water Decrees, Vol 2, District 5-6, 1869-1896, pg 482
Date of appropriation, 1 Apr 1878
General Course is SE
Natural Stream is Dry Creek, a tributary of the St Vrain Creek
Headgate is located, on the Groesbeck place in Boulder County
Length, 2 mi
Width, 2 ft
Depth, 12 in
Grade, 1/2 in per rod
Capacity, 50 customary inches, increased to 288 customary inches
Acres under irrigation, 300 acres, actual 50 acres requiring 1 in to irrigate

Pella Ditch, No. 10 Amended
Water District No. 5
First Judicial District
Jurisdiction, Boulder, Larimer and Weld counties
Owner, Pella Ditch Company
Boulder District Court Judgment Book, Water Decrees, Vol 2, District 5-6, 1869-1896, pg 486
Date of appropriation, 20 Mar 1862
General Course is SE
Natural Stream is St Vrain Creek
Headgate is located, south bank of St Vrain Creek in Sec 36, T3N, R70W
Length,
Width, 3 ft
Depth, 18 in
Grade, 1/4 in per rod
Capacity, 640 customary inches, enlarged to 1072 in
Acres under irrigation,
First Enlargement, 10 May 1867, No. 35
Second Enlargement, 1 June 1873, No. 56

WATER DISTRICT NO. 6

Jones & Donnelly Ditch, Corrected
Water District No. 6 First Judicial District
Jurisdiction, Boulder, Larimer and Weld counties
Owner, John A Ellet and Mrs L C Donnelly, by Charles W Campbell their attorney
Boulder District Court Judgment Book, Water Decrees, Vol 2, District 5-6, 1869-1896, pg 488
Natural Stream is South Boulder Creek [not Boulder Creek]

Boulder & White Rock Ditch, No 1
Water District No. 6
First Judicial District
Jurisdiction, Boulder, Larimer and Weld counties
Respondents, Hugh McCammon, Elijah Autrey
Owner, [petitioner] Boulder & White Rock Ditch Company
Boulder District Court Judgment Book, Water Decrees, Vol 2, District 5-6, 1869-1896, pg 491
Date of appropriation, 29 Nov 1873
Natural Stream is Goose Creek from Boulder Creek and Tyler Lake
Headgate is located, NW 1/4, NW 1/4 Sec 29, T1N, R70W
Capacity, 1000 in
Priority No 1 from Goose Creek

Rea Ditch No 1 and Rea Ditch No 2, No 1
Water District No. 6
First Judicial District
Jurisdiction, Boulder, Larimer and Weld counties
Owner, [petitioner] Lucy N Rea
Boulder District Court Judgment Book, Water Decrees, Vol 2, District 5-6, 1869-1896, pg 492
Case Number, 3737
Date of appropriation, 1 Mar 1884
Natural Stream is Gregory Canon Creek
Headgate is located, SW 1/4, SE 1/2, Sec 32, T1N, R71W
Capacity, 45 inches per second
Priority No 1 from Gregory Canon Creek

Marshall Ditch No. 1, Marshall Ditch No. 2, Marshall Reservoir No. 1
Water District No. 6
Eighth Judicial District
Jurisdiction, Boulder, Larimer and Weld counties
Owner, [petitioner] James Marshall, residing near the mouth of South Boulder Canyon
Witnesses, W H Brown, James Marshall, C M Pruden, George Teal

Boulder District Court Judgment Book, Water Decrees, Vol 2, District 5-6, 1869-1896, pg
Case Number,
Date of appropriation, Ditch No. 1: June 1887; Ditch No. 2: June 1892; Reservoir No. 1: 15 May 1895
General Course is Ditch No. 1 N; Ditch No. 2 N
Natural Stream is Spring Creek [Spring Brook]
Headgate is located, Ditch No. 1, right bank of Spring Brook, SW 1/4, NW 1/4, Sec 32
Ditch No. 2, left bank of Spring Brook, SE 1/4, SE 1/4, Sec 31, T1S, R70W, about 1200 ft south of the W 1/4 corner, Sec 32
Reservoir is located, NW 1/4, NW 1/4, Sec 32 T1S R70W
Length, Ditch No. 1: 1/2 mi, Ditch No. 2: 1/2 mi
Width, Ditch No. 1: 12 in; Ditch No. 2: 2 ft
Depth, Ditch No. 12: 6 in; Ditch No. 2: 1 ft
Grade, Ditch No 1: 3 ft per mile; Ditch No. 2: 3 ft per mile
Capacity, Ditch No. 1: 1.29 ct ft water per second; Ditch No. 2: 3.44 ct ft per second
Reservoir, 191,600 cu ft
Acres under irrigation, Ditch No 1 irrigates the W 1/2, NW 1/4, Sec 32, 10 acres
Ditch No. 2 irrigates W 1/2, NW 1/4 Sec 32, constructed across land belonging to M P Fox, 20 acres
Reservoir irrigates W 1/2, Sec 32

WATER DISTRICT NO. 5

Coffin Meadow Ditch, No 3 Decree Reopened

Water District No. 5
First Judicial District
Jurisdiction, Boulder, Larimer and Weld counties
Owner, George W Coffin
Boulder District Court Judgment Book, Water Decrees, Vol 2, District 5-6, 1869-1896, pg 495
Case Number, 1325
Date of appropriation, 1 May 1860
General Course is
Natural Stream is St Vrain Creek
Headgate is located, Sec 8, T2N, R68W
Length,
Width,
Depth,
Grade, 1/4 in to the rod
Capacity, appropriated 300 in
Acres under irrigation, [not given]
Ordered that there be allowed to flow into the ditch 300 in running on a grade of 1/4 in to the rod.

Highland Reservoir, No. 2 (enlarged) No. 10

Water District No. 5
First Judicial District
Jurisdiction, Boulder, Larimer and Weld counties
[Petitioner] Oligarchy Ditch Company, represented by B L Carr, Esq, F P Secor, Esq
Owner, Highland Ditch Company, represented by S A Giffin, Esq
Witness, George A Starbird, civil engineer
Boulder District Court Judgment Book, Water Decrees, Vol 2, District 5-6, 1869-1896, pg 500
Case Number,
Date of appropriation, [enlargement]
Natural Stream is st Vrain Creek
Reservoir is located, Secs 5 and 6, T3N, R69W
Capacity, 119,118,680 cu ft, enlargement of 49,252,600 cu ft on 1 Aug 1888
Decreed that surplus waters of the St Vrain Creek be allowed to flow into the enlarged Highland Reservoir as of 28 June 1889, priority No. 10 senior to the Oligarchy Ditch Company and their reservoir

Oligarchy Reservoir [and Palmerton Ditch], No 5

Water District No. 5
First Judicial District
Jurisdiction, Boulder, Larimer and Weld counties
[Petitioner] Oligarchy Ditch Company, represented by B L Carr, Esq, F P Secor, Esq
Owner, Highland Ditch Company, represented by S A Giffin, Esq
Witness, George A Starbird, civil engineer, Charles E Baker, Secretary for Oligarchy Ditch Company
Boulder District Court Judgment Book, Water Decrees, Vol 2, District 5-6, 1869-1896, pg 500
Case Number,
Date of appropriation, 7 Apr 1884
General Course is [NA]
Natural Stream is st Vrain Creek through the Palmerton Ditch [St Vrain & Palmerton Ditch Company]
Reservoir is located, Secs 25 and 26, T3N, R70W, north bank
Length, [not given]
Width, [Palmerton Ditch] 4 2/3 ft
Depth, [Palmerton Ditch] 3 2/3 ft
Grade, [Palmerton Ditch] 1/4 in to the rod
Capacity, 47,440,800 cu ft; [Palmerton Ditch] 47 cu ft per second
Decreed that surplus waters of the St Vrain Creek be allowed to flow into Oligarchy Reservoir as of 2 July 1889, priority No. 11 for reservoir purposes

Belcher Spring Gulch Ditch, No. 1
Water District No. 5
First Judicial District
Jurisdiction, Boulder, Larimer and Weld counties
Owner, [claimant] William J Longfellow
Boulder District Court Judgment Book, Water Decrees, Vol 2, District 5-6, 1869-1896, pg 506
Case Number, 4586
Date of appropriation, 1 Sept 1873
General Course is [not given]
Natural Stream is Spring Gulch, a tributary of the St Vrain River
Headgate is located, north line, NW 1/4, SE 1/4, Sec 7, T2N, R58W
Length,
Width,
Depth,
Grade,
Capacity,
Acres under irrigation, 30 acres, requiring 1 cu ft per second to irrigate

Coffin Spring Gulch Ditch, No. 2,
Water District No. 5
First Judicial District
Jurisdiction, Boulder, Larimer and Weld counties
Owner, Morse H Coffin, Julia D Coffin
Boulder District Court Judgment Book, Water Decrees, Vol 2, District 5-6, 1869-1896, pg 507
Case Number, 4586
Date of appropriation, [Priority No. 2] 1 May 1875; [Priority No. 5] 1 Jan 1884
General Course is [not given]
Natural Stream is Spring Gulch
Headgate is located, NW corner of the SE 1/4, SE 1/4, Sec 7, T2N, R68W
Length,
Width,
Depth,
Grade,
Capacity, [Priority No. 2] 1/2 cu ft per second; [Priority No. 5]; [Priority No. 5] 1/2 cu ft per second
Acres under irrigation, 15 acres, requiring 1 cu ft per second to irrigate
Priority No. 2 and Priority No. 5 (first enlargement)

Hansen Ditch, No. 3,
Water District No. 5
First Judicial District
Jurisdiction, Boulder, Larimer and Weld counties
Owner, Bryant Newby
Boulder District Court Judgment Book, Water Decrees, Vol 2, District 5-6, 1869-1896, pg 507
Case Number, 4586
Date of appropriation, 3 May 1878
General Course is
Natural Stream is Spring Gulch
Headgate is located, SE corner S 1/2, SW 1/4, Sec 25, T3N, R69W
Length,
Width,
Depth,
Grade,
Capacity, 1 1/2 cu ft per second
Claimed, 100 customary inches
Acres under irrigation, 50 acres, requiring 1 1/2 cu ft per second to irrigate

Last Chance Ditch, No. 4
Water District No. 5
First Judicial District
Jurisdiction, Boulder, Larimer and Weld counties
Owner, Benjamin W Calkins, J W Redd, L V Nichols
Boulder District Court Judgment Book, Water Decrees, Vol 2, District 5-6, 1869-1896, pg 507
Case Number, 4586
Date of appropriation, 30 June 1878
General Course is
Natural Stream is Spring Gulch
Headgate is located, 1224 ft north and 1009 ft W, SE corner, SW 1/4, Sec 25, T3N, R69W
Length,
Width,
Depth,
Grade,
Capacity, 10 cu ft per second
Acres under irrigation, 500 acres requiring 10 cu ft per second to irrigate

Spring Gulch Ditch No. 5
Water District No. 5
First Judicial District
Jurisdiction, Boulder, Larimer and Weld counties
Owner, William H Dickens, Charles J Gregg
Boulder District Court Judgment Book, Water Decrees, Vol 2, District 5-6, 1869-1896, pg 5070
Case Number, 4586
Date of appropriation, 2 Jan 1884
General Course is
Natural Stream is Spring Gulch
Headgate is located, east bank near NE corner, SW 1/4, Sec 6, T2N, R68W

Length,
Width,
Depth,
Grade,
Capacity, 10 cu ft per second
Acres under irrigation, 320 acres, requiring 10 cu ft per second to irrigate
Priority No. 6 [?? earlier described as no. 5]

Calkins Lake Reservoir, No. 1
Water District No. 5
First Judicial District
Jurisdiction, Boulder, Larimer and Weld counties
Owner, Benjamin W Calkins
Boulder District Court Judgment Book, Water Decrees, Vol 2, District 5-6, 1869-1896, pg 507
Case Number, 4586
Date of appropriation, 1 June 1879
General Course is
Natural Stream is Spring Gulch through Last Chance Ditch
Reservoir is located, NE 1/4, Sec 36; SE 1/4 Sec 25, both T3N, R69W
Length,
Width,
Depth,
Grade,
Capacity, 5,924,160 cu ft
Acres under irrigation,

Davidson's Dry Creek Ditch
Water District No. 5
First Judicial District
Jurisdiction, Boulder, Larimer and Weld counties
Owner, Benjamin W Calkins
Boulder District Court Judgment Book, Water Decrees, Vol 2, District 5-6, 1869-1896, pg 508
Case Number, [not given]
Date of appropriation, 1 June 1879
General Course is [not given]
Natural Stream is South Boulder Creek
[petitioner] Davidson Ditch Co, Downer & Hawkins appearing for the ditch company
Owner, E C Lewis
[respondant] South Boulder and Rock Creek Ditch Company, R H Whitely, Giffin & Rowland appearing for the ditch company
30 cu ft per second with a priority of 1 Apr 1865, out of the water decreed to the Leyner Ditch Company on 2 June 1882, should be turned into headgate of the Cottonwood No. 1 Ditch
Headgate of the Cottonwood No. 1 Ditch, east bank of Dry Creek, 1/2 west of the center of Sec 30, T1N, R69W

Longmont Supply Ditch
Lucian H Richardson, Trustee of the Farm Investment Company vs Longmont Supply Ditch Company [defendant]
Boulder District Court Judgment Book, Water Decrees, Vol 2, District 5-6, 1869-1896, pg 508
Case Number, 3865
Edward D Upham, attorney for Farm Investment Company
Decrees that 15 share of stock in the Longmont Supply Ditch Company in the name of Lucian H Richardson, Trustee for Middlesex Banking Company is valid

Last Chance Reservoir No 1
Water District No. 5
First Judicial District
Jurisdiction, Boulder, Larimer and Weld counties
Owner
Boulder District Court Judgment Book, Water Decrees, Vol 2, District 5-6, 1869-1896, pg 576, 514
Case Number,
Date of appropriation,
General Course is
Natural Stream is south bank of Coal Creek, N 1/2, NW 1/4
Headgate is located,
Length,
Width,
Depth,
Grade,
Capacity,
Acres under irrigation,
Reservoir priority No. 7 by reason of enlargement, 1,051,000 cu ft at the rate of 10.78 cu ft per second (appropriation 15 Sept 1885)
Reservoir priority No. 3, 1,983,000 cu ft at the rate of 10.78 cu ft per second (1 Apr 1872)

Last Chance Reservoir No 2
Water District No. 5
First Judicial District
Jurisdiction, Boulder, Larimer and Weld counties
Owner
Boulder District Court Judgment Book, Water Decrees, Vol 2, District 5-6, 1869-1896, pg 514
Case Number,
Date of appropriation,

General Course is
Natural Stream is
Headgate is located, Coal Creek by means of Last Chance Ditch
Length,
Width,
Depth,
Grade,
Capacity,
Acres under irrigation,
Located in the SW 1/4 of Section 19, SW 1/4 of the NW 1/4 of Section 30 T2S, R69W, county of Jefferson
Reservoir priority No. 4, by reason of original construction, 2.972,000 cu ft at the rate of 10.78 cu ft per second (1 Apr 1876)
Reservoir priority No 6, by reason of enlargement, 1,888,000 cu ft at a rate of 10.78 cu ft per second (15 Sept 1884)

Smart Reservoir
Water District No. 5
First Judicial District
Jurisdiction, Boulder, Larimer and Weld counties
Owner
Boulder District Court Judgment Book, Water Decrees, Vol 2, District 5-6, 1869-1896, pg 514
Case Number,
Date of appropriation,
General Course is
Natural Stream is Coal Creek by means of Last Chance Ditch
Headgate is located, south bank of Coal Creek on Sec 18 T2S R70W
Reservoir is located, S 1/2 Sec 16, T2S, R70W, Jefferson County
Length,
Width,
Depth,
Grade,
Capacity,
Acres under irrigation,
Reservoir Priority No. 5 by reason of original construction, 10,305,000 cu ft at the rate of 18 cu ft per second (1 Sept 1882)
Reservoir Priority No. 9, by reason of enlargement, 4,125,000 cu ft at the same rate (1 Sept 1892)

Ditch No. 1, Community Ditch, Marshall Reservoir, West Lake Reservoir, Section 19 Reservoir, Section 9 Reservoir, Section 15 Reservoir
Water District No. 5
First Judicial District
Jurisdiction, Boulder, Larimer and Weld counties
Owner
Boulder District Court Judgment Book, Water Decrees, Vol 2, District 5-6, 1869-1896, pg 514-515-516
Case Number,
Date of appropriation,
General Course is
Natural Stream is South Boulder Creek
Headgate is located, south bank of South Boulder Creek, 1188 ft west of the east line and 1500 ft north of the south line of Section 25, T1S R71S
Length,
Width,
Depth,
Grade,
Capacity,
Acres under irrigation,
Priority No. 1, by reason of original construction, 83.3 cu ft per second (6 June 1885)
Marshall Reservoir, South Boulder Creek, located Sec 22, T1S R70W, Reservoir Priority No. 1, 58,768,000 cu ft at the rate of 83.3 cu ft per second (6 June 1885).
West Lake Reservoir, South Boulder Creek, located Sec 29, T1S R68W, Reservoir Priority No. 2, 30,452,000 cu ft at the rate of 83.3 cu ft per second (6 June 1885).
Section 19 Reservoir, South Boulder Creek, located NW 1/4 Sec 19, T1S R68W, Reservoir Priority No. 3, 3,520,000 cu ft at the rate of 83.3 cu ft per second (1 May 1888).
Section 9 Reservoir, South Boulder Creek, located N 1/2 Sec 9, T1S R68W, Reservoir Priority No. 4, 927,000 at the rate of 83.3 cu ft per second (15 Dec 1889).
Section 15 Reservoir, South Boulder Creek, Located NE 1/4 NW 1/4 Sec 15, T1S R68W, Reservoir Priority No. 5,

Allen-Hayden Ditches No 1, 2, 3 and 4 (being Ditches No. 3, 4, 5, and 6) Decree
Water District No. 5
First Judicial District
Jurisdiction, Boulder, Larimer and Weld counties
Owner
Boulder District Court Judgment Book, Water Decrees, Vol 2, District 5-6, 1869-1896, pg 516
Case Number,

Date of appropriation,
General Course is
Natural Stream is
Headgate is located,
Length,
Width,
Depth,
Grade,
Capacity,
Acres under irrigation,
Ditch No. 3 (called Allen-Hayden Ditch No. 1), Four Mile Creek, located south bank of Four Mile Canon Creek, at the NE Corner of the SE 1/4 of the SE 1/4 of Section 17, T1N R70W bears north 3 dgrees east 985 ft1 cu ft per second (2 Sept 1878)
Ditch No. 4 (called Allen-Hayden Ditch No. 2), Four Mile Creek, irr 40A, located south bank of Four Mile Canon Creek, at the NE corner of the NW 1/4 of Section 21 T1N R70W, bears south 83 degrees 45 ft east 1013 ft, 1 cu ft per second (3 Apr 1878)
Ditch No. 5 (called Allen-Hayden Ditch No. 3), Four Mile Creek, irr 60A, located north bank of Four Mile Canon Creek, NE corner NE 1/4 Section 21, T1N R70W, bears south 50 degrees 15 minutes east 560 ft, 1/2 cu ft per second (4 Apr 1878)
Ditch No. 6 (called Allen-Hayden Ditch No. 4), Four Mile Creek, irr 10A, located north bank of Four Mile Canon Creek, NW corner NE 1/4 Section 21, T1N R70W, bears south 40 degrees 10 minutes west 1233 ft, 1/2 cu ft per second (5 Apr 1878)

Low Ditch No. 1
Water District No. 5
First Judicial District
Jurisdiction, Boulder, Larimer and Weld counties
Owner
Boulder District Court Judgment Book, Water Decrees, Vol 2, District 5-6, 1869-1896, pg
Case Number,
Date of appropriation,
General Course is
Natural Stream is Four Mile Creek
Headgate is located, north bank of Four Mile Creek, T1N R70W, bear 32 degrees 45 minutes west 341.5 ft
Length,
Width,
Depth,
Grade,
Capacity,
Acres under irrigation,
Priority No. 7 by construction, 2 cu ft per second (1 July 1882)

McKay Reservoir and Ditch
Water District No. 5
First Judicial District
Jurisdiction, Boulder, Larimer and Weld counties
Owner
Boulder District Court Judgment Book, Water Decrees, Vol 2, District 5-6, 1869-1896, pg
Case Number,
Date of appropriation,
General Course is
Natural Stream is Coal Creek
Headgate is located,
Length,
Width,
Depth,
Grade,
Capacity,
Acres under irrigation,
Was not constructed with reasonable diligence, water claim denied

WATER DISTRICT NO. 6

Willis Ditch
Water District No. 6
District Court of Boulder County
Owner, W A Willis, Thos Harris, George Harris, J W Jacobs of Louisville
Boulder District Court Judgment Book, Water Decrees, Vol 2, District 5-6, 1869-1896, pg 518-519
Case Number,
Date of appropriation, 5 May 1870
General Course is northeasterly
Natural Stream is Coal Creek
Headgate is located, NW 1/4 of SE 1/4 of SE 1/4 Sec 9 T1S R69W bears north 86 degrees 23 minutes for 714.7 ft
Length,
Width, 4 ft
Depth, 2 ft (1 ft)
Grade, 1/2 in to the rod
Capacity, 9 cu ft per second
Acres under irrigation, 200A
Ditch Priority No. 66

Eggleston Reservoir No. 3
Water District No. 6
District Court of Boulder County
Owner, George W Eggleston

Boulder District Court Judgment Book, Water Decrees, Vol 2, District 5-6, 1869-1896, pg 520-521-522
Case Number,
Date of appropriation, 1 Jan 1874
General Course is easterly
Natural Stream is Coal Creek
Headgate is located, 2360 ft SW of NE corner, Sec 33, T1S T70W
Length,
Width, 2 ft
Depth, 1 ft
Grade, 1/2 in per rod
Capacity, 1,015,860 cu ft, 9 cu ft per second
Acres under irrigation, 75A
Reservoir Priority No. 2

Eggleston Reservoir No. 4
Water District No. 6
District Court of Boulder County
Owner, Geo W Eggleston, Wm Hughes, W H English
Boulder District Court Judgment Book, Water Decrees, Vol 2, District 5-6, 1869-1896, pg 523-524-525
Case Number,
Date of appropriation, 1 Oct 1879
General Course is north easterly
Natural Stream is Coal Creek
Headgate is located, 518 ft NW of NE corner Sec 32, T1S R70W
Length,
Width, 4 ft
Depth, 1 ft
Grade, 1/2 in to the rod
Capacity, 8,000,000 cu ft
Acres under irrigation, 200A
Reservoir Priority No. 3

Moffat Ditch
Water District No. 6
District Court of Boulder County
Owner, Lathan W Jones, William R Moffat (his heirs) Anna M Moffat, Annie E Connell, Rosalie W Jones, Ruth R See, George W Moffat, Addie W Ramage, Sarah C Stevens, William R Moffat, Martin A Moffat
Witnesses, Lathan W Jones, Geo W Eggleston
Boulder District Court Judgment Book, Water Decrees, Vol 2, District 5-6, 1869-1896, pg 526-527-528
Case Number,
Date of appropriation, 4 Feb 1889
General Course is easterly
Natural Stream is Coal Creek
Headgate is located, SE 1/4 S 1/2 NE 1/4, Sec 26; NW 1/4 NW 1/4 Sec 25, T1S R70W,
Length, 1 1/2 mi
Width, 1 ft
Depth, 2 1/2 ft
Grade, 1/2 in to the rod
Capacity, 3 cu ft per second
Acres under irrigation, 375A
Priority No. 67

Kerr Ditch No. 1 and No. 2
Water District No. 6
District Court of Boulder County
Owner, Louisville Coal Mining Company, David Kerr, Thomas Bell
Boulder District Court Judgment Book, Water Decrees, Vol 2, District 5-6, 1869-1896, pg 529-530-531
Case Number,
Date of appropriation, No 1. 15 Apr 1861; No. 2, 15 Apr 1868
General Course is north easterly
Natural Stream is Coal Creek
Headgate is located, No. 1 north side of Coal Creek NW corner of Section 16 T1S R69W bears north 16 degrees 10 minutes west 828 ft; No. 2, south side of Coal Creek NW corner of Sec 16 bears north 48 degrees west 114 ft
Length, No 1. 5280 ft; No. 2 3/4 mi
Width, No 1, 2 ft; No. 2, 2 ft
Depth, No 1, 1 ft; No 2, 1 ft
Grade, No 1, 422 ft per 100 ft, No 2, .75 ft per 100 ft
Capacity, No. 1, 7.68 cu ft per second, No. 2, 3.24 cu ft per second
Acres under irrigation, No. 1, 45A req 1 1/2 in per acre, No. 2, 37 1/2 A req 1 1/2 in per acre
Priority No. 64 (No. 1), No. 65 (No. 2)

WATER DISTRICT NO. 5

Bonus Lateral Ditch (crossed out)
Water District No. 5
Eighth Judicial District
Jurisdiction, Boulder, Larimer and Weld counties
Owner, Freeman Belcher
Boulder District Court Judgment Book, Water Decrees, Vol 2, District 5-6, 1869-1896, pg 532-533
Case Number,
Date of appropriation, 1 Mar 1870
General Course is southeasterly
Natural Stream is Dry Creek
Headgate is located, SW 1/4 Sec 7, T2N R68W

Length,
Width,
Depth,
Grade, 1/8 in per rod
Capacity, 75 in
Acres under irrigation,
Appropriation No. 1

Rice Ditch (crossed out)
Water District No. 5
Eighth Judicial District
Jurisdiction, Boulder, Larimer and Weld counties
Owner
Boulder District Court Judgment Book, Water Decrees, Vol 2, District 5-6, 1869-1896, pg 533
Case Number,
Date of appropriation,
General Course is
Natural Stream is
Headgate is located,
Length,
Width,
Depth,
Grade,
Capacity,
Acres under irrigation,

Bonus Lateral Ditch
Water District No. 5
Eighth Judicial District
Jurisdiction, Boulder, Larimer and Weld counties
Owner, Freeman Belcher
Boulder District Court Judgment Book, Water Decrees, Vol 2, District 5-6, 1869-1896, pg 534-535
Case Number,
Date of appropriation, construction began 1 Apr 1868, completed 1 Mar 1870
General Course is south easterly
Natural Stream is Dry Creek
Headgate is located, SW 1/4 Sec 7, T2N R68W
Length, 1/2 mi
Width, 3 ft bottom, 3 1/2 ft top
Depth, 8 in
Grade, 1/8 in to the rod
Capacity, 75 customary in
Acres under irrigation, 60A
Appropriation No. 1

Rice Ditch and Mill Ditch (enlargement)
Water District No. 5
Eighth Judicial District
Jurisdiction, Boulder, Larimer and Weld counties
Owner, Georgiana Rice, Kate Rice
Boulder District Court Judgment Book, Water Decrees, Vol 2, District 5-6, 1869-1896, pg 537-538
Case Number,
Date of appropriation, 1 Mar 1872, enlargement 1 May 1884
General Course is north easterly
Natural Stream is Dry Creek
Headgate is located, near E and W 1/4, Sec 14, T2N R69W
Length,
Width, enlargement 5 ft bottom. 5 ft top
Depth, enlargement, 3 ft
Grade, 1/2 in to the rod
Capacity, 150 customary in, enlarged to 200 customary in
Acres under irrigation, 150A
Appropriation No. 2, for the enlargement Appropriation No. 6

John Rice Ditch
Water District No. 5
Eighth Judicial District
Jurisdiction, Boulder, Larimer and Weld counties
Owner, Brunhilde Ottens, Georgiana Rice, Kate Rice
Boulder District Court Judgment Book, Water Decrees, Vol 2, District 5-6, 1869-1896, pg 540-541
Case Number,
Date of appropriation, 1 Apr 1884
General Course is easterly
Natural Stream is Dry Creek
Headgate is located, NW 1/4 Sec 14, T2N 469W
Length,
Width,
Depth,
Grade, 1/4 in per rod
Capacity, 300 customary in
Acres under irrigation, 200A, req 1 1/2 in per acre

Lower Baldwin Ditch
Water District No. 5
Eighth Judicial District
Jurisdiction, Boulder, Larimer and Weld counties
Owner, Freeman Belcher, Brunhilde Ottens, Nettie Baldwin, William Butler, M S Belcher, James Kearns
Boulder District Court Judgment Book, Water Decrees, Vol 2, District 5-6, 1869-1896, pg 543-544
Case Number,
Date of appropriation, 1 Apr 1873
General Course is north easterly
Natural Stream is Dry Creek

Headgate is located, MW 1/4, Sec 29, T2N, R69W
Length,
Width, 3 ft bottom
Depth, 42 in
Grade, 1/4 in per rod
Capacity, 175 customary in
Acres under irrigation,
Appropriation No. 4

Upper Baldwin Ditch (Stipulation and Ammended Findings)
Water District No. 5
Eighth Judicial District
Jurisdiction, Boulder, Larimer and Weld counties
Owner, Freeman Belcher, S H Standart
Boulder District Court Judgment Book, Water Decrees, Vol 2, District 5-6, 1869-1896, pg 545-552
Case Number,
Date of appropriation, 1 Apr 1872
General Course is north easterly
Natural Stream is Dry Creek
Headgate is located, Sec 29, T2N R69W
Length,
Width, 5 ft
Depth,
Grade, 1/4 in per rod
Capacity, 360 customary in
Acres under irrigation, req 1 in per acre
Appropriation No. 3

WATER DISTRICT NO.6

Kinnear Reservoir
Water District No. 6
Eighth Judicial District
Jurisdiction, Boulder, Larimer and Weld counties
Owner, John S Kinnear
Boulder District Court Judgment Book, Water Decrees, Vol 2, District 5-6, 1869-1896, pg 553-554, 561
Case Number,
Date of appropriation, work commenced 1 Sept 1869, completed 20 May 1872
General Course is
Natural Stream is Coal Creek
Headgate is located, 2 1/2 of the SW 1/4, Sec 20, S 1/2 SW 1/4, SW 1/4, NW 1/4, SW 1/4, W 1/2, SE 1/4, SE 1/4 SE 1/4 Sec 21, NW 1/4 NW 1/4, NE 1/4 NE 1/4, Sec 28, T2S, R69W
Length,
Width,
Depth,
Grade,
Capacity, 40,962,478 cu ft, 40.47 cu ft per second
Acres under irrigation, 1360A
Reservoir Priority No. 9, later Reservoir Priority No. 1

Church's Upper Lake
Water District No. 6
Eighth Judicial District
Jurisdiction, Boulder, Larimer and Weld counties
Owner
Boulder District Court Judgment Book, Water Decrees, Vol 2, District 5-6, 1869-1896, pg 554-555, 561
Case Number,
Date of appropriation, work commenced 20 May 1870, completed 1871, enlargement commenced 1 Nov 1891, completed 1 Apr 1892
General Course is easterly
Natural Stream is Coal Creek
Headgate is located, SW 1/4 Sec 3, T2S R69W
Length,
Width,
Depth,
Grade,
Capacity, 5,216,000 cu ft, enlarged to 1,910,000 cu ft, 18.11 cu ft per second
Acres under irrigation,
Reservoir Appropriation No. 8, later Reservoir Priority No. 2

Last Chance Reservoirs No. 1 and No. 2
Water District No. 6
Eighth Judicial District
Jurisdiction, Boulder, Larimer and Weld counties
Owner
Boulder District Court Judgment Book, Water Decrees, Vol 2, District 5-6, 1869-1896, pg 555, 561-562
Case Number,
Date of appropriation, work commence on No. 1 on 1 Apr 1872, completed 1 Apr 1873, enlargement began 15 Sept 1885, completed Oct 1887, No. 2 commenced 1875, copleted 1 Apr 1876, enlargement 15 Sept 1884, completed 15 Oct 1887
General Course is
Natural Stream is Coal Creek
Headgate is located, No. 1 N 1/2 NE 1/4 Sec 30, T2S R69W; No. 2 SW 1/4 Sec 19, SW 1/4 NW 1/4 Sec 30, T2S R69W
Length,
Width,
Depth,
Grade,
Capacity, No. 1 13A high water line, 8.62 at low water

line, 1,963,000 cu ft, enlarged to 13.79A at high water line, same low water line, enlargement to 1,933,200 cu ft; No. 2 1263 A at high water line, 8.37A at low water line, 2,972,000 cu ft, enlargement to 13.95A high water line, 1,888,000 cu ft, 10.79 cu ft per second
Acres under irrigation,
Reservoir Appropriation No. 3 and No. 4, enlargement Appropriations No. 6 and No. 7
Later Reservoir Priority No. 3 and 4

Smart Reservoir
Water District No. 6
Eighth Judicial District
Jurisdiction, Boulder, Larimer and Weld counties
Owner
Boulder District Court Judgment Book, Water Decrees, Vol 2, District 5-6, 1869-1896, pg 556-557, 562
Case Number,
Date of appropriation, work commenced 1 Sept 1882, completed 1 June 1883, enlargement commenced 1 Sept 1892, completed Dec 1892
General Course is
Natural Stream is Coal Creek via the Last Chance Ditch
Headgate is located, S 1/2 Sec 16, T2S R70W
Length,
Width,
Depth,
Grade,
Capacity, 24.37 acres at high water, 15.06 acres at low water, 10,305,000 cu ft, enlargement 26.55 acres at high water line, 4,125,000 cu ft
Acres under irrigation, 200A
Reservoir Appropriation No. 9, Later Reservoir Priority No. 5

Community Ditch and Reservoir
Water District No. 6
Eighth Judicial District
Jurisdiction, Boulder, Larimer and Weld counties
Owner
Boulder District Court Judgment Book, Water Decrees, Vol 2, District 5-6, 1869-1896, pg 557, 562-563
Case Number,
Date of appropriation, work commenced 6 June 1885, completed 1 June 1886
General Course is easterly
Natural Stream is South Boulder Creek
Headgate is located, south side of South Boulder Creek, 1188 ft west of the east line and about 1500 north of the south line of Section 25, T1S, R71W
Length, 33 mi
Width, 6 ft bottom, 16 ft top
Depth,
Grade, 5 ft per mi
Capacity, 83.3 cu ft per second
Acres under irrigation, 2670A
Priority on South Boulder Creek, No. 1

Marshall Reservoir
Water District No. 6
Eighth Judicial District
Jurisdiction, Boulder, Larimer and Weld counties
Owner
Boulder District Court Judgment Book, Water Decrees, Vol 2, District 5-6, 1869-1896, pg 557, 563
Case Number,
Date of appropriation,
General Course is
Natural Stream is South Boulder Creek
Headgate is located, Sec 22, T1S R70W
Length,
Width,
Depth, 14.28 ft
Grade,
Capacity, 94.6 acres at high water, 58,768,627 cu ft
Acres under irrigation,
Reservoir Priority No. 1
Priority on South Boulder Creek, No. 1

West Lake Reservoir
Water District No. 6
First Judicial District
Jurisdiction, Boulder, Larimer and Weld counties
Owner
Boulder District Court Judgment Book, Water Decrees, Vol 2, District 5-6, 1869-1896, pg 557, 563
Case Number,
Date of appropriation, work commence 6 June 1885, completed 1886
General Course is
Natural Stream is South Boulder Creek
Headgate is located,
Length,
Width,
Depth, 9.75 ft
Grade,
Capacity, 71.7 acres at high water, 30,452,000 cu ft
Acres under irrigation,
Reservoir Priority No. 2

Section Nineteen (19) Reservoir
Water District No. 6
Eighth Judicial District
Jurisdiction, Boulder, Larimer and Weld counties
Owner
Boulder District Court Judgment Book, Water Decrees, Vol 2, District 5-6, 1869-1896, pg 557, 563
Case Number,
Date of appropriation, work commened 1 Mar 1888, completed 1888
General Course is
Natural Stream is South Boulder Creek
Headgate is located, NW 1/4 Sec 19, T1S R68W
Length,
Width,
Depth, 4.05 ft
Grade,
Capacity, 19.95 acres at high water, 3,520,000 cu ft
Acres under irrigation,
Reservoir Priority No. 3

Section Nine (9) Reservoir
Water District No. 6
Eighth Judicial District
Jurisdiction, Boulder, Larimer and Weld counties
Owner
Boulder District Court Judgment Book, Water Decrees, Vol 2, District 5-6, 1869-1896, pg 557-558, 563-564
Case Number,
Date of appropriation, work commenced 15 Dec 1889, completed 1 Apr 1900
General Course is
Natural Stream is South Boulder Creek
Headgate is located, NE 1/4 NW 1/4 Sec 9, T1S R68W
Length,
Width,
Depth, 2 ft
Grade,
Capacity, 10.65 acres at high water, 927,000 cu ft
Acres under irrigation,
Reservoir Priority No. 4

Section Fifteen (15) Reservoir
Water District No. 6
Eighth Judicial District
Jurisdiction, Boulder, Larimer and Weld counties
Owner, Community Ditch & Reservoir Company
Boulder District Court Judgment Book, Water Decrees, Vol 2, District 5-6, 1869-1896, pg 558, 564
Case Number,
Date of appropriation, work commenced 1 May 1898, completed Man 1898
General Course is
Natural Stream is South Boulder Creek
Headgate is located, NE 1/4 NE 1/4 Sec 15, T1S R68W
Length,
Width,
Depth, 2.87 ft
Grade,
Capacity, 6.14 acres, 707,900 cu ft
Acres under irrigation,
Reservoir Priority No. 5

Allen-Hayden Ditch No. 1
Water District No. 6
First Judicial District
Jurisdiction, Boulder, Larimer and Weld counties
Owner
Boulder District Court Judgment Book, Water Decrees, Vol 2, District 5-6, 1869-1896, pg 558, 564
Case Number,
Date of appropriation, work commenced 1864
General Course is easterly
Natural Stream is Four Mile Canon Creek
Headgate is located, south side of Four Mile Creek, NE corner SE 1/4 Sec 17, T1N R70W bears north 3 degrees east 985 ft
Length, 2412 ft
Width, 3 1/2 ft
Depth, 13 in
Grade, 3 in per 100 feet
Capacity, 45 cu ft per second
Acres under irrigation, 40A
Priority from the Four Mile Canon Ditch is No. 1
Priority from the Ford Ditch is No. 2

Allen-Hayden Ditch No 2
Water District No. 6
Eighth Judicial District
Jurisdiction, Boulder, Larimer and Weld counties
Owner
Boulder District Court Judgment Book, Water Decrees, Vol 2, District 5-6, 1869-1896, pg 559, 564
Case Number,
Date of appropriation, work commenced 1866
General Course is easterly
Natural Stream is Four Mile Canon Creek
Headgate is located, south bank of Four Mile Canon Creek, NW corner of the NE 1/4 Sec 21, T1N R70W bears south 83 degrees 45 minutes east 1013 ft
Length, 2630 ft

Width, 4 ft 4 in
Depth, 13 in
Grade, 3 in per 100 ft
Capacity, 4 cu ft per second
Acres under irrigation, 40A
Priority from Four Mile Canon Creek, No. 4

Allen-Hayden Ditch No 3
Water District No. 6
Eighth Judicial District
Jurisdiction, Boulder, Larimer and Weld counties
Owner
Boulder District Court Judgment Book, Water Decrees, Vol 2, District 5-6, 1869-1896, pg 559, 564-565
Case Number,
Date of appropriation, work commenced 1867, completed 1867
General Course is easterly
Natural Stream is Four Mile Canon Creek
Headgate is located, north side of Four Mile Creek, NW corner of the NE 1/4, Sec 21, T1N R70W bears south 56 degrees 15 minutes east 560 ft
Length, 2760 ft
Width, 40 in
Depth, 13 in
Grade, 3 in per 100 ft
Capacity, 4 cu ft per second
Acres under irrigation, 40A
Priority from Four Mile Canon Creek, No. 5

Allen-Hayden Ditch No 4
Water District No. 6
Eighth Judicial District
Jurisdiction, Boulder, Larimer and Weld counties
Owner
Boulder District Court Judgment Book, Water Decrees, Vol 2, District 5-6, 1869-1896, pg 559-560
Case Number,
Date of appropriation, work commenced 1867, completed 1867
General Course is easterly
Natural Stream is Four Mile Canon Creek
Headgate is located, north side of Four Mile Canon Creek, NW corner NE 1/4 Sec 21, T1N R70W, bears south 40 degrees 10 minutes west 785 ft
Length, 1233 ft
Width, 40 in
Depth, 13 in
Grade, 3 in per 100 ft
Capacity, 4 cu ft per second
Acres under irrigation, 10A
Priority from Four Mile Canon Creek, No. 6

Low Ditch No. 1
Water District No. 6
Eighth Judicial District
Jurisdiction, Boulder, Larimer and Weld counties
Owner
Boulder District Court Judgment Book, Water Decrees, Vol 2, District 5-6, 1869-1896, pg 560, 564
Case Number,
Date of appropriation, work commenced 1 July 1882
General Course is easterly
Natural Stream is Four Mile Canon Creek
Headgate is located, north side of Four Mile Canon Creek, SW corner Sec 15, T1N R70W bears south 32 degrees 45 minutes west 341.5 feet
Length, less than a mile
Width, 1 ft
Depth, 7 in
Grade, 13 ft per mile
Capacity, 2 cu ft per second
Acres under irrigation, 45A
Priority from Four Mile Canon Creek, No. 7

McKay Reservoir and Ditch (Dismissed the Claim)
Water District No. 6
Eighth Judicial District
Jurisdiction, Boulder, Larimer and Weld counties
Owner
Boulder District Court Judgment Book, Water Decrees, Vol 2, District 5-6, 1869-1896, pg 560
Case Number,
Date of appropriation, never completed
General Course is
Natural Stream is Coal Creek
Headgate is located, NW 1/4 Sec 21, T1S R68W, south bank of Coal Creek, SE 1/4 NW 1/4 Sec 18, T2S R69W
Length,
Width,
Depth,
Grade,
Capacity,
Acres under irrigation,

WATER DISTRICT No 5

Peck and Metcalf Ditch
Water District No. 5
Eighth Judicial District
Jurisdiction, Boulder, Larimer and Weld counties

Owner, Clara C Butterworth
Boulder District Court Judgment Book, Water Decrees, Vol 2, District 5-6, 1869-1896, pg 566
Case Number,
Date of appropriation, 15 May 1867
General Course is north easterly
Natural Stream is Dry Creek
Headgate is located, Sec 7, T2N R69W
Length,
Width, 4 1/2 ft
Depth, 18 In
Grade, 1/2 in per rod
Capacity, 180 customary in
Acres under irrigation, 110A, req 1 1/2 in per acre
Priority No. 1

Oscar Beckwith Ditch
Water District No. 5
Eighth Judicial District
Jurisdiction, Boulder, Larimer and Weld counties
Owner, Oscar F Beckwith, Elmer F Beckwith
Boulder District Court Judgment Book, Water Decrees, Vol 2, District 5-6, 1869-1896, pg 566
Case Number,
Date of appropriation, May 1878
General Course is south easterly
Natural Stream is Dry Creek
Headgate is located, SE 1/4 SE 1/4 Sec 8, T2N R69W
Length, 200 rods
Width, 4 ft
Depth, 1 ft
Grade, 1/3 in per rod
Capacity, 400 customary in
Acres under irrigation, 200A, 2 in per acre
Priority No. 2

Clover Basin Ditch
Water District No. 5
Eighth Judicial District
Jurisdiction, Boulder, Larimer and Weld counties
Owner, Clover Basin Ditch Company (Taylor Ditch No. 1, Taylor Ditch No. 2)
Boulder District Court Judgment Book, Water Decrees, Vol 2, District 5-6, 1869-1896, pg 566
Case Number,
Date of appropriation, 1 June 1879, enlargement 2 June 1879
General Course is northeasterly
Natural Stream is Dry Creek
Headgate is located,
Length, No. 1, 20 rods
Width, No. 1, 3 ft
Depth, No. 1, 20 in
Grade, No. 1, 1 1/2 in per rod
Capacity, No. 1, 382 customary in,
Acres under irrigation, 610A, 1 1/4 to 1 1/2 in per acre
Priority No. 3

William H Dickens Ditch
Water District No. 5
Eighth Judicial District
Jurisdiction, Boulder, Larimer and Weld counties
Owner, William H Dickens
Boulder District Court Judgment Book, Water Decrees, Vol 2, District 5-6, 1869-1896, pg 567
Case Number,
Date of appropriation, 1 Nov 1882
General Course is
Natural Stream is Dry Creek
Headgate is located, 4 rods north and east of the center of Sec 10, T2N R69W
Length,
Width, 4 ft
Depth, 1 ft
Grade,
Capacity, 400 customary in
Acres under irrigation, 125A, 2 to 2 1/2 in per acre
Priority No. 4

Anderson Ditch
Water District No. 5
Eighth Judicial District
Jurisdiction, Boulder, Larimer and Weld counties
Owner, Swan Anderson, Hugo Anderson
Boulder District Court Judgment Book, Water Decrees, Vol 2, District 5-6, 1869-1896, pg 567
Case Number,
Date of appropriation, 1883
General Course is north easterly
Natural Stream is Dry Creek
Headgate is located, NW 1/4 of Sec 14, T2N R69W
Length, 1 mi
Width, 2 ft
Depth, 1 1/2 ft
Grade,
Capacity, 75 customary in
Acres under irrigation, 40A
Priority No. 5

Niwot Irrigating Ditch
Water District No. 5
Eighth Judicial District
Jurisdiction, Boulder, Larimer and Weld counties
Owner, Niwot Irrigating Ditch Company
Boulder District Court Judgment Book, Water Decrees, Vol 2, District 5-6, 1869-1896, pg 567
Case Number,
Date of appropriation, Oct 1889
General Course is
Natural Stream is Dry Creek
Headgate is located, SW corner NW 1/4 NW 1/4 Sec 9, T2N R69W
Length,
Width, 3 1/2 ft
Depth, 3 ft
Grade, 1/4 in per rod
Capacity, 500 in
Acres under irrigation,
Priority No. 6

Wiswall Ditch
Water District No. 5
Eighth Judicial District
Jurisdiction, Boulder, Larimer and Weld counties
Owner, F Wiswall, Charles Mowrey, Alice P Laybourn, J M Randall, Everett Whipple, W D Whipple, John Brailey, George Bloom
Boulder District Court Judgment Book, Water Decrees, Vol 2, District 5-6, 1869-1896, pg 567-568
Case Number,
Date of appropriation, 10 Nov 1892
General Course is south easterly
Natural Stream is Dry Dreek
Headgate is located, NW corner SW 1/4 SE 1/4 Sec 9, T2N R69W
Length, 1 1/2 mi
Width, 3 1/2 ft
Depth, 1 ft
Grade, 1 in per rod
Capacity, 300 customary in
Acres under irrigation, 60A
Priority No. 7

WATER DISTRICT No. 6

Kinnear Reservoir
Water District No. 6
Eighth Judicial District
Jurisdiction, Boulder, Larimer and Weld counties
Owner
Boulder District Court Judgment Book, Water Decrees, Vol 2, District 5-6, 1869-1896, pg 569-570, 576
Case Number,
Date of appropriation, work commenced 1 Sept 1869, completed 20 May 1872
General Course is
Natural Stream is Coal Creek
Headgate is located, S 1/2 SE 1/4 Sec 20, S 1/2 SW 1/4, NW 1/4 SE 1/4, W 1/2 SE 1/4, SE 1/4 SE 1/4 Sec 21, NW 1/4 NE 1/4, NE 1/4 NE 1/4 Sec 28, T2N R69W
Length,
Width,
Depth,
Grade,
Capacity, 40,962,478 cu ft
Acres under irrigation,
Priority No. 1

Church's Upper Lake Reservoir
Water District No. 6
Eighth Judicial District
Jurisdiction, Boulder, Larimer and Weld counties
Owner
Boulder District Court Judgment Book, Water Decrees, Vol 2, District 5-6, 1869-1896, pg 570, 576
Case Number,
Date of appropriation, work commenced 20 May 1870, finished 1881, enlargement 1 Nov 1891, completed 1 Apr 1892
General Course is
Natural Stream is Coal Creek
Headgate is located, SW 1/4 Sec 3, T2S R69W
Length,
Width,
Depth,
Grade,
Capacity, 5,216,000 cu ft, enlargement addl 1,910,000 cu ft, 18.11 cu ft per second
Acres under irrigation, 125A
Reservoir Priority No. 2, Enlargement Priority No. 8

Last Chance Reservoirs No. 1 and No. 2
Water District No. 6
Eighth Judicial District
Jurisdiction, Boulder, Larimer and Weld counties
Owner
Boulder District Court Judgment Book, Water Decrees, Vol 2, District 5-6, 1869-1896, pg 571, 576
Case Number,
Date of appropriation, work commenced 1 Apr 1872, completed 1 Apr 1873, enlargement commenced

15 Sept 1885, completed Oct 1887, No. 2 work commenced 1875 completed 1 Apr 1876, enlargement commenced 15 Sept 1884, completed 15 Oct 1887
General Course is
Natural Stream is
Headgate is located, No. 1, N 1/2 NE 1/4 Sec 30, T2S R69W; No. 2 SW 1/4, Sec 19, SW 1/4 NW 14 Sec 30, T2S R69W
Length,
Width,
Depth,
Grade,
Capacity, No. 1, 13 acres at high water, 8.68 acres at low water, 1,983,200 cu ft, enlargement No. 1 13.79 acres at high water line, 1,051,000 cu ft; No. 2 12.63 acres at high water, 8.37 acres at low water, 2,972,900 cu ft, enlargement 13.96 acres at high water line, 1,888,000 cu ft, 10.78 cu ft per second
Acres under irrigation,
Reservoir Priority No. 6 and No. 7

Smart Reservoir
Water District No. 6
Eighth Judicial District
Jurisdiction, Boulder, Larimer and Weld counties
Owner
Boulder District Court Judgment Book, Water Decrees, Vol 2, District 5-6, 1869-1896, pg 572
Case Number,
Date of appropriation, work commenced 1 Sept 1882, completed 1 June 1883, enlargement commenced 1 Sept 1892, completed Dec 1892
General Course is
Natural Stream is
Headgate is located, S 1/2 Sec 16, T2S, R70W
Length,
Width,
Depth,
Grade,
Capacity, 24.37 acres at high water, 15.06 at low water, 10,305,000 cu ft, enlargement 26.55 acres at high water, addl 4,125,000 cu ft, 28.78 cu ft per second
Acres under irrigation,
Reservoir Priority No. 5 and No. 9

Community Ditch and Reservoir
Water District No. 6
Eighth Judicial District
Jurisdiction, Boulder, Larimer and Weld counties
Owner
Boulder District Court Judgment Book, Water Decrees, Vol 2, District 5-6, 1869-1896, pg 572
Case Number,
Date of appropriation,
General Course is easterly
Natural Stream is South Boulder Creek
Headgate is located, south bank of South Boulder Creek, 1188 ft west of the east line, 1500 ft north of the south line of Sec 25, T1S R71W
Length, 33 mi
Width, 6 ft bottom, 16 ft top
Depth,
Grade, 5.6 ft per mi
Capacity, 83.3 ct ft per second
Acres under irrigation, 2670A

Marshall Reservoir
Water District No. 6
Eighth Judicial District
Jurisdiction, Boulder, Larimer and Weld counties
Owner
Boulder District Court Judgment Book, Water Decrees, Vol 2, District 5-6, 1869-1896, pg 572
Case Number,
Date of appropriation, work commenced 6 June 1885, complete 1 June 1886
General Course is
Natural Stream is Boulder Creek
Headgate is located, Sec 22, T1S R70W
Length,
Width,
Depth,
Grade,
Capacity, 94.6 acres at high water, 14.28 ft can be drawn, 58,768,627 cu ft
Acres under irrigation,
Reservoir Priority No. 1

West Lake Reservoir
Water District No. 6
Eighth Judicial District
Jurisdiction, Boulder, Larimer and Weld counties
Owner
Boulder District Court Judgment Book, Water Decrees, Vol 2, District 5-6, 1869-1896, pg 573
Case Number,
Date of appropriation, work commenced 6 June 1885, completed 1886
General Course is
Natural Stream is South Boulder Creek
Headgate is located, NW 1/4 Sec 29, T1S R69W

Length,
Width,
Depth,
Grade,
Capacity, 71.7 acres at high water, 9.75 can be drawn, 30,452,000 cu ft
Acres under irrigation,
Reservoir Priority No. 2

Section Nineteen (19) Reservoir
Water District No. 6
Eighth Judicial District
Jurisdiction, Boulder, Larimer and Weld counties
Owner
Boulder District Court Judgment Book, Water Decrees, Vol 2, District 5-6, 1869-1896, pg 573
Case Number,
Date of appropriation, work commenced 1 May 1888, completed 1888
General Course is
Natural Stream is South Boulder Creek
Headgate is located, NW 1/4 Sec 19, T1S R68W
Length,
Width,
Depth,
Grade,
Capacity, 19.95 acres, 4.05 ft can be drawn, 3,520,000 cu ft
Acres under irrigation,
Reservoir Priority No. 3

Section Nine (9) Reservoir
Water District No. 6
Eighth Judicial District
Jurisdiction, Boulder, Larimer and Weld counties
Owner
Boulder District Court Judgment Book, Water Decrees, Vol 2, District 5-6, 1869-1896, pg 573
Case Number,
Date of appropriation, work commenced 15 Dec 1889, completed 1 Apr 1890
General Course is
Natural Stream is South Boulder Creek
Headgate is located, NW 1/4 Sec 9, T1S R69W
Length,
Width,
Depth,
Grade,
Capacity, 16.65 acres, 2 ft may be drawn, 927,000 cu ft
Acres under irrigation,
Reservoir Priority No. 4

Section Fifteen (15) Reservoir
Water District No. 6
Eighth Judicial District
Jurisdiction, Boulder, Larimer and Weld counties
Owner
Boulder District Court Judgment Book, Water Decrees, Vol 2, District 5-6, 1869-1896, pg 573
Case Number,
Date of appropriation, work commenced 1 May 1898, completed May 1898
General Course is
Natural Stream is South Boulder Creek
Headgate is located, NW 1/4 NE 1/4 Sec 15, T1S R69W
Length,
Width,
Depth,
Grade,
Capacity, 6.14 acres, 2.87 ft may be drawn, 767,900 cu ft
Acres under irrigation,
Reservoir Priority No. 5

Allen-Hayden Ditch No. 1
Water District No. 6
Eighth Judicial District
Jurisdiction, Boulder, Larimer and Weld counties
Owner
Boulder District Court Judgment Book, Water Decrees, Vol 2, District 5-6, 1869-1896, pg 574
Case Number,
Date of appropriation, 1 Apr 1875
General Course is easterly
Natural Stream is Four Mile Creek
Headgate is located, south side of Four Mile Creek, NE corner SE 1/4 Sec 17, T1N R70W bears north 3 degrees east 985 ft
Length, 2412 ft
Width, 3 1/2 ft
Depth, 13 in
Grade, 3 in per 100 ft
Capacity, 45 cu ft per second
Acres under irrigation, 40A
Priority No. 2

Allen Hayden Ditch No. 2
Water District No. 6
Eighth Judicial District
Jurisdiction, Boulder, Larimer and Weld counties
Owner
Boulder District Court Judgment Book, Water Decrees, Vol 2, District 5-6, 1869-1896, pg 574
Case Number,

Date of appropriation, 1866
General Course is easterly
Natural Stream is Four Mile Creek
Headgate is located, southside of Four Mile Creek, south bank NW corner of the NE 1/4 Sec 21, T1S R70W bears 83 degrees 45 minutes east 1013 ft
Length, 2630 ft
Width, 4 ft 4 in
Depth, 13 in
Grade, 3 in per 100 ft
Capacity, 4 cu ft per second
Acres under irrigation, 40A
Priority No. 4

Allen-Hayden Ditch No. 3
Water District No. 6
Eighth Judicial District
Jurisdiction, Boulder, Larimer and Weld counties
Owner
Boulder District Court Judgment Book, Water Decrees, Vol 2, District 5-6, 1869-1896, pg 574-575
Case Number,
Date of appropriation, 1867
General Course is easterly
Natural Stream is Four Mile Creek
Headgate is located, north side Four Mile Creek NW corner NE 1/4 Sec 21, T1N R70W bears south 56 degrees 15 minutes east 560 ft
Length, 2760 ft
Width, 40 in
Depth, 13 in
Grade, 3 in per 100 ft
Capacity, 4 cu ft per second
Acres under irrigation, 6A
Priority No. 5

Allen-Hayden Ditch No. 4
Water District No. 6
Eighth Judicial District
Jurisdiction, Boulder, Larimer and Weld counties
Owner
Boulder District Court Judgment Book, Water Decrees, Vol 2, District 5-6, 1869-1896, pg 575
Case Number,
Date of appropriation, 1867
General Course is easterly
Natural Stream is Four Mile Creek
Headgate is located, north side Four Mile Creek, NW corner NE 1/4 Sec 21, T1N R70W bears south 40 degrees 10 minutes west 785 ft
Length, 1233 ft
Width, 40 in
Depth, 13 in
Grade, 3 in per 100 ft
Capacity, 4 cu ft per second
Acres under irrigation, 10A
Priority No. 6

Low Ditch No. 1
Water District No. 6
Eighth Judicial District
Jurisdiction, Boulder, Larimer and Weld counties
Owner
Boulder District Court Judgment Book, Water Decrees, Vol 2, District 5-6, 1869-1896, pg
Case Number,
Date of appropriation, 1 July 1882
General Course is
Natural Stream is Four Mile Creek
Headgate is located, north side Four Mile Creek, SW corner Sec 15, T1N R70W
Length, less than 1 mi
Width, 1 ft
Depth, 7 in
Grade, 13 ft per mile
Capacity, 2 cu ft per second
Acres under irrigation, 45A
Priority No. 7

McKay Reservoir and Ditch
Water District No. 6
Eighth Judicial District
Jurisdiction, Boulder, Larimer and Weld counties
Owner
Boulder District Court Judgment Book, Water Decrees, Vol 2, District 5-6, 1869-1896, pg
Case Number,
Date of appropriation, 1881 never completed
General Course is
Natural Stream is Coal Creek
Headgate is located, NW 1/4 Sec 21, T1S R68W; south bank of Coal Creek, SE 1/4 NW 1/4 Sec 18, T1S R69W
Length,
Width,
Depth,
Grade,
Capacity,
Acres under irrigation,
Priority Rights:

Index

C

D

E

F

G

H

I

J

K

N

O

P

R

S

T

U

V

W

Y

Z

Additional Titles

If you borrowed this copy from a library and would like to order a copy, please send a check or money order to: Iron Gate Publishing, P.O. Box 999, Niwot, CO 80544. Our research books are available online to institutions and individuals at Amazon.com and on our website:

www.irongate.com

Colorado's Historical Assets: A Research Guide for Genealogists, Local Historians and History Buffs Containing a Treasure Trove of Museums, Ghost Towns, Courthouses, Historic Homes and Hotels, along with the Libraries and Archives Holding Colorado's History
ISBN 978-1-68224-044-1 $35.00 + $5.00 S&H

Digging Up Dirt: The Gold Hill Cemetery, Gold Hill, Colorado
ISBN 978-1-68224-037-3 $34.95 + $5.00 S&H

Rocky Ford, Colorado—A Walk Past Local Doors: Businesses and Residences from the Fairgrounds to Reservoir Hill, US 50 Curve to Curve
ISBN 978-1-68224-025-0 $34.95 + $6.00 S&H

Walking Rocky Ford and the Arkansas Valley: A Tour of Rocky Ford, Colorado and Vicinity
ISBN 978-1-68224-180-6 $29.95 + $6.00 S&H

Colorado's Historical Assets: A Research Guide for Genealogists, Local Historians and History Buffs Containing a Treasure Trove of Museums, Ghost Towns, Courthouses, Historic Homes and Hotels, along with the Libraries and Archives Holding Colorado's History
ISBN 978-1-68224-044-1 $35.00 + $5.00 S&H

Digging Up Dirt: The Gold Hill Cemetery, Gold Hill, Colorado
ISBN 978-1-68224-037-3 $34.95 + $5.00 S&H

Rocky Ford, Colorado—A Walk Past Local Doors: Businesses and Residences from the Fairgrounds to Reservoir Hill, US 50 Curve to Curve
ISBN 978-1-68224-025-0 $34.95 + $6.00 S&H

Walking Rocky Ford and the Arkansas Valley: A Tour of Rocky Ford, Colorado and Vicinity
ISBN 978-1-68224-180-6 $29.95 + $6 S&H

Cemeteries and Remote Burials in Larimer County, Colorado, Volume I: The Poudre and North, Including the Laramie River Valley and Livermore
ISBN 978-1-68224-010-6 $44.95 + $5.00 S&H

Cemeteries and Remote Burials in Larimer County, Colorado, Volume II: South of the Poudre, Including Fort Collins, Loveland, and Berthoud
ISBN 978-1-68224-012-0 $41.95 + $5.00 S&H

Cemeteries and Remote Burials in Larimer County, Colorado, Volume III: Estes Park Area and the Rocky Mountain National Park, Including Park Property in Grand County
ISBN 978-1-68224-014-4 $23.95 + $5.00 S&H

Taxpayer Series

Boulder County, Colorado Taxpayers, 1866-1867: An Index
ISBN 978-1-68224-184-4 $11.95 + $5.00 S&H

Boulder County, Colorado Taxpayers, 1868-1869: An Index
ISBN 978-1-68224-186-8 $11.95 + $5.00 S&H

Boulder County, Colorado Taxpayers, 1870-1871: An Index
ISBN 978-1-68224-187-5 $11.95 + $5.00 S&H

Boulder County, Colorado Taxpayers, 1872-1873: An Index
ISBN 978-1-68224-188-2 $11.95 + $5.00 S&H

Boulder County, Colorado Taxpayers, 1874: An Index
ISBN 978-1-68224-189-9 $11.95 + $5.00 S&H

Boulder County, Colorado Taxpayers, 1875: An Index
ISBN 978-1-68224-190-5 $11.95 + $5.00 S&H

Boulder County, Colorado Taxpayers Assessment Roll, 1872-1873: An Index
ISBN 978-1-68224-191-2 $11.95 + $5.00 S&H

Boulder County, Colorado Taxpayers Assessment Roll, 1874: An Index
ISBN 978-1-68224-192-9 $11.95 + $5.00 S&H

Boulder County, Colorado Taxpayers Assessment Roll, 1876: An Index
ISBN 978-1-68224-193-6 $11.95 + $5.00 S&H

School District Series

Boulder County, Colorado School Census Records 1875–1885: An Annotated Index
ISBN 978-1-68224-175-2 $35.95 + $5.00 S&H

Boulder County, Colorado School Census Records 1886–1890: An Annotated Index
ISBN 978-1-68224-174-5 $45.95 + $5.00 S&H

Boulder County, Colorado School Census Records 1891–1895: An Annotated Index
ISBN 978-1-68224-173-8 $55.95 + $6.00 S&H

Boulder County, Colorado School Census Records 1896–1900: An Annotated Index
ISBN 978-1-68224-172-1 $65.95 + $6.00 S&H

Boulder County, Colorado District 1—Superior School Census Records 1876–1900: An Annotated Index
ISBN 978-1-68224-114-1 $9.95 + $4.00 S&H

Boulder County, Colorado District 2—Shamrock School Census Records 1876–1900: An Annotated Index
ISBN 978-1-68224-115-8 $9.95 + $4.00 S&H

Boulder County, Colorado District 3—Boulder School Census Records 1877–1900: An Annotated Index
ISBN 978-1-68224-113-4 $35.95 + $6.00 S&H

Boulder County, Colorado District 4—Valmont School Census Records 1879–1900: An Annotated Index
ISBN 978-1-68224-116-5 $9.95 + $4.00 S&H

Boulder County, Colorado District 5—Davidson School Census Records 1879–1900: An Annotated Index
ISBN 978-1-68224-117-2 $9.95 + $4.00 S&H

Boulder County, Colorado District 6—Burlington School Census Records 1875–1900: An Annotated Index
ISBN 978-1-68224-118-9 $9.95 + $4.00 S&H

Boulder County, Colorado District 7—Niwot School Census Records 1876–1900: An Annotated Index
ISBN 978-1-68224-119-6 $14.95 + $4.00 S&H

Boulder County, Colorado District 8—Montgomery School Census Records 1879–1900: An Annotated Index
ISBN 978-1-68224-120-2 $9.95 + $4.00 S&H

Boulder County, Colorado District 9—Pella School Census Records 1880–1900: An Annotated Index
ISBN 978-1-68224-121-9 $9.95 + $4.00 S&H

Boulder County, Colorado District 10—Baseline School Census Records 1879–1900: An Annotated Index
ISBN 978-1-68224-122-6 $11.95 + $4.00 S&H

Boulder County, Colorado District 11—Jamestown School Census Records 1879–1900: An Annotated Index
ISBN 978-1-68224-123-3 $14.95 + $4.00 S&H

Boulder County, Colorado District 12—Ward School Census Records 1879–1900: An Annotated Index
ISBN 978-1-68224-124-0 $11.95 + $4.00 S&H

Boulder County, Colorado District 13—Bader School Census Records 1879–1900: An Annotated Index
ISBN 978-1-68224-125-7 $9.95 + $4.00 S&H

Boulder County, Colorado District 14—White Rock School Census Records 1879–1900: An Annotated Index
ISBN 978-1-68224-126-4 $9.95 + $4.00 S&H

Boulder County, Colorado District 15—Marshall School Census Records 1879–1900: An Annotated Index
ISBN 978-1-68224-127-1 $14.95 + $4.00 S&H

Boulder County, Colorado District 16—Pleasant View School Census Records 1883–1900: An Annotated Index
ISBN 978-1-68224-128-8 $11.95 + $4.00 S&H

Boulder County, Colorado District 17—Longmont School Census Records 1883–1900: An Annotated Index
ISBN 978-1-68224-129-5 $32.95 + $5.00 S&H

Boulder County, Colorado District 18—Middle Boulder School Census Records 1884–1900: An Annotated Index
ISBN 978-1-68224-130-1 $9.95 + $4.00 S&H

Boulder County, Colorado District 19—Caribou School Census Records 1879–1900: An Annotated Index
ISBN 978-1-68224-131-8 $11.95 + $4.00 S&H

Boulder County, Colorado District 20—Batchelder School Census Records 1884–1900: An Annotated Index
ISBN 978-1-68224-132-5 $9.95 + $4.00 S&H

Boulder County, Colorado District 21—Hygiene View School Census Records 1885–1900: An Annotated Index
ISBN 978-1-68224-133-2 $11.95 + $4.00 S&H

Boulder County, Colorado District 22—Altona School Census Records 1885–1900: An Annotated Index
ISBN 978-1-68224-134-9 $9.95 + $4.00 S&H

Boulder County, Colorado District 23—Armstrong School Census Records 1885–1900: An Annotated Index
ISBN 978-1-68224-135-6 $11.95 + $4.00 S&H

Boulder County, Colorado District 24—Gold Hill School Census Records 1885–1900: An Annotated Index
ISBN 978-1-68224-136-3 $11.95 + $4.00 S&H

Boulder County, Colorado District 25—Bashor School Census Records 1884–1900: An Annotated Index
ISBN 978-1-68224-137-0 $9.95 + $4.00 S&H

Boulder County, Colorado District 26—Ryssby School Census Records 1885–1900: An Annotated Index
ISBN 978-1-68224-138-7 $9.95 + $4.00 S&H

Boulder County, Colorado District 27—Wallstreet School Census Records 1886–1900: An Annotated Index
ISBN 978-1-68224-139-4 $9.95 + $4.00 S&H

Boulder County, Colorado District 28—Sunshine School Census Records 1885–1900: An Annotated Index
ISBN 978-1-68224-140-0 $9.95 + $4.00 S&H

Boulder County, Colorado District 29—Louisville School Census Records 1885–1900: An Annotated Index
ISBN 978-1-68224-141-7 $24.95 + $5.00 S&H

Boulder County, Colorado District 30—Pine Grove School Census Records 1885–1900: An Annotated Index
ISBN 978-1-68224-142-4 $9.95 + $4.00 S&H

Boulder County, Colorado District 31—Salina School Census Records 1884–1900: An Annotated Index
ISBN 978-1-68224-143-1 $11.95 + $4.00 S*H

Boulder County, Colorado District 32—Crisman School Census Records 1886–1900: An Annotated Index
ISBN 978-1-68224-144-8 $9.95 + $4.00 S&H

Boulder County, Colorado District 33—Silver Spruce School Census Records 1886–1900: An Annotated Index
ISBN 978-1-68224-145-5 $9.95 + $4.00 S&H

Boulder County, Colorado District 34—Sugarloaf School Census Records 1886–1900: An Annotated Index
ISBN 978-1-68224-146-2 $9.95 + $4.00 S&H

Boulder County, Colorado District 35—Chapman School Census Records 1886–1900: An Annotated Index
ISBN 978-1-68224-147-9 $9.95 + $4.00 S&H

Boulder County, Colorado District 36—Eldorado Springs School Census Records 1886–1900: An Annotated Index
ISBN 978-1-68224-148-6 $9.95 + $4.00 S&H

Boulder County, Colorado District 37—Culver School Census Records 1885–1900: An Annotated Index
ISBN 978-1-68224-149-3 $9.95 + $4.00 S&H

Boulder County, Colorado District 38—Magnolia School Census Records 1884–1900: An Annotated Index
ISBN 978-1-68224-150-9 $9.95 + $4.00 S&H

Boulder County, Colorado District 39—Rowena School Census Records 1884–1900: An Annotated Index
ISBN 978-1-68224-151-6 $9.95 + $4.00 S&H

Boulder County, Colorado District 40—Springdale School Census Records 1886–1900: An Annotated Index
ISBN 978-1-68224-152-3 $9.95 + $4.00 S&H

Boulder County, Colorado District 41—Fairview School Census Records 1885–1900: An Annotated Index
ISBN 978-1-68224-153-0 $9.95 + $4.00 S&H

Boulder County, Colorado District 42—Beasley School Census Records 1885–1900: An Annotated Index
ISBN 978-1-68224-154-7 $9.95 + $4.00 S&H

Boulder County, Colorado District 43—Broomfield School Census Records 1884–1900: An Annotated Index
ISBN 978-1-68224-155-4 $11.95 + $4.00 S&H

Boulder County, Colorado District 44—Potato Hill School Census Records 1885–1900: An Annotated Index
ISBN 978-1-68224-156-1 $9.95 + $4.00 S&H

Boulder County, Colorado District 45—Pleasant View Ridge School Census Records 1885–1900: An Annotated Index
ISBN 978-1-68224-157-8 $9.95 + $4.00 S&H

Boulder County, Colorado District 46—Canfield School Census Records 1880–1900: An Annotated Index
ISBN 978-1-68224-158-5 $11.95 + $4.00 S&H

Boulder County, Colorado District 47—Lyons School Census Records 1885–1900: An Annotated Index
ISBN 978-1-68224-159-2 $14.95 + $4.00 S&H

Boulder County, Colorado District 48—Nelson School Census Records 1886–1900: An Annotated Index
ISBN 978-1-68224-160-8 $9.95 + $4.00 S&H

Boulder County, Colorado District 49—Bunce School Census Records 1886–1900: An Annotated Index
ISBN 978-1-68224-161-5 $9.95 + $4.00 S&H

Boulder County, Colorado District 50—Lee Hill School Census Records 1887–1900: An Annotated Index
ISBN 978-1-68224-162-2 $9.95 + $4.00 S&H

Boulder County, Colorado District 51—Sunset School Census Records 1888–1900: An Annotated Index
ISBN 978-1-68224-163-9 $9.95 + $4.00 S&H

Boulder County, Colorado District 52—Lafayette School Census Records 1888–1900: An Annotated Index
ISBN 978-1-68224-164-6 $24.95 + $5.00 S&H

Boulder County, Colorado District 53—Noland School Census Records 1891–1900: An Annotated Index
ISBN 978-1-68224-165-3 $9.95 + $4.00 S&H

Boulder County, Colorado District 54—Eggleston School Census Records 1892–1900: An Annotated Index
ISBN 978-1-68224-166-0 $9.95 + $4.00 &H

Boulder County, Colorado District 55—Stony Lake School Census Records 1893–1900: An Annotated Index
ISBN 978-1-68224-167-7 $9.95 + $4.00 S&H

Boulder County, Colorado District 56—Eldora School Census Records 1896–1900: An Annotated Index
ISBN 978-1-8224-168-4 $9.95 + $4.00 S&H

Boulder County, Colorado District 57—Pine Cliff School Census Records 1896–1900: An Annotated Index
ISBN 978-1-68224-169-1 $9.95 + $4.00 S&H

Boulder County, Colorado District 58—Pine Glade School Census Records 1897–1900: An Annotated Index
ISBN 978-1-8224-170-7 $9.95 + $4.00 S&H

Boulder County, Colorado District 59—Allenspark School Census Records 1897–1900: An Annotated Index
ISBN 978-1-68224-171-4 $9.95 & $4.00 S&H

Additional Boulder County Titles

Boulder County, Colorado Payments, Accounts, Burial Permits and Licenses, 1879-1893: An Annotated Index
ISBN 978-1-68224-185-1 $11.95 + $5.00 S&H

Boulder County, Colorado Specialized Land Grants, 1857-1909, Agricultural Scrip Patents, Military Warrant Patents, State Volume Patents & Timber Culture Patents: An Annotated Index
ISBN 978-1-68224-194-3 $13.95 + $5.00 S&H

Boulder County, Colorado Probate Case Files Index: 1862–1978
ISBN 978-1-68224-112-7 $49.95 + $6.00 S&H

Boulder County, Colorado Lodged Wills and Inheritance Tax Waivers, 1899-1975: An Annotated Index
ISBN 978-1-68224-109-7 $11.95 + $4.00 S&H

Boulder County, Colorado School Census 1877: An Annotated Index
ISBN 978-1-68224-035-9 $15.95 + $4.00 S&H

Boulder County, Colorado, District Court, Petit Jury Lists, 1883-1910: An Annotated Index
ISBN 978-1-68224-034-2 $11.95 + $4.00 S&H

Boulder County, Colorado District Court, Petit Jury Records, 1867-1936: An Annotated Index
ISBN 978-1-68224-031-1 $24.95 + $5.00 S&H

Boulder County, Colorado District Court, Grand Jury Records, 1867-1922: An Annotated Index
ISBN 978-1-68224-032-8 $11.95 + $4.00 S&H

Boulder County, Colorado Surveys and Mineral Claims at the General Land Office, 1859-1876: An Annotated Index
ISBN 978-1-68224-030-4 $15.95 + $4.00 S&H

Boulder County, Colorado Clerk & Recorder, Loose Papers Box 1, 1861-1878: An Annotated Index
ISBN 978-1-68224-029-8 $21.95 + $5.00 S&H

Boulder County, Colorado Clerk & Recorder, Loose Papers Box 2, 1861-1878: An Annotated Index
ISBN 978-1-68224-028-1 $21.95 + $5.00 S&H

Boulder County, Colorado District Court Judge's Docket, Vol 1, 1867-1871: An Annotated Index
ISBN 978-1-68224-026-7 $15.95 + $4.00 S&H

Boulder County, Colorado District Court Record, June 1862 to March 1866: An Annotated Transcription
ISBN 978-1-68224-024-3 $11.95 + $4.00 S&H

Boulder County, Colorado Treasurer, Register of Accounts, 1867-1880: An Annotated Index
ISBN 978-1-68224-023-6 $19.95 + $5.00 S&H

Boulder County, Colorado County Court Index Book I, Plaintiffs and Defendants: An Annotated Index
ISBN 978-1-68224-021-2 $34.95 + $5.00

Minutes of the Board of Trustees of the University of Colorado, 1870-1876: An Annotated Index
ISBN 978-1-68224-020-5 $11.95 + $4.00 S&H

Boulder County, Colorado District Court Civil Appearance Docket, 1878-1882: An Annotated Index
ISBN 978-1-68224-019-9 $19.95 + $5.00 S&H

Boulder County, Colorado County Court Will Record, Volume A, 1875-1889: An Annotated Index
ISBN 978-1-68224-018-2 $11.95 + $4.00 S&H

Boulder County, Colorado, County Court Probate Record, Vol 1, 1875-1884: An Annotated Index
ISBN 978-1-68224-017-5 $11.95 + $4.00 S&H

Early Land Owners Along the St. Vrain Creek, Colorado Territory, 1860-1861: An Annotated Index
ISBN 978-1-68224-006-9 $11.95 + $4.00 S&H

Boulder County, Colorado District Court Widow's Relinquishment, Volumes 1 & 2, 1889–1937: An Annotated Index
ISBN 978-1-68224-009-0 $11.95 + $4.00 S&H

Boulder County, Colorado, District Court Guardians Bonds, Vol. A, 1876-1902: An Annotated Index
ISBN 978-1-879579-78-1 $11.95 + $4.00 S&H

Boulder County, Colorado Probate Court Fee Book, 1874-1890: An Annotated Index
ISBN 978-1-879579-88-0 $11.95 + $4.00 S&H

Boulder City Town Company Lot Sales 1859-1864: An Annotated Map Guide
ISBN 978-1-879579-87-3 $15.95 + $5.00 S&H

Brainard's Hotel Register, Boulder, Colorado, 1880: An Annotated Index
ISBN 978-1-879579-86-6 $15.95 + $5.00 S&H

Boulder County Commissioners Journal, 1861-1871: An Annotated Transcription
ISBN 978-1-879579-77-4 $45.99 + $5.00 S&H

Boulder County Commissioners Journal, 1871-1874: An Annotated Transcription
ISBN 978-1-879579-91-0 $39.95 + $5.00 S&H

Boulder, Colorado Teachers, 1878-1900: An Annotated Index
ISBN 978-1-879579-93-4 $11.95 + $4.00 S&H

Boulder County, Colorado District Court Execution Docket, 1875-1885: An Annotated Index
ISBN 978-1-879579-94-1 $11.95 + $4.00 S&H

Boulder, Colorado Births 1892–1906: An Annotated Index
ISBN 978-1-879579-79-8 $11.95 + $4.00 S&H

Boulder County Probate Court Appraisement Record A, 1875-1888: An Annotated Index
ISBN 978-1-879579-72-9 $11.95 + $4.00 S&H

Boulder County Assessor's Tax List, 1875: An Annotated Index
ISBN 978-1-879579-55-2 $11.95 + $4.00 S&H

Boulder County Assessor's Tax List, 1876: An Annotated Index
ISBN 978-1-879579-56-9 $11.95 + $4.00 S&H

Boulder Valley Presbyterian Church Records, 1863-1900: An Annotated Index
ISBN 978-1-879579-58-3 $11.95 + $4.00 S&H

Boulder's Masonic Pioneers, 1867-1886: Members of Columbia Lodge No. 14, Boulder County, Colorado Territory
ISBN 978-1-879579-57-6 $15.95 + $4.00 S&H

Map: Boulder City Town Company 1859 Original Survey Map
ISBN 978-1-68224-000-7 $24.95 (PAPER) + $7.00 S&H
ISBN 978-1-68224-001-4 $74.95 (MYLAR) + $7.00 S&H

Map: Boulder City Town Company, 11 Aug 1859 Land Lottery Map Showing Lot Purchases
ISBN 978-1-68224-002-1 $24.95 (PAPER) + $7.00 S&H
ISBN 978-1-68224-003-8 $74.95 (MYLAR) + $7.00 S&H

Map: Boulder City Town Company 20 Sept 1859 Map Showing Stock Certificates Issued by Lot
ISBN 978-1-68224-004-5 $24.95 (PAPER) + $7.00 S&H
ISBN 978-1-68224-005-2 $74.95 (MYLAR) + $7.00 S&H

Additional Titles from Around Colorado

Inventors in the Colorado Territory and their U.S. Patents, 1861-1876: An Annotated Index
ISBN 978-1-68224-022-9 $54.95 + $5.00 S&H

Colorado Territorial Penitentiary, Board of Managers Reports, 1871-1877: An Annotated Index of Marshals, Wardens, Guards, Board Members, Prisoners, and Local Businesses
ISBN 978-1-68224-039-7 $11.95 + $4.00 S&H

Colorado's Territorial Masons: An Annotated Index of the Proceedings of the Grand Lodge of Colorado, 1861–1876
ISBN 978-1-879579-85-9 $29.95 + $5.00 S&H

Denver, Colorado Territory Wagon Sales & Repair Ledger 1867-1870: An Annotated Index
ISBN 978-1-68224-040-3 $12.95 + $4.00 S&H

Denver, Colorado Police Force Record, 1879-1903: An Annotated Index
ISBN 978-1-879579-81-1 $11.95 + $4.00 S&H

Arapahoe County, Colorado Territory Criminal Court Index, 1862-1879: An Annotated Index
ISBN 978-1-879579-70-5 $11.95 + $4.00 S&H

General Research Titles

Map Your U.S. Research: A Workbook for Genealogists
ISBN 978-1-68224-041-0 $27.95 + $5.00 S&H

Make the Most of Your Genealogical Research Trip: Battle Plan—Washington, D.C.
ISBN 978-1-68224-027-4 eBook $5.95
ISBN 978-1-68224-38-0 print $12.95 + $4.00

These titles are also available through Ingram.

Directory of Genealogical and Historical Societies, Libraries and Archives in the US and Canada 2022 (2 Vols)

Vol 1, ISBN 978-1-68224-178-3 $125.00 + $10.00 S&H

Vol 2, ISBN 978-1-68224-179-0 $125.00 + $10.00 S&H

Publishing Titles

If you would like to order one of these books, please send a check or money order to: Iron Gate Publishing, P.O. Box 999, Niwot, CO 80544. Our books are available online to institutions through Ingram, to individuals at Amazon.com and on our website:

www.irongate.com

Set Yourself Up to Self-Publish: A Genealogist's Guide
ISBN 978-1-879579-99-6 $19.95 + $5.00 S&H

Set Yourself Up to Self-Publish: A Local Historian's Guide
ISBN 978-1-879579-98-9 $19.95 + $5.00

Publish Your Genealogy: A Step-by-Step Guide for Preserving Your Research for the Next Generation
ISBN 978-1-879579-62-0 $24.95 + $5.00 S&H

Publish Your Family History: A Step-by-Step Guide to Writing the Stories of Your Ancestors
ISBN 978-1-879579-63-7 $24.95 + $5.00 S&H

Publish a Local History: A Step-by-Step Guide from Finding the Right Project to Finished Book
ISBN 978-1-879579-64-4 $24.95 + $5.00 S&H

Publish a Memoir: A Step-by-Step Guide to Saving Your Memories for Future Generations
ISBN 978-1-879579-65-1 $24.95 + $5.00 S&H

Publish a Biography: A Step-by-Step Guide to Capturing the Life and Times of an Ancestor or a Generation
ISBN 978-1-879579-66-8 $24.95 + $5.00 S&H

Publish a Photo Book: A Step-by-Step Guide for Transforming Your Genealogical Research into a Stunning Family Heirloom
ISBN 978-1-879579-67-5 $24.95 + $5.00 S&H

Publish a Source Index: A Step-by-Step Guide to Creating a Genealogically Useful Index, Abstract or Transcription
ISBN 978-1-879579-68-2 $24.95 + $5.00 S&H

Publish Your Specialty: A Step-by-Step Guide for Imparting Your Research Expertise to Others
ISBN 978-1-879579-76-7 $24.95 + $5.00 S&H

www.ingramcontent.com/pod-product-compliance
Lightning Source LLC
LaVergne TN
LVHW061247100826
845148LV00008B/1047

* 9 7 8 1 6 8 2 2 4 2 0 1 8 *